WOMEN'S MOVEMENTS IN INTERNATIONAL PERSPECTIVE

LATIN AMERICA AND BEYOND

Women's Movements in International Perspective
Latin America and Beyond

Maxine Molyneux

Institute of Latin American Studies
31 Tavistock Square, London WC1H 9HA
www.sas.ac.uk/ilas/publicat.htm

First published in 2001 by Palgrave Macmillan

This edition published in 2003 by
Institute of Latin American Studies
School of Advanced Study
University of London

British Library Cataloguing-in-Publication Data
A catalogue record for this book is available
from the British Library

ISBN 1 900039 58 3

For A.M.H and F.H

Contents

Acknowledgements

There are many debts of gratitude to those who helped in different ways to bring this book to fruition. It was the Director of ILAS, James Dunkerley, who made it a possibility first by suggesting that I publish this collection and then by giving his support to its materialisation.

I would also like to thank those who have in various ways helped in the writing of these chapters: Amalia Chamorro, Nikki Craske, Ana Criquillon, Elisabeth Croll, Elisabeth Dore, Barbara Einhorn, Maria Carmen Feijoó, Ann Marie Goetz, Jon Halliday, Hermione Harris, Elisabeth Jelin, Deniz Kandiyoti, Saul Landau, Sian Lazar, Emily Morris, Ruth Pearson, Shirin Rai, Sheila Rowbotham, Jennifer Schirmer, Deborah Steinberg, Jean Stubbs, Barbara Taylor, Paul Thompson, Virginia Vargas, Margarita Velázquez, Nira Yuval Davis, the late Harold Wolpe, the late Gordon White and my Masters and PhD students for their insights and shared enthusiasms. A special thanks, too, to all those who so generously gave their time in interviews and conversations in many different situations and parts of the world.

My thanks for financial and institutional support go to: the Fuller Bequest at the University of Essex for helping to sponsor research on Cuba, Ethiopia and the Soviet Union; to the ESRC for a grant to run the seminar series on Gender, Class and Ethnicity in Post-Communist States; to the Nuffield Foundation for funding a research in Nicaragua; to IDS for funding a Research Fellowship to do comparative work on state socialism; to UNRISD for supporting work on post communist states; the DFID for sponsoring research on rights-based approaches to development in Latin America; and, not least, to ILAS for sustained support and for sponsoring trips to Cuba, Central America, Peru and Bolivia. Thanks too, to former colleagues at Essex University and Birkbeck College and to former co-editors of *Feminist Review*, as well as to colleagues at ILAS and co-editors of *Economy and Society*, for providing a context for stimulating discussion and debate. At ILAS thanks to the editorial team, John Maher and Melanie Jones; to Tony Bell, to Alan Biggins and Valerie Cooper of the ILAS Library and to Anna Hayes.

Finally, thanks to my partner Fred Halliday to whom I owe a special debt of gratitude for so many things and to my son Alex, who made his own mark on this project and whose IT expertise came to my rescue on many an occasion.

Introduction

Conflict over gender and political power has been central to the history of the modern world. While this was true for Europe and North America, it was in the developing world where these conflicts – over gender, as over nation and class – were often most acute. It is the analysis of this interaction of gender and politics in the developing countries, on the basis of debates within development and political sociology, that is the focus of this book. In the interdisciplinary approach adopted here, the analysis of gender has also drawn on other adjacent, but not always accommodating, interlocutors, whether these be within the shifting optics of academic disciplines, or within the equally changeable and sometimes overlapping terrains of critical theory and radical politics.

The chapters that follow are both comparative and international. They seek to relate the experience of individual countries to that of others and at the same time to explore the degree to which what may appear as processes specific to a particular country are in significant degree international. The majority of these chapters arose from a set of interrelated research projects, which sought to analyse gender politics and policy issues in relation to states, state policies and revolutions in the countries of the South. The attempt to develop a gender analysis of revolutions was encouraged by involvement in two comparative projects supported by the Institute of Development Studies at the University of Sussex. One was the 'Subordination of Women Project', which provided a pioneering context for the analysis of gender and development,[1] the other was a project developed by the late Gordon White analysing the variant forms of state socialism. At the same time, I undertook a number of research projects for international development agencies – ILO, UNDP, UNFPA – as part of the monitoring exercise carried out during and after the UN Decade for Women (1976–85). The collapse of communism in

1

1989 launched a new project supported by UNRISD on the social effects of adjustment in the former communist states of Eastern Europe and the Soviet Union. These various research contexts provided an opportunity to develop a comparative and critical approach to development policy and practice. The combination of these interests – feminism and social theory, on the one hand, development theory and policy, on the other – brought both comparative and international issues into sharper focus.[2]

In reflecting these influences, the chapters assembled here address two interrelated themes. Chapters 1–4 are concerned with specific cases of feminist politics within the context of revolutionary movements in Latin America. Chapters 5–7 are more comparative, examining the experience of state socialist regimes, the variability of women's movements and the changing claims that women have made on citizenship in Latin America. Together these individual and comparative analyses address broader theoretical issues concerning the structural and political dimensions of gender inequality and of organised action to oppose it, both from above, by states, and from below, by social movements.

While these questions have long been at the centre of debates in the social sciences, the focus of this book represents a significant decentring from the mainstream European and North American analysis of gender issues. In the 1970s and 1980s the empirical and theoretical focus of much of this latter scholarship was on the industrialised regions of the West. As a consequence, it was also concerned almost wholly with developed capitalism, from which case theories and generalisations about the social condition of women or their politics were all too frequently drawn. Area specialists and those in the development field apart, few who wrote on gender relations took much account of the experience of the developing countries. Equally, the record of state socialism, the only significant alternative yet seen to capitalism, and one with its own distinctive approach to gender inequality, remained on the margins of scholarly interest, a neglect compounded by the inhospitable conditions for independent, let alone critical, feminist, scholarship which prevailed in these states. Yet the experience of countries which underwent radical social upheaval, as well as the policies subsequently adopted by post-revolutionary regimes, is an essential part of any overall analysis of gender and power. As I argue, these states exhibited significant continuities and contrasts with the developed countries and brought about a substantial and in some ways distinctive mobilisation of women in their efforts to promote social change. No account of gender and politics, of women's social movements or of policies to address gender inequality is complete without considering their distinctive evolution.

Movements and States

These two overarching themes, the political sociology of women's movements and gender–state relations, define the contours of this book. Women's movements, understood as female collective action in pursuit of social and political goals, are, like other such social movements, essentially modern phenomena. They have generally arisen in the context of modern state-formation and economic change and have represented a response to the social and political conditions that have accompanied them. Women's movements and states have therefore tended to exist in mutual recognition, albeit one which has often been antagonistic and contestatory. This pertains to a recurrent theme in the chapters that follow – the inherently *political* character of women's movements. While autonomy has long been a principle of feminist organisation, in practice women's movements have been associated with a variety of forms of political linkage, within as well as outside the institutions of party and state. If this was true in the period of the radical movements of the past, be they nationalist, populist or socialist, it is equally so today in the context of a democratic opening, in Latin America and the former communist states alike, where the possibilities, and pitfalls, of interaction with the state lie at the centre of political debates. This debate over the degree to which such interaction is necessary or desirable is nowhere more acute than within women's movements, especially those of Latin America.

Chapter 1 provides an account of one unambiguous response to this question. It contains a discussion of a women's movement that emerged, as was characteristic of early anarchism, in outright rejection of the state. It comprises an account of a feminist paper, *La Voz de la Mujer* (Women's Voice), that arose out of the sizeable anarchist movement which had developed in Argentina by the 1880s, itself strongly influenced by anarchism in Spain and Italy. A passing reference to *La Voz* by the three major historians of Argentine anarchism – Max Nettlau, Diego Abad de Santillán and Iaâcov Oved – led me to discover nine editions of the paper in the archives of the Institute of Social History in Amsterdam. The research for this project was conceived, in common with the spirit of the times, as work aiming to uncover a piece of 'hidden history'. The existence of this current, active within the Argentine working-class movement, not only illustrated the early presence of radical women's movements long before the developments of the 1970s and 1980s, but also revealed the degree to which feminist ideas had become internationalised. From the 1890s in Argentina the anarchist press carried regular columns about '*feminismo*',[4] and reported enthusiastically on its fortunes in Europe and North America.

The research on *La Voz*, therefore, served not only to recover a lost history but also to refute the view, prevalent in much of the left in Latin America and elsewhere, that feminism was a 'bourgeois', 'reformist' movement and its demands of concern only to women of the privileged classes. The militant anarchist feminists of Argentina passionately identified with the female working-class as they denounced the dual oppression of marriage and work and railed against the hypocrisy of the Church in matters of sexuality. In so doing they formed part of the vibrant history of socialist feminism in the subcontinent. That this history is still in the process of being recovered by Latin American historians is shown by the fact that in 1997 Maria Carmen Feijoó, then at the University of Quilmes in Argentina, was able, much to my delight, to publish a facsimile edition of the nine extant copies of the paper with a translation of this chapter as the introduction.[3]

Chapters 2 and 3 analyse the tensions that arose between feminism and socialism in post-1979 revolutionary Nicaragua. Here theoretical questions posed within gender and development approaches, on the one hand, and within the study of gender and social revolution, on the other, were raised particularly sharply in a country where revolution coincided with the emergence, in both Latin America and the developed West, of an international women's movement. Chapter 2 explores some of the theoretical issues raised in the analysis of state policies through a reconceptualisation of the question of 'interests'. In examining the Nicaraguan Revolution, I argue that some account of women's interests had been taken by the Sandinista government, as was evident in the policies it pursued. However, it was important to take the argument a stage further and to question the ways in which women's interests were conceptualised. I argue that there was no theoretical basis for assuming a uniformity of interests among women. Women's interests should be disaggregated and differentiated in order to establish analytic criteria for distinguishing between the goals pursued by women's movements, or on behalf of women, by parties and governments.

The twofold distinction that was developed in this chapter between women's and gender interests, and between what I term 'strategic' and 'practical' interests, was to be assimilated into the gender and development policy literature that followed the UN Decade for Women. It formed part of the ongoing debate over the appropriateness and effectiveness of 'mainstreaming' feminist priorities into development policies as the issue of 'integrating women into development' acquired momentum in international policy arenas. The question posed then, as it is now, of how best to confront those forces that aim to instrument-alise and demobilise movements for social change, is also explored in several later chapters in this volume.

Chapter 3 examines the tension between women's demands and interests of state in Nicaragua, with reference to the issue of abortion. It addresses the way in which an issue that had been central to second-wave feminism in the developed countries, not least Britain, was resignified in the very different context of Nicaragua. Here a combination of conservative religious forces and popular religious sentiment, abetted by counter-revolutionary influences from outside, confronted both the revolutionary party and women's movements alike. While this analysis seeks to contextualise the process of feminist demand-making, it also highlights both the conflicts over policy that frequently arise over women's issues and the tendency of governing parties, even those with a commitment to 'women's emancipation', to subordinate women's rights to other priorities. This was starkly rendered in a subsequently notorious speech by the Sandinista leader Daniel Ortega to an assembly of women in 1987. While he castigated those demanding reproductive rights, Ortega deployed the authority of the revolution to underline women's moral obligation to bear more children to replace those fallen in the Contra War, only a few years before the FSLN would be voted out of power in the elections of 1990.

Chapter 4 develops a gendered analysis of state socialism in Latin America in relation to Cuba, by examining the state-sponsored women's union, the Federación de Mujeres Cubanas (FMC). It reviews the record of almost 40 years of state policy on gender issues and women's mobilisation in Cuba. While acknowledging the positive changes brought about by the revolutionary regime, and the social entitlements enjoyed by the population, the chapter focuses on the issue of organisational autonomy which has been central to feminist politics. It examines the consequences of the limits on such activity by women and the limits placed on policy by considerations of broader state interest. Here I resist the temptation to treat Cuba as being, in terms of the comparative study of state socialism, a unique case. In beginning its life via popular revolution, in advancing a project of social equality, in satisfying the basic needs of its population and in facing the hostile and revanchist polices of its powerful neighbour, Cuba has rightly elicited considerable regional and international sympathy. Yet, as much as its counterparts in Eastern Europe, Africa or the Far East, its trajectory also poses questions of critical analysis in relation to the enduring lack of genuinely representative political institutions. The Cuban leadership was justified in claiming that the revolution enabled it to meet some of the social and economic dimensions and prerequisites of social justice: but those within Cuba who have sought, in the 1990s, to defend the gains of the revolution while criticising the party's monopoly of political power have been silenced.

In Cuba, as elsewhere in the communist and former communist bloc, the issue of democracy and political power is strongly linked to that of gender inequality and the collapse of its former ally in 1990 placed its system under acute tension. The second half of this chapter therefore examines the gendered effects of Cuba's economic crisis and considers the limits here as in other respects of Cuban exceptionalism. It is impossible to say whether, with regard to party policies on women, popular evaluations of the Castro regime will turn out to be significantly different from those that emerged in other parts of the post-communist world. In Russia and Eastern Europe, there was considerable criticism of the nature of the official project of women's 'emancipation'. Such a programme for all its undoubted social achievements, redounded less to the credit of these regimes than was supposed by many analysts, especially under conditions perceived as dependent on an unacceptable concentration of political power at the centre.

The following chapters, 5–7, are more comparative in scope. Chapter 5 places the experience of state socialism in an international and historical perspective. Within the political sociology of gender, and within development studies, the communist project of women's emancipation was, for a long time, largely unanalysed. While some writers of second-wave feminism had argued for such a critical, comparative analysis of the socialist record, they were exceptional.[4] Yet such analysis could serve as a means of testing the theoretical concepts elaborated within 'Western' feminism against a distinct, revolutionary but undemocratic, alternative.

Chapter 5 revisits and revises the issue of the gendered character of socialism, and of the relationship between socialism and feminism. It engages with the question of how these states embarked on a programme of social change that differed substantially from that of the capitalist states and which had as one of its central components a project to 'emancipate' women. Yet the claims made by communist parties regarding their record of achievement on gender matters, notably of having achieved sex equality, were erroneous and in some ways misconceived. Inequalities persisted and were sustained by policies, not only in the domestic sphere but also in the main areas of public life.

Although what was gained through the socialist programme did reflect demands that issued from feminist movements in many parts of the world, this process was limited – in sum, women were mobilised but far from emancipated. This apparent paradox can be explained, I suggest, not through the analysis of the gendered relations present in socialist societies alone, but through a reading of state socialism as having sought a specific form of modernity premised on a distinctive development model. No adequate account of what these states did, and did not, achieve with regard to women can be abstracted from this development project.

State socialism rejected liberal capitalism and pursued an alternative route to modernity, one which envisaged a different and superior place for women within the society it sought to create. Yet the political economy that it fashioned in order to achieve its goals proved neither a match for capitalism, nor a sustainable alternative to it. Over time this became evident: by the mid-1980s, the Soviet model had begun to unravel. Elsewhere in the communist and non-communist worlds confidence in the possibility of a viable alternative to capitalism had waned. Research visits I made to the Soviet Union at the time revealed a tired population and a disheartened intellectual elite. In conversations with Soviet sociologists of the family, I learnt that they had been positioned as those whose work would help to 'solve' the problems of a failing system – of family dissolution, alcoholism and youth unrest – and that communism had not escaped any more than capitalism. In the event, the accumulated dissatisfaction and frustration with the system expressed itself in complaints about the quality of daily life, which the disciplinary intent of Soviet sociology had by then little means of assuaging.

Such an analysis of state socialism – specific in the Nicaraguan and Cuban cases, more general in Chapter 5 – demonstrates some of the ways in which gender relations are shaped by broader state and international forces. Given the collapse of the communist project as a whole, and the evolution of social science analysis of gender stratification, the optic of current analysis may diverge considerably from that through which the earlier literature was produced. The question that prompted much previous writing, of whether or not the socialist societies could provide a resolution for the oppression of women, has been answered in the negative, ultimately by the foundering of these societies themselves.

The chapters on state socialism focus predominantly on the policies of states and their gendered character, seen 'from above'. Chapters 6 and 7 examine gender–state relations from a different perspective, showing how, across a century of Latin American history, women's movements operating 'from below' have interacted with states. In Chapter 6, 'Analysing Women's Movements', I consider some prevailing definitions of women's movements and critique the common assumption that women's movements are necessarily autonomous, self-directed and acting to advance women's interests. Here I also revisit and develop the concerns of my earlier work on interests, to reflect on the uses that were made in the policy arena of the distinctions I had originated. In responding to the critique of the concept of interests that emerged in other approaches to social movements, I enter a defence of the concept of interests as a construct essential to political analysis. The chapter elaborates some additional distinctions between the varied forms of female collective action that have arisen, and so continues the process of analysis and disaggregation of women's movements that was begun in Chapter 2.

Chapter 7, on the women's movement in Latin America, was prompted by a conference in Mexico on Gender and Citizenship in 1996. It considers the distinctive characteristics of Latin American feminist and women's movements through a discussion of their historical evolution and of some of their political gains in the 1990s. In particular, it engages with some of the debates over citizenship that entered Latin American women's movements with the return to democracy in the 1980s. The end of authoritarian regimes of left and right, and the opening up of new political opportunities, led to some convergence of attitudes towards liberal democracy in Latin America. Within the region's feminist movements, the division which pervaded much of the twentieth century – between those who sought an improvement in women's position *within* capitalism and those who made such a change conditional on its overthrow – was superseded by a more differentiated debate on the political and social modalities of liberalism and on the relation between gender rights and political democracy as a whole. As such, it is perhaps an appropriate concluding chapter; not, however, one that signals a feminist 'end of history' so much as one which opens with a different set of challenges.

Feminism and its Futures

It is the persistence of such challenges that links the issues explored in this book to contemporary theoretical and policy debates. Since the first of the chapters included here was written, scholarly and political interest has moved towards a more international or global perspective. As the dynamic of feminism shifted in the mid-1970s from the North to the countries of the South, and as the study of gender itself became increasingly internationalised, even as it became more pluralised and more aware of ethnic and cultural differences within the North, interest in questions of difference and commonality brought the study of 'other' societies and political movements into sharper focus. This has been paralleled by the growing number of contributions to the scholarly literature from within these countries themselves as well as from their diasporas.

As has occurred in relation to feminism itself, so the countries seen as constituting the 'periphery' have moved from the margins to occupy at least an honorific place within contemporary social science. If no social science textbook is today without its chapter on gender, nor is it without an international, global perspective. No state or people is, at least in theory, outside its purview. The teaching of sociology in one country has been joined, where not replaced, by approaches that acknowledge international processes of change. The *maquila* or the export processing zone, analysed and written about since the 1970s by feminists in the development field, may now be as familiar to today's sociology students as the Dagenham shopfloor or the housing classes of Birmingham to those of the 1970s. Yet, for all this apparent internationalisation, the countries of the periphery and the social movements they have generated are still rarely studied in the depth that they deserve, while the most sustained alternative model of the twentieth century, that of state socialism, has all too often remained outside the scope of the theoretical and historical mainstream.

If scholarly interest has shifted towards an appreciation of international processes and has thereby converged with earlier concerns within development studies, there has been a similar movement with regard to some areas of feminist scholarship. Not only has the study of gender relations, politics and policies in developing societies received more attention in recent years but some of the earlier work within gender and development has itself eventuated in positions that many now claim, from different theoretical traditions, as axiomatic: that social theories are limited by their gender-blind and androcentric character; that no category of 'women' can be constructed on an unquestioned commonality of circumstance or interest; that reductive accounts of inequality based on economic relations cannot do justice to the multiplicity of determinations which operated to sustain it; that states are important sites in the reproduction of gender inequalities; and that an analysis of the work and power relations in the home is essential for policy and political interventions aimed at securing sex equality.

Looking back on that body of earlier work, it is striking that although the Marxist structuralism that influenced so much of it ceased to be a theoretical referent for feminist analysis of development, the efforts to theorise a gendered political economy nonetheless continued apace, and have indeed met with some success in regard to international policy debates. The critique of development policy from a gender perspective revealed its masculinist rationale as regards structural adjustment and in its treatment of poverty and households. Rendering visible the work that women did in the reproductive sphere and in the community challenged prevalent assumptions about social and economic relations. The emphasis on the material inequalities found in the family, and in the social division of labour more broadly, entered the calculations of such international policy instruments as the UNDP's *Human Development Report*. The demand from women's movement activists to have the activities carried out in the reproductive sphere fully acknowledged in the formulation and implementation of development policy has been integrated into countless guidelines for development agencies and government departments alike. Within development practice issues of gender have acquired considerable salience, even as they have increasingly and sometimes problematically become matters of state concern. In one way or another these chapters return to the dilemmas posed for women's movements as much by their demands being ignored by the institutional agencies of power as by being only *partially* met.

The themes which run through this book result from an engagement with some of the concerns that have arisen within the social sciences in recent decades, where they form part of a collective effort to develop a gender analysis of socialist revolutions, women's and feminist movements, states and their policies in developing countries. However, these are not only issues of scholarly interest, and in dealing with questions of power and politics they have lain at the heart of the struggles by women's movements to secure greater equality and recognition. It is against the background of that history, and as a participant in it, that I draw out some more general conclusions intended to demonstrate the relevance of the analysis of women's movements and revolutionary experiences to the continuing debate on equality and rights.

The interaction between feminism and socialism, one which endured for much of the twentieth century, is the theme of many of the chapters in this selection. State socialism disappointed the hopes invested in it, even as it fulfilled some of feminism's historic demands. But if the revolutionary perspective has been abandoned, this has been accompanied by a stronger, often more exigent, view of what is necessary, and possible, under liberal democracy itself. The feminist advocacy of gender equality, in law and public life, proceeds in the recognition of the limits of formal equality. Here the insights of class analysis, and of the parallel analysis of racism, have rendered more complex the awareness of inequality and its workings within developed democratic societies. At the same time, what is understood as equality between the sexes has itself been made the subject of extensive discussion and debate.

These issues lie at the centre of a worldwide involvement of women's movements in the formulation of policy goals in the 1980s and 1990s, one which found expression in the Fourth World Women's Conference held in Beijing in 1995, attended by 30 000 women. Among other things, the conference resolved to promote women's human rights and the political and economic conditions under which greater sex equality could be achieved. If women's demands at the end of the century have retained a striking consistency with those made at the beginning, this is because they have found no adequate resolution in the intervening decades.

Feminism's original goal, adopted by state socialism – the 'emancipation of women' – now seems utopian, unrealisable and, for some, tarred as much by its origins in the West and its colonising pretensions as by its authoritarian application in the socialist world. Yet the aspirations that it expressed, together with its cognate 'liberation', implied support for a process by which people were freed, individually and collectively, from the oppressive relations that restrained them, and that had, in so doing, denied them their rights. The emancipation of collective entities – classes, nations, women, followed by ethnic groups and sexual minori-' ties – was, it was argued, consonant with that of each individual member of that group. The emancipation of women depended upon the removal of socially constructed constraints – legal, economic, domestic, social, later psychological. In this perspective, be it in liberal or revolutionary visions, the emancipation of women appeared to be not merely a matter of acquiring rights, but to be embedded in a double relationship. It was, on the one hand, part of a process of social individuation that accompanied economic change, and it was at the same time a goal to be fought for.

This perspective, and the language associated with it, pervaded much of post-Enlightenment, nineteenth- and twentieth-century thought. Right through the 1970s and 1980s, when many other established ideas were rejected, the goals of 'emancipation' and 'liberation' were invoked in both developed and developing societies. Yet, in more recent times, the claim of emancipation has come under sustained criticism. In the crisis of nationalist and revolutionary authoritarian regimes, it has come to sound ideological and hollow. For some, 'emancipation' and 'liberation' should be thrown in the foundationalist dustbin, a relic of a now outmoded rationalist, and Enlightenment, discourse.

The argument on these issues is not, however, as final as might be claimed. 'Emancipation', understood as a project of freeing people from multiple forms of oppression, as a set of universal criteria for assessing such a freeing, and as a connection between this, as a realisable goal, and the broader condition of modernity, has far from lost its significance. Too easily dismissed by writers located within generally comfortable democratic societies and by those unengaged with the politics of women's movements, the criteria of equality, rights and citizenship are of enduring, direct relevance to those in societies where such entitlements do not prevail, and where the preconditions for effective collective action are not given. They are equally relevant to those in post-communist societies which are afflicted by new forms of gendered inequality, from the States of the former USSR, to China, as well as South Yemen and Nicaragua, and where, in the case of the former Soviet Union, a generalised economic collapse has exacerbated social inequalities. There is little reason, in the wake of the twentieth century, to abandon the aspiration to emancipation, or to forgo indignation at the denial of rights. Across the world violations of women's rights continue, some traditional and long-standing, some sanctioned by modern states, some by new forms of communalism, identity politics and ethnic authoritarianism, from the incidence of rape in the wars of former Yugoslavia to the terrorist patriarchy of the Taliban in Afghanistan. In the face of such sustained, worldwide violation of women's rights there seems little place for metropolitan agnosticism.

1

'No God, No Boss, No Husband!' Anarchist Feminism in Nineteenth-Century Argentina

This chapter examines anarchist feminism, a tendency within the nineteenth-century anarchist movement in Argentina, through a study of the content and social context of the newspaper *La Voz de la Mujer*.[1] There are two main reasons for examining this phenomenon. The first is one familiar to feminist historians – that of making visible what, in Sheila Rowbotham's phrase (1973), has been 'hidden from history'. The full history of anarchist feminism in Argentina has never been written; nor has it been acknowledged as a distinct tendency within the anarchist movement or the Latin American women's movements. The major historians of Argentine anarchism – Max Nettlau, Diego Abad de Santillán and Iaâcov Oved[2] – do little more than note the existence of *La Voz*, leaving its content unanalysed and its significance unexplored.

A second reason concerns the political implications of such phenomena within feminist debate, especially in the Latin American context. *La Voz de la Mujer* was a newspaper written by women for women and the editors claimed that it was the first of its kind in Latin America. Although they were mistaken about this,[3] *La Voz* could claim originality in being an independent expression of an explicitly feminist current within the continent's labour movement. As one of the first recorded instances in Latin America of the fusion of feminist ideas with a revolutionary and working-class orientation, it differs from the feminism found elsewhere in Latin America during the initial phases of industrialisation, which centred on educated middle-class women and to some extent reflected their specific concerns. In the Latin American context, in which feminism is all too often dismissed by radicals as a 'bourgeois' or 'reformist' phenomenon, the example of *La Voz* constitutes a challenge to this essentialising of the movement. Although empirical investigation cannot be the exclusive terrain for debate about the nature and effectiveness of feminism, a consideration of the facts can inform that debate.

The Context

Anarchist feminism emerged in Buenos Aires in the 1890s within a context shaped by three factors that distinguished Argentina among nineteenth-century Latin American states: rapid economic growth, the influx of large numbers of European immigrants and the formation of an active and radical labour movement. During the second half of the nineteenth century the Argentine economy was undergoing a spectacular expansion. In the period between 1860 and 1914, its growth rates were among the highest in the world, giving Argentina a lead over the rest of Latin America that it was to retain until the 1960s. The basis of this expansion was the exploitation of the fertile pampas, the rolling plains of the interior, which produced cheap wheat and meat for the European markets. As demand for these products grew and Argentina's productive capacity increased, the area of land under cultivation rose from 200 000 acres in 1862 to 60 million in 1914.[4]

The growth of the economy increased the demand for labour and this was satisfied through immigration on a vast scale. From the 1870s, special bureaux were set up in Italy, Spain, France and Germany to lure immigrants to Argentina with the promise of cheap land, fares and loans. The response in the depressed areas of Europe was overwhelmingly positive, and the rate of immigration achieved was unequalled anywhere on the subcontinent. Overall, between 1857 and 1941, when immigration all but ceased, over 6.5 million migrated to Argentina, and of these nearly 3.5 million stayed. From 1857 to 1900 there were 1.93 million arrivals, of whom 1.13 million stayed.[5] By 1914 Argentina was the country with the highest ratio of immigrants to indigenous population in the world.[6] In 1895 they represented 20 per cent of Argentina's nearly 4 million inhabitants and 52 per cent of the population of Buenos Aires, the capital city.[7]

The largest ethnic group comprised Italians, who in 1895 accounted for 52 per cent of the total number of immigrants. Spaniards made up the second largest grouping with 23.2 per cent of the total, and French immigrants accounted for 9.6 per cent. Smaller percentages of Germans, British, Austrians, Uruguayans, Arabs, Swiss and East Europeans made up the remainder. It was among these immigrant communities that the group producing *La Voz de la Mujer* arose and was active. Anarchism as a political ideology was originally imported by immigrants from the

European countries in which the anarchist movement was strong – Italy, Spain and France.[8] Anarchist groups and publications, many of them founded by political refugees from Europe, first emerged in the 1860s and the 1870s.

Despite anarchism's alien origins, there can be little doubt that the material conditions encountered by the immigrants in Argentina provided fertile soil for its appeal. On their arrival in Buenos Aires, about half the immigrants initially sought their fortunes on the land, whereas the rest found work in the expanding port economy and in other urban centres such as Rosario and La Plata. They became day labourers and artisans, domestic servants and public employees engaged in the numerous state-funded building projects. While some had capital to invest in businesses and in real estate, the majority were members of the rural or urban working class, who had come to Argentina to escape the hardships of their own countries and make their fortunes.

Few immigrants managed to achieve the social mobility they aspired to. Most remained workers; an estimated 70 per cent of the immigrants were concentrated in the city of Buenos Aires, and of the working class as a whole about 60 per cent were foreign-born. The frustrated desire for some improvement in their means was probably a major cause of immigrant discontent.[9] For many of these workers, conditions were dismal. In Buenos Aires, where the population doubled between 1869 and 1887 and again between 1887 and 1904, housing was scarce and of poor quality. Many workers lived in *conventillos,* or tenements, where the average immigrant family of five persons shared a 12-foot by 12-foot room.[10] Although wages were not low by the standards of other Latin American countries, they were constantly eroded by devaluation. Workers were frequently cheated in deals with their bosses and employment conditions were harsh, a ten-hour day, six-day week schedule being the norm.[11]

These material difficulties were compounded by political conditions that did nothing to lessen immigrant dissatisfaction. Although in theory Argentina's was a constitutional government in which popular sovereignty prevailed, in practice there existed a system of bloc votes, clientelistic relations and informal alliances with local *caudillos* (bosses). This denied real political representation to most Argentine residents, whether native-born or immigrant. As the immigrants became more vocal and working-class militancy increased, immigrants appeared to threaten the very economic prosperity they had helped engender. In order to increase control over them, citizenship laws made it almost impossible for immigrants to become naturalised, although their children were considered Argentine citizens by right of birth. It is therefore not surprising that in 1895, of a total of 345 493 foreigners in Buenos Aires, only 715 had become citizens.[12]

This policy of restricted enfranchisement enabled successive governments to postpone some of the consequences of immigration for two decades. The immigrant population was kept in a precarious situation economically and politically. The dual disqualification (electoral and national) that allowed minimal political expression of its aspirations encouraged it to take a combative and often revolutionary form. Immigrant discontent was evident in the strikes of the late 1880s and reached a crescendo in a general strike of 1902. But the force the government wished to contain was one it needed to continue creating.

The immigrant communities formed an integral part of the nascent working class in Argentina and played a prominent role in shaping its ideologies and the character of its struggles. They brought from Europe a political culture that arose from their experience of working-class organisations and forms of action, transposing the debates over anarchism, socialism and trade union organisation to the shopfloors, tenements and cafés of Buenos Aires, Rosario and La Plata. The first strike, in 1878, was organised by the printers' union, established 20 years before by Spanish cooperativists. By the 1880s forms of working-class organisation and resistance were widespread, and this growth was accelerated by the onset of a severe recession, known as the Baring Crisis, which gripped Argentina from 1889 to 1891. The economic collapse precipitated a governmental crisis, an uprising by supporters of the embryonic Radical Party, and the first extensive wave of strike action, by the end of which there were few branches of employment that had escaped the effects of workers' discontent.

In the climate of growing working-class militancy in the 1880s and 1890s, revolutionary groups were active producing pamphlets and newspapers, organising mass meetings, putting on theatre performances and participating in strikes and demonstrations. Until the emergence of the Socialist Party as a significant force at the turn of the century, much of this activity was undertaken by anarchists, many of them, like Ettore Mattei and Enrico Malatesta, exiles from Europe. They enjoyed significant support within the working class and controlled several powerful unions, among them the bakers (organised by Mattei) and the bricklayers. In the 1880s and 1890s there were sometimes as many as 20 anarchist newspapers being published at any one time, in French, Spanish and Italian; occasionally, articles in each language appeared in the same newspaper.

Anarchism in Argentina reached its peak in the first two decades of the twentieth century, and the earlier history of this movement can be seen as a slow and often interrupted advance toward this climax. *La Voz de la Mujer* thus appeared after half a century of tentative and continuous anarchist activity and as one of the first expressions of what was to be Argentina's anarchist heyday.

The ebb and flow of Argentine anarchism and its preferred forms of organisation and struggle followed a pattern similar to that in Europe, and by the 1890s it was, as elsewhere, largely under the influence of the anarchist communism propagated by Peter Kropotkin and Elysée Reclus in Europe, and Emma Goldman and Alexander Berkman in the United States. This was the tendency to which *La Voz de la Mujer* belonged. Anarchist communism was a fusion of socialist and anarchist ideas. It was dedicated to the violent overthrow of the existing society and the creation of a new, just and egalitarian social order organised on the principle of 'from each according to ability, to each according to need'. Internationally, the movement was divided over whether the revolution was to occur through a popular uprising or through a mass strike. There were also disagreements over the degree to which the anarchist movement should itself be organised and over the appropriateness of employing individual acts of violence against the state for propaganda purposes. Both socialism and anarchism focused on the working class, but also expressed some sympathy for the principle of women's emancipation. By the 1880s there had emerged within the European anarchist movement a distinctive feminist current, represented by writer-activists such as Teresa Mañé ('Soledad Gustavo')[13] and Teresa Claramunt, just as within the movement in North America these ideas were developed by Voltairine de Cleyre, Emma Goldman and others. The writings of some of these figures were already being published in Argentina in the 1880s, and in the anarchist press critiques of the family appeared together with editorials supporting 'feminism', by then a term in current usage. The main impulse for anarchist feminism came from Spanish activists, but Italian exiles like Malatesta and Pietro Gori gave support to feminist ideas in their journals and articles.

In the 1880s and 1890s one of the main forms of anarchist activity was the editing, printing and distribution of newspapers, leaflets and pamphlets. Indeed, there was apparently as much anarchist literature circulating in Buenos Aires by the last years of the century as there was in the anarchist stronghold of Barcelona.[14] In the early years, much of the editorial content of these papers was imported from Europe, but as time went on the content reflected an increasingly local involvement.

Very little is known about how these publishing ventures were financed, but from the information available it seems that some of the funds came in the form of small donations raised at meetings and lectures. Printing costs were relatively low; according to the accounts listed at the back of the publications, the cost in 1897 of printing 2000 copies of a newspaper was in the region of 45 pesos – a little over twice the weekly wage. The subscription lists show that individual donations were normally about 20 centavos, but there were usually three or four groups, some in the provinces, who regularly sent sums of up to 5 pesos each. Donors were usually identified by false names, evocative *noms de guerre* (such as 'Firm in the Breach', 'Less Asking, More Taking', 'A Bomb-Thrower'), or by their trades; the latter, which included shoemakers, street sweepers, prostitutes, waiters and bus drivers, together with the small sums donated, are some indication of the class identification of the readership.[15] Pamphlets and newspapers were often given away. Because of the irregularity with which these newspapers appeared, the precariousness of their existence and their susceptibility to police crackdowns, the institution of the regular subscription was not effected.

La Voz de la Mujer was typical of the small circulation, semi-clandestine and ephemeral newspapers of the anarchist-communist tendency that advocated 'propaganda by deed'. Although addressed to the working class, it appeared to have few organic links to it and its militant anti-reformist stance further weakened its capacity for political intervention in the struggles of the day. Yet its feminism must have aroused some response among women workers in the cities of Buenos Aires, La Plata and Rosario, for it lasted a year and printed between 1000 and 2000 copies of each issue – a respectable number for an anarchist newspaper of its time.

It was among the women workers of the urban centres that *La Voz de la Mujer* arose and campaigned for support. Its editors were drawn from the large Spanish and Italian communities and identified themselves with the women of the working class. There was certainly a constituency of urban working-class women in nineteenth-century Argentina, and many of these women were immigrants. The 1895 census reports that there were 368 560 immigrant women (just over half the number of men, though women constituted the majority of the native-born population), 37 per cent of whom were in Buenos Aires. We do not know what percentage of this total were workers, but immigrant women were the majority of the economically active population of Buenos Aires and made up 40 per cent of the 21 571 domestic servants, 66.1 per cent of the dressmakers, 56.9 per cent of the seamstresses, 16.9 per cent of the cooks,

23 per cent of the teachers and 34 per cent of the nurses. Overall, immigrant women constituted approximately half of the 66 068 women registered as employed in the capital and were concentrated in domestic service, the sewing and textile industries and cooking.[16]

The little information available on women's wages and working hours shows that they suffered systematic discrimination, low pay and long hours. The average working day for the domestic servants of Buenos Aires was well over twelve hours in the mid-1890s, despite a strike by domestic servants over the denial of rest periods in 1888. A second domestic servants' strike is reported from the 1890s, this time in protest against employers' practice of issuing servants conduct books in which judgements of them were recorded; possession of such a book was required for employment and a negative judgement made it almost impossible to find another job. It appears that women in the textile industry worked an eight-and-a-half-hour day, which was below the average. Female workers in such trades received wages lower than the average: dressmakers and seamstresses received between 50 centavos and 1.00 peso per day, when the average wage for men workers was between 1.50 and 2.50 pesos. The wages of domestic servants were generally even lower, if they were paid at all.[17]

This discrimination in employment was not primarily due to limited educational opportunities for girls and women. In Argentina the sexual disparity in education was very small compared with that of many developing countries, and the literacy rate was similar to that in many European countries at the time. In 1895, 49 per cent of all men and 41.5 per cent of all women were literate. In Buenos Aires the rates were 6 per cent and 10 per cent higher, respectively. Gender inequality was even less marked with regard to access to primary and secondary education. It was with pride that the editors of the 1895 census reported that Argentina was distinguished among the nations of the world for the fact that there was no significant discrimination against the female sex as far as schooling was concerned. Whatever the qualitative differences concealed behind the numerical equality, there can be no doubt that there was less sex discrimination in education in Argentina than in most countries of the world at the time. The 1895 census reports 298 boys per 1000 at school, compared with 294 girls per 1000.[18]

This relatively high rate of participation coupled with equal opportunities for girls in education meant that the radical press had a potential readership that was not confined to the upper classes. *La Voz de la Mujer* could count on the existence of significant numbers of women with literacy and at least some education among the workers to whom they addressed their propaganda. The poorer immigrant women, however, were often uneducated. These women were generally attached as wives or mothers to their husbands and families, yet many of them must have suffered the usual problems associated with upheaval and adjustment to an alien culture, even if alleviated somewhat by continuities in language and religious values. For women, migration, whether internal or international, was both an effect and a cause of changes in the family and in their position in the wider society. As the socioeconomic structure of the Old World decomposed, relations in the family were redefined and, among some groups, liberalised. Yet it would appear that most immigrant women remained trapped within their own communal cultures in sexual and family matters and that the traditions and prejudices of Southern Europe continued to exert an influence. Despite the tumultuous conditions of the capital in this period, women were kept within traditional social and economic roles and forced to work under the discriminatory structures prevailing elsewhere in the industrialising world. *La Voz de la Mujer*, therefore, arose in the context of decomposition and recomposition of the traditional role divisions.

Feroces de Lengua y Pluma (Ferocious of Tongue and Pen)

The distinctiveness of *La Voz de la Mujer* as an anarchist newspaper lay in its recognition of the specificity of women's oppression. It called upon women to mobilise against their subordination both as women and as workers. Its first editorial was a passionate rejection of women's lot:

> Compañeros y compañeras! Greetings!
> So: fed up as we are with so many tears and so much misery; fed up with the neverending drudgery of children (dear though they are); fed up with asking and begging; of being a plaything for our infamous exploiters or vile husbands, we have decided to raise our voices in the concert of society and demand, yes, demand our mite of pleasure in the banquet of life.[19]

The appearance of this first issue received a mixed response from the rest of the anarchist movement, ranging from silence and hostility to praise. *El Oprimido*, edited by 'an amiable Englishman' called Dr Creaghe,[20] extended a particularly warm welcome in its issue of November 1895:

> By giving it this name, a group of militant women has unfurled the red flag of anarchy and intends to publish a magazine for propaganda

among those who are their comrades both in work and in misery. We greet the valiant initiators of this project, and at the same time we call on all our comrades to support them.

A substantial section of the anarchist press was sympathetic to feminist issues at this time. The mid-1890s in Argentina saw increasing coverage of issues relating to women's equality; particularly marriage, the family, prostitution and the domination of women by men. Some newspapers even published special series of pamphlets devoted to 'the woman question'. *La Questione Sociale,* the Italian-language newspaper founded by Malatesta when he came to Argentina in 1883, published a series of pamphlets 'especially dedicated to an analysis of women's issues', including writings by 'Soledad Gustavo' on women and education and on the sufferings of poor and proletarian women. These two pamphlets were well enough received to merit republishing, the latter claiming a print run of 4000. The Science and Progress Press, a venture of Dr Creaghe linked to *La Questione Sociale,* also produced numerous pamphlets on women, including the texts of a series of lectures given by 'Dr Arana' in the province of Santa Fe. These included an 87-page dissertation based on the work of Morgan called *Woman and the Family,* published in 1897, and a shorter work drawn from Maine entitled *Slavery Ancient and Modern* that included in its examples of the latter type the institution of marriage. These pamphlets were first printed in editions of 500 but were reprinted three times before the end of the century, indicating some considerable interest in the subject. Ruvira (1971) notes that the first all-woman groups that emerged in 1895 were adherents of *La Questione Sociale* and that it was these groups that produced 'the real militants' – 'Pepita Gherra', Virginia Bolten, Teresa Marchisio, Irma Ciminaghi, and Ana López.

The journal *Germinal,* which first appeared in 1897, was, like *El Oprimido,* particularly concerned with 'the woman question'; it carried several articles under the general heading of 'Feminism', and it defended 'the extremely revolutionary and just character of feminism' against the charge that it was merely a creation of 'elegant little ladies'. Much if not all of the feminist material in the anarchist press appears to have been written by women, although this is impossible to verify because the use of pseudonyms was common practice. *La Voz de la Mujer* enjoyed cordial relations with at least some of its contemporaries, particularly those belonging to the more extreme propaganda-by-deed tendency such as *El Perseguido* and *La Voz de Ravachol.* It also had relations with the Spanish newspapers *El Esclavo, La Voz del Rebelde* and *El Corsario,* with the New

York newspaper *El Despertar* and with the Uruguayan newspaper *Derecho a la Vida*.

Yet this apparent sympathy for feminism in principle within the anarchist ranks was matched by substantial opposition in practice. Since there appear to be no traces of this opposition in the anarchist press of the period, it is probable that these criticisms had been expressed orally. The first issue of *La Voz de la Mujer* seems to have aroused considerable hostility because in the following issue the editors attacked the 'anti-feminist attitudes' prevalent among men in the movement in no uncertain terms.

> When we women, unworthy and ignorant as we are, took the initiative and published *La Voz de la Mujer*, we should have known, Oh modern rogues, how you would respond with your old mechanistic philosophy to our initiative. You should have realised that we stupid women have initiative and that is the product of thought. You know – we *also* think ... The first number of *La Voz de la Mujer* appeared and of course, all hell broke loose: 'Emancipate women? For what?' 'Emancipate women? Not on your nelly!' ... 'Let our emancipation come first, and then, when we men are emancipated and free, we shall see about yours'.

The editors concluded that women could hardly rely upon men to take the initiative in demanding equality for women, given such hostile and hypocritical attitudes.[21] The same issue of the newspaper contains a second article on the question, entitled 'To the Corrupters of the Ideal'. In it men are warned, 'You had better understand once and for all that our mission is not reducible to raising your children and washing your clothes and that we also have a right to emancipate ourselves and to be free from all kinds of tutelage, whether economic or marital.'

We can, however, assume that the polemic did not subside, because the editorial in the third issue is addressed 'To Our Enemies' and states that despite 'the veritable tempest [which] has broken over *La Voz de la Mujer*', the editors (who had apparently been referred to as 'savages of tongue and pen') were still 'firm in the breach'. A slight retreat is indicated in their concern to emphasise that they were attacking not male anarchist comrades in general but only those 'false anarchists' who failed to defend 'one of anarchism's most beautiful ideals – the emancipation of women'.

The editors' outrage at the hypocrisy they saw in the movement was justified in that anarchism advocated freedom and equality for *all* humankind. Women as an oppressed group could rightly demand support from fellow anarchists in their struggle for emancipation. But although anarchism's principles had attracted many free-thinking women to its ranks and parts of the movement took feminism seriously, there was a certain ambivalence over the precise status of the struggle for women's emancipation *per se*. Women were welcomed as militants in 'the cause of anarchy', as *El Oprimido* had put it, but they were given somewhat less encouragement to struggle for feminist demands and none at all to form autonomous feminist groups. Anarchist doctrine was itself somewhat ambivalent about feminism, and there was remarkably little theoretical debate about the subject. Although Bakunin had included in the programme of his International Alliance of Social Democracy the explicit aim of abolishing sexual inequality along with class inequality, the anarchist record on women's rights was an uneven one. The French Proudhonists had opposed the demands of feminists for equal pay and equal work and thought women's natural place was in the bosom of the family.[22] The chief inspiration of the anarchist communism of the 1880s and 1890s, Peter Kropotkin, encouraged women's activism within the movement but disapproved of feminism. He saw the struggle of the working class for liberation as primary; women's specific interests were to be subordinated to the achievement of this goal.

In Argentina, as anarchists began to take up some of the practical demands of the working class toward the end of the century, one of the latter's most vigorous campaigns was for protective legislation for women. When, for the first time, equal pay for women was raised as a demand and supported by a significant number of labour unions in the Argentine Workers' Federation in 1901, Pietro Gori, a renowned anarchist propagandist, moved that 'women should be prohibited from working in those areas which could be dangerous to maternity and which could undermine their morals; and children under 15 should be stopped from working altogether'. The concern with women's morality and the juxtaposition of women and children in this paternalistic formulation is telling.[23] The committee voted unanimously to 'organise women workers in order that they might raise their moral, economic and social conditions'.[24]

Yet it is not difficult to see why feminists were attracted to anarchism. Its key tenets stressed the struggle against authority, and anarchist feminism focused its energies on the power exercised over women in marriage and the family, seeking their freedom to have relationships outside these institutions. The anarchist emphasis on oppression and on power relations, albeit largely untheorised, opened up a space within which women could be seen simultaneously as victims of society and victims of male authority. As *La Voz de la Mujer* expressed it in issue no. 5, 'We hate authority because we aspire to be human beings and not machines directed by the will of "another", be this authority, religion or any other name.' One of *La Voz's* supporters elaborated on this 'any other name' when she signed herself: 'No God, No Boss, No Husband'.

Thus anarchism, perhaps more than socialism with its emphasis on economic exploitation, was able to accommodate some aspects of feminism, even though feminist ideas did not meet with wide acceptance in themselves either within or beyond the anarchist movement. This tension between the movement as a whole and the feminists within it was reflected in the trajectory of *La Voz*.

As far as we know, *La Voz de la Mujer* was published only nine times; the first issue appearing on 8 January 1896 and the last almost exactly one year later, on New Year's Day. It may well have been revived at a later date and may have had sister publications elsewhere in Argentina and even in Uruguay. The standard sources on the anarchist movement of this period date its existence from 1896–7 but tell us little more. The editorials of *La Voz* refer to three changes of editorship, but, on account of the semi-clandestine nature of the group, no names are mentioned. However, in an issue of a periodical called *Caras y Caretas* published in 1901, mention is made of the 'two beautiful women who edit *La Voz de la Mujer*'. An unnamed actress is also alluded to as one of the collaborators. A series of photographs accompanying the article shows three women named as editors of *La Voz* – Teresa Marchisio, María Calvía and Virginia Bolten.[25] Unfortunately, no further light is cast on these women and we are left with the intriguing possibility that *La Voz de la Mujer'* was revived after its closure in 1897 and was again being published in 1901. Whether this was the same newspaper with the same editors is impossible to say.

It is also reported that another version of the newspaper and bearing its name was published in the provincial town of Rosario by Virginia Bolten.[26] She was said to be a 'great orator' and indefatigable organiser and she is the only woman known to have been deported in 1902 under the Residence Law, which gave the government the power to expel immigrants active in political organisations. It also appears that yet another *La Voz de la Mujer* was published in Montevideo (Diego Abad de Santillán, personal communication), and because this was where Virginia Bolten was exiled it is reasonable to suppose that she may have been involved in establishing this Uruguayan version.

Like many other anarchist newspapers of the period, *La Voz* appeared sporadically, bearing on its cover the words *'Sale cuando puede'* ('Appears when it can'); at first this was about once every three weeks, and then the time between issues lengthened to six weeks and then to two months. It was published in newspaper format and contained four pages of copy. Nos 1–4 claimed a print run of 1000; nos 5, 7 and 8, 2000, and no. 9, 1500.[27] As was normal for these anarchist newspapers, it was financed by voluntary subscription, and a list of donors was printed at the back of each issue. An indication of the temper of its readership can be gained from the following donors' names: 'Women Avengers Group', 'One Who Wants to Fill a Cannon with the Heads of the Bourgeoisie', 'Long Live Dynamite', 'Long Live Free Love', 'A Feminist', 'A Female Serpent to Devour the Bourgeoisie', 'Full of Beer', 'A Man Friendly to Women'.

The newspaper's contents were presented in a number of different ways; the main form was the article, varying in length from one or two columns to a page and a half. Each issue usually contained an editorial, a poem[28] and a moral tale about the 'martyrs' of bourgeois society (the poor, the workers, the prostitutes) or their adversaries (judges, priests, the police). In addition, translations and articles from the European movement were reproduced as they were elsewhere in the anarchist press of the time, among them the writings of 'Soledad Gustavo', Laurentine Sauvrey, Teresa Claramunt, A. María Mozzoni, and María Martínez. The editors of *La Voz de la Mujer* actively sought the cooperation of prominent women anarchists and, according to a note in no. 5, were in communication with Emma Goldman and Louise Michel. The back page of the newspaper contained a section entitled 'Round Table' in which small items of news from Europe and Argentina were discussed. It was here too that the Socialist Party of Argentina was regularly berated for its reformist politics – in regard to the working-class movement, *not* the woman question – and that topical issues relating to women were reported. We hear, for instance, of the spirited intervention of a young woman anarchist in a workers' meeting on behalf of women's emancipation.

Most of the signed articles bore the names of women, and most were written in Spanish, with only occasional items in Italian. Although the newspaper accepted articles in either language, the names of the editors, collaborators and contributors indicated the newspaper's affiliations with Spanish anarchism and with the Spanish immigrant community.[29] This is not surprising, as it was primarily from Spain that anarchist feminism came to Argentina. Even the feminist material in the Italian press was written largely by Spanish authors.

Themes and Politics

La Voz de la Mujer described itself as 'dedicated to the advancement of communist anarchism'. Because its politics were of the militant anarchist variety that defended acts of violence, it was published semi-clandestinely. It was addressed to a working-class readership and its editors wrote frequently and passionately about the misery and poverty endured by women of this class, to which they claimed to belong. The mood of the newspaper was one of fiery optimism, as exemplified in the following verse from a poem entitled 'A Toast', by Josefa M. R. Martínez: 'Greetings, *compañeras!* Anarchy/Hurrah, dear brothers and sisters, to the fight/ Strong of arm, serene of heart'. In common with the rest of the anarchist movement, the editors were bitterly opposed to the authority of religion and the state and uncompromisingly hostile to the police and other representatives of the law. They tended to offer robust advice to strikers on how to handle police harassment, urging them to 'knock off a few' in order to teach the police a lesson.

The central theme running through *La Voz,* however, is that of the multiple nature of women's oppression. The 'storm' in the anarchist movement that greeted the newspaper's appearance seems to have been caused by the militant feminism of the first editorial, which took the distinctive and, for many Argentine anarchists and socialists of the time, heretical position that women were the most exploited section of society. A later editorial asserted, 'We believe that in present-day society nothing and nobody has a more wretched situation than unfortunate women.' According to the editors women were doubly oppressed – by bourgeois society and by men.

The specifically feminist development of anarchist theory lay in its libertarian stance on marriage and its attack upon male power over women. Anarchist communism had taken over from Engels the critique of bourgeois marriage as a means of safeguarding capitalist property transmission. It also reiterated his view that the family was the site of women's subordination. The writers in *La Voz de la Mujer,* like anarchist feminists elsewhere, went on to develop a concept of oppression that focused on gender relations. Marriage was not just a bourgeois institution; it also restricted women's freedom, including their sexual freedom. *La Voz* attacked the 'conjugal onanism' of marriage as a central cause, along with class oppression, of misery and despair. Marriages entered into without love, fidelity maintained through fear rather than desire, oppression of women by husbands they hated – all were seen as symptomatic of the coercion implied by the marriage contract. People were not free to do as they pleased, even less so because divorce was illegal in Argentina. It was this lack of autonomy and alienation of the individual's will that the anarchist feminists deplored and sought to remedy, initially through free love and then, and more thoroughly, through social revolution.

La Voz de la Mujer was a keen supporter of free love. This was an issue that had been taken up by both the North American and Spanish anarchist movements by the 1890s and remained an anarchist ideal for decades afterwards. An advocacy of free love and a hostility to marriage were shared by other anarchist and libertarian groups in Latin America, some of which went further than *La Voz* in both elaborating the ideas and putting them into practice. Literature on the benefits of free and multiple relationships was circulating in the movement in Argentina, as was information and propaganda on the free-love communes that had come into existence among the immigrant communities in some Latin American countries.[30] *La Voz de la Mujer* offered its readers few practical guidelines for living out their ideal, and it is not clear what social arrangements were envisaged for those who practised free love or for their probable offspring.

What the editors had in mind appears to have been a liberal variant of sequential heterosexual monogamy, their ideal consisting in 'two comrades freely united'. In a context in which contraception was at best minimally available, the editors had little to say about children, and what they did say represented a variety of views. There is only one reference to family planning, of which the writer expressed approval on the grounds that too many children increased the poverty of the poor (a position that was to gain ground with the spread of eugenicist ideas). There is no explicit discussion of abortion, and the few references to it reveal the ambivalence of the editors. Abortion is mentioned as something nuns and bourgeois women resorted to, and was seen as evidence of their hypocrisy. We are left uncertain as to whether the act itself was to be deplored or only the people performing it. Attitudes toward children ranged from extremes of sentimentality to angry denunciation of the mother's lot. The editors adopted the conventional anarchist position on illegitimacy, deploring it as an irrational social prejudice and expressing sympathy for its victims. In general, and especially in the later issues of *La Voz,* children were written about with great feeling for their sufferings, and considerable stress was laid on the emotional bond between mother and child. In an article on the horrors of war, the focus was upon the mother's fear of losing her son in combat. Mothers were held up as the main repositories of parental affectivity. The editors' hostility to the family and to marriage, then, was tempered by respect for at least some of its conventions. The fact that they at no point proposed the more obvious forms of alleviation of the problem of childcare, through nurseries or collective organisation, is significant. Childcare must have represented a problem for a readership of women workers, and the absence of any discussion on the matter suggests that traditional attitudes toward motherhood may have been stronger than the more radical of the editors would have wished.

There is a silence, too, on the entire question of domestic work. Although the editors attacked the oppression of women and their entrapment in the home and in drudgery, they never proposed either that men should share this labour in the household or that it should be more equally administered. It may well be that they were prevented by their particular variant of anarchist ideology from proposing any solution that would have involved the state or private capital (with nurseries, for example) or that could have been considered a purely reformist measure. Nonetheless, the fact that they did not argue for an equal distribution of labour within the home or communal responsibility indicates that they could not break with prevailing notions of the place of women within the traditional division of labour.

La Voz's position on free love, although more cautious than that of some of its contemporaries, did amount to a rejection of men's traditional authority over women and control of their sexuality. In the context of Southern European machismo, in which virginity, fidelity and the double standard were the common currency of male privilege, such demands for female autonomy were certain to arouse a hostile response. An item in issue no. 7 of *La Voz* shows that the editors' ideal of free union and dissolution, with women taking the initiative, was far from acceptable to men, even within the anarchist movement itself. The article deplored the action of the male anarchist activist, F. Denanbride, who had shot his lover five times as she was attempting to leave him. (The woman, a collaborator on *La Voz de la Mujer* called Anita Lagouardette, had miraculously survived.) The newspaper's treatment of this episode illustrates a flaw in its anarchist feminist reasoning. The editors saw free love as the solution to the problem of male–female relations; when marriage, the cause of misery and despair, was abolished, the home would become 'a paradise of delights'. Men and women would be free to enter into relationships with whomever they chose and to dissolve them at will, without the corrosive effects of law, state or custom. This view ignored both the complex and internalised subordination of women and the modes of oppression and sense of superiority internalised by men.

Free union could only have been an adequate solution if the interests of both parties involved had been identical or if the party whose wishes were contradicted had no feelings. In any situation in which partners to a conflict differed in strength, the weaker would obviously lose, and in a world in which people were socialised along lines of male–female inequality, the stronger – the male – would be able to use slogans of 'freedom' to impose his will on his female companion – either by leaving her when she did not want to be left or by forcing her to remain. Moreover, in a world in which women, especially those with children, had few alternatives to dependence on men through marriage, the bid for independence probably seemed not only romantic but also a more realistic possibility for men; hence it may have been seen as threatening rather than liberating to the least advantaged women.

For all its radicalism, the free-love slogan was still tempered by the conventions of its day, and this was especially true of its implications for sexual practice. The demand for free love had to do with personal autonomy, but while it involved a greater measure of sexual freedom, it did not mean sexual libertarianism. The caution that characterised the editors' free-love advocacy can partly be explained by the ambivalence they expressed about sexuality. Their writings on the subject, like those found in Spain at the time, reveal a combination of vulgarity, radicalism and shocked prudery. Marriage, for instance, was attacked because it corrupted those involved and led to degenerate sexual practices. In a particularly florid passage, it was denounced as harbouring 'coital fraud and aberrations', with all its attendant 'disgusting diseases and its thousands and thousands of loathsome and repugnant practices which convert the marriage bed into a trough of disgusting obscenities – and from there to adultery!' In similar vein, 'degenerate' sex, including masturbation, was associated with the enemy, especially priests and the bourgeoisie, who were berated as homosexuals and pederasts. The limits of the editors' radicalism on this issue were clear; they were not advocating sexual permissiveness and were not, it seems, even sure that they liked sex very much. Their free-love slogans signified a desire for freedom from certain legal and personal constraints, but sexuality was to be confined to the realm of normative practice.

This reflects the cultural context from which these women emerged. They saw the main problem in terms of freeing themselves from the power of men and questioned the privileges that men enjoyed at women's expense. Moreover, given the existing moral climate and the power relations between men and women, the latter frequently found themselves the victims of sexual exploitation for which they paid the social cost in terms of damaged reputation and illegitimate children. It is therefore not surprising that sexual exploitation is a recurrent theme of anarchist feminism: sex was a threat to women. *La Voz de la Mujer*, therefore, combines various anarchist elements, such as hatred of the Church and of class exploitation, with a specifically feminist critique of the sexual exploitation of women. A powerful illustration of this, addressed in quite explicit language, is contained in issue no. 3, in which the Church is attacked with all the venom of Spanish anarchism for the hypocrisy of its functionaries in relation to sexuality. 'Luisa Violeta' gives an allegedly autobiographical account of an incident between a priest and herself in a confessional. The priest rebukes her for not attending mass. She explains that her mother has been ill and she has had to care for her, but the priest will have none of it: 'Disgraceful girl, don't you know that it is the soul first and then the body ... ?' In the course of the confession Luisa asks forgiveness for masturbating, a subject that provokes a keen interest on the other side of the grille. The priest wants to know exactly what parts of her body she touches and whether she performs these acts alone; then he asks her whether she was taught to do this by someone else. She retorts that it was none other than the priest himself. At this point, he invites her into his cubicle and tries to rape her.

Insistence on the profanity of the priesthood was a recurrent theme, together with a more general attack on the hopelessness of looking to religion for a salvation that can only come through social revolution. Given that the prevailing view of women was conditioned by expectations of their religiosity, piety and chastity, this kind of critique must have been particularly scandalous at the time.

Hostility to the Church eclipsed even such sororal sympathy as the editors of *La Voz de la Mujer* might have mustered for their cloistered sisters, the nuns. These women were originally just as much the victims of the lack of opportunities as were the prostitutes to whom, in one article, they were likened. In issue no. 4, nuns were bitterly criticised not so much for their ideological role as the purveyors of religious values as for their hypocrisy and deceit concerning sexuality: 'parasites of society, who after satisfying your carnal appetites with your saintly men – the priests – cast the fruits of your entrails in the streets or bury them in your convent gardens'. Not surprisingly, these articles appear to have aroused criticism from readers of *La Voz de la Mujer*, and they prompted a reply in no. 5. The author insisted that the allegations were true and in her defence cited newspaper reports of a young girl being raped by a priest and the disposal of unwanted babies by nuns.

Hypocrisy, the double standard and the sexual exploitation of women formed the basis of the editors' feminist sympathy for prostitutes. Prostitutes were 'fallen women', innocents who had been corrupted, doubly betrayed on the basis of their sex and their class. An article by 'Pepita Gherra' in issue no. 4 contains this description of the ideal-typical prostitute: 'Yes, I know, poor child, the priest was your lover and the monk bought you for four coins. Your father was sacked, your mother is ill and your little brothers and sisters are suffering agonies of hunger.' In keeping with the Romantic tradition, the prostitute was considered 'the martyr of society': as the creation of social corruption, she occupied a central place in the anarchist critique of class and gender injustice. The editors held that prostitution was forced on women through poverty, men's rapacity and the lack of realistic alternatives for earning their living, and was reinforced by the double standard and the institution of marriage, which trapped people in empty and unfulfilling relationships and drove men to look for their pleasures elsewhere.

In the late nineteenth century, Buenos Aires was already in the process of becoming the Latin American vice capital. Although fewer than 700 prostitutes were registered in the 1895 census, this was a considerable understatement if other contemporary accounts are to be believed. It appears from the figures that a large percentage of the prostitutes in Argentina were immigrants, and this is consistent with reports of a white slave trade at this time.[31] No. 8 of *La Voz de la Mujer* carries a long discussion of a pamphlet, apparently written by women who had been shipped to Buenos Aires by a 'well-known entrepreneur' in this trade, calling for police intervention to stop the traffic in women. *La Voz de la Mujer* supported the women in mobilising against the practice, but considered it futile and incorrect to ask the police to intervene.

Shifts in Orientation and Demise

Changes in editorship with numbers 5 and 7 are associated with a shift in political emphasis – a gradual retreat from the militant feminism of the first few issues in favour of more orthodox anarchist concerns. When, in its early issues, *La Voz* vigorously defended a feminist position against the criticisms of men in the movement, it was careful to point out that it was not against men but against those who opposed the idea of women's emancipation. After issue no. 3 there were no further explicit allusions to recalcitrant men, and this may bear some relation to the significant editorial change that took place with issue no. 5. The latter appeared in a different, larger format, apparently part of a campaign to increase the readership. This was necessary because there was 'still great prejudice against women and against the great headway made by women's propaganda'. The articles of 'Pepita Gherra' were now prominently featured, and more articles tended to be on general anarchist themes rather than specifically women's questions. The tone of the writing was less militantly feminist, less analytical and less critical of men than before. Another significant index of the editors' increasing defensiveness was their denial that the newspaper was in the hands of the Grupito Amor Libre (Free-Love Sect), and, indeed, from this issue on, there was no more discussion of free love. However, the slogan 'Long Live Free Love' continued to be included along with 'Social Revolution' and 'Long Live Anarchy' in the programmatic calls that ended editorials.

Despite the change in editorship, there was no explicit criticism of the previous editorial line of the newspaper, and the new editors affirmed their intention to follow 'the path of the old editors, that is, to fight ceaselessly against bourgeois society: we shall fight without compromise against those prejudices and preoccupations inculcated in us during our childhood by stupid men and fanatical women, and by others who place their pens at the disposal of scoundrels'. With the seventh issue there appears to have been a further editorial change. According to a small announcement on the last page, a new group was now running the newspaper; as in the earlier case, no reasons were given for the change and no criticisms made of previous policy. The only indication of a change of line is given by the contents of the newspaper; it was now being written, apparently, almost entirely by 'Pepita Gherra', and these last three issues were even less concerned with feminist issues than the previous two. They were characterised by a concern with general anarchist themes such as anti-patriotism and anti-clericalism.

The appearance of an appeal for help in issue no. 9 indicates that the newspaper had entered a crisis. The print run for this number dropped from 2000 to 1500, and the issue was dominated by a disquisition on the Spanish-Cuban War reportedly printed in *La Voz* because of lack of funds to publish it as a pamphlet. The appeal for support that reviewed the newspaper's development reads as follows:

TO OUR READERS

A year has passed since the first number of *La Voz de la Mujer* appeared. It has been a year of struggles, of sacrifices, of cruel choices, of expectations and failures, which have only been alleviated to some extent by the rewards of struggle.

Two editorial groups have undertaken the work of producing this paper, and they have both placed all their limited knowledge and their energies at the disposal of the cause which they defend: Anarchy. Throughout this year, the life of this paper has been precarious and uncertain, so much so that we must confess and emphasise that (1) comrades who like our propaganda work must help us a bit more efficiently, because otherwise our efforts will be useless and we shall have to stop bringing out *La Voz de la Mujer*; and that (2) this will mean the end of the ONLY paper in the Americas and perhaps in the whole world that is propagating our ideals about women and that is particularly for women.

Compañeros y compañeras: we must repeat that we are not lacking in enthusiasm and will, but our resources are very few. Therefore, if we cannot go on, we shall retreat until we can return once again to the breach and shall always be ready, when the hour of combat sounds from the clock of human consciousness, to run forward and either win or die for anarchy; for this cause we shall give all our intellectual and bodily energies and our final breath.

The Editors of *La Voz de la Mujer*

Notes
(1) Therefore we say: given the state of ignorance in which women are kept, we believe that our role as journalists is to break open the ground of women's minds; another paper, or this one some time in the future, will sow and cultivate the seeds. This is why our propaganda work is as it is; every paper has its own role.
(2) Alternatively, we may have to hand it over to other women comrades who are more capable or have more resources.

Despite this appeal, however, it appears that, with issue no. 9, *La Voz de la Mujer* ceased to exist. The difficulties faced by such a newspaper were formidable. It readily acknowledged its failure to generate sufficient support, and there were a variety of reasons for this, both practical and political. Among the practical difficulties can be listed all the problems of publishing under clandestine or semi-clandestine conditions. *La Voz* used a variety of different presses and probably relied on the collaboration of sympathetic men, who may in turn have forced the editors to moderate their more unacceptable views. There are indications that the newspaper was distributed mainly by male activists and that these men were not very diligent in ensuring that it was circulated or that the funds it raised were delivered to the editors. This raises the more complex political reasons for *La Voz de la Mujer*'s decline: if it was circulated mostly by men, then there were either few women to whom anarchism appealed in nineteenth-century Argentina or few sympathetic to the project of *La Voz*.

There are two separate but related issues here concerning the political appeal of anarchist and feminist ideas. Anarchism clearly enjoyed fairly widespread sympathy among immigrant workers in the late nineteenth and early twentieth centuries, but support for it was gradually eroded by changes in the immigrant communities themselves. It seems to have been initially popular among immigrants, especially the least advantaged, because its unanchored cosmopolitanism, idealism and militant opposition to all forms of authority were expressive of the frustrations of a displaced rural Southern European labour force faced with the realities of urban poverty in an alien land. Disappointed hopes and political disenfranchisement fuelled these immigrants' militancy and confirmed their disengagement from their host country. Many left, but those who stayed through choice or circumstance had to survive within Argentine society. About half of the male migrants married Argentine women and established a less attenuated relationship with their adopted country. Meanwhile, both male and female Argentine workers as well as some immigrants were, by the 1890s, committed to the struggle for practical reforms to ameliorate the condition of the working class. Some of the anarchist groups entered into these struggles and gave them a militant edge. These groups remained, at least until the first decades of the twentieth century, serious rivals of the more avowedly reformist Socialist Party.

The revolutionary currents of anarchism, such as *La Voz*, remained aloof from the reformist tendencies; whereas some sectors of the working class, both national and immigrant, were demanding an eight-hour day, higher wages and better conditions, many anarchists derided such struggles and called instead for direct action against the state and its institutions. The anarchist press of *La Voz de la Mujer*'s disposition was particularly disengaged from the struggles of its day. The newspaper's contents scarcely mention strikes or repression, working-class demands or action. Instead, the main concern was with ideological struggle.

La Voz de la Mujer's militant stance against what it saw as reformism probably marginalised it from the women workers it sought to influence. Its semi-clandestine nature made organisation and public meetings difficult. The newspaper appeared infrequently and circulated mainly among the radical members of the various immigrant communities.

Thus, by far the greatest proportion of the material printed in *La Voz de la Mujer* could have been written in almost any Spanish-speaking country at any time between 1870 and 1930; ironically, the section of the newspaper that gives the most vivid indications of life in Argentina at this time is the subscription list, with its fleeting references to trades, living conditions, regions of the country and leisure activities. Overall, its contents suggest that links with the realities of working class and immigrant women's lives in Argentina were extremely attenuated.

Even in the 1890s, the splits that had developed in the movement reflected the direction events were taking. The more militant variants of anarchist communism, such as *La Voz* and the *Voice of Ravachol* (named after a bomb-thrower), soon lost out to those tendencies that were more responsive to the working class and embraced its struggles. The anarchist movement was henceforth characterised by a growing support for anarcho-syndicalist ideas. This was, however, a question of too little and too late, and anarchism, even in its more syndicalist form, was within a few decades a spent force. The Socialist Party, founded in 1894, committed as it was to electoral participation and labour reform, had by the second decade of the twentieth century overtaken the anarchists, and both were eclipsed by the liberal populism of the Radical Party.

La Voz de la Mujer was, therefore, already a minority tendency within the anarchist movement as a whole, a movement which was being challenged to adapt to both the needs of the immigrants who were planning to stay in Argentina and those of the indigenous working class. But *La Voz* lost the contest twice over. Not only did its politics marginalise it from the working class, but it also gained insufficient support from women.

In one sense, *La Voz* was not particularly concerned to attract a wide readership. Its variety of anarchist feminism sought to develop small groups of dedicated activists rather than a mass movement. Its politics were avowedly sectarian and its sympathies reserved exclusively for working-class and poor women. There was little or no cooperation with other radical groups that shared *La Voz*'s concern for the working-class. The Socialist Party was reviled in much the same terms as the bourgeoisie, its newspaper *La Vanguardia* being described by one writer, presumably on account of its reformism, as 'socialistic(sic)-bourgeois filth'. Although the women workers to whom they addressed their writings had many a cause for grievance, the editors' commitment to militant anarchism made it virtually impossible for them to involve themselves in any discussion of the practical issues they faced.

There was, therefore, a tendency to avoid formulating any precise strategies for change and action, even when certain more practical demands can be seen as emerging from working women. Apart from the abolition of marriage, the editors called for an end to restricted opportunities for women, domestic slavery, discrimination against women at work, unequal access to education and men's 'uncontrolled' sexual demands upon women. But these issues were merely signalled, with little or no discussion. Given the expressed concern for women workers, there were surprisingly few references to the employment and work conditions prevailing in Argentina at the time. *La Voz* was opposed to strikes for better wages and conditions. Its only intervention on behalf of women workers was to point out to laundresses the futility of boycotting the washhouses in an attempt to bring down the price of admission; instead it advised them to smash the machinery. Even when considerable space was allotted to a theme, as in the case of free love, the editors, as noted earlier, offered their readers few practical guidelines for realising their ideal.

From the turn of the century onwards, a different variant of feminism emerged that did take up such issues, that of the Socialist Party. Such women as Cecilia Grierson, Alicia Moreau de Justo and Juana Rouco Buela launched the struggle for equal rights, better educational opportunities and reform of the Civil Code, and in so doing they redefined the politics, strategy and terrain of feminist struggle.[32]. Unlike *La Voz* and those of its persuasion, the Argentine Socialist Party, influenced by the gradualist vision of Eduard Bernstein, was committed to a programme of demands formulated principally in terms of concessions that could be won from the state.

Although the socialist programme was directed at achieving more tangible results than that of anarchism, it lacked the fiery feminist radicalism of the anarchist feminists. More important, in their tendency to derive women's oppression primarily from capitalism or to see it as mediated by the discriminatory practices of the state, the socialists did not develop, as the anarchists had done, a radical critique of the family, machismo and authoritarianism in general. Nor did sexuality occupy the same place within socialist feminist discourse. The free-love slogans of anarchism were replaced by more traditional notions of women's 'natural' moral superiority, with all its connotations of hearth, home and virtuous motherhood.[33] The insights of the anarchist feminists had to wait half a century to be given theoretical substance and even longer to form the basis of a distinctive practice.

The recovery of this feminist current within the nineteenth-century anarchist movement indicates that there was greater diversity of feminist

discourse in Latin America than is commonly supposed. It also underlines the point that the individuals who make up a social movement
enter it from different social positions and therefore have specific needs
as well as, on occasion, conflicting interests. Women and men anarchists, though united in a common cause, entered politics from different
positions in the sexual and social divisions of labour. This shaped both
their experience and, in the case of women, their specific demands. The
tension between men's and women's needs in a political movement with
universal goals was clearly experienced by the editors of *La Voz de la
Mujer*, as it has been by their successors in different epochs and national
contexts.

Yet for all this, *La Voz* failed to universalise its feminist appeal.
Although it had its supporters among the women of Argentina's urban
centres, it could not sustain a readership of any size. This was not,
however, because its targets were misconceived or because it had
'imported' an alien and inappropriate vision from Europe. Women suffered as much in Argentina as in Spain or Italy from sexual exploitation,
the double standard and oppressive family situations that expressed
both the inequality and the power relations between the sexes. The
problem was rather that its message was expressed in terms too out-
rageous for the cultural context and for the times. Argentina may have
been a more secular society than many other countries in Latin America,
but most women, whether native or immigrant, would have been
scandalised by attacks on the Church and family and by the explicit
discussion of sexuality.[34] To many women, the family may have been
experienced as a site of oppression, but it was also a locus of relative
security in a rapidly changing world in which they had few alternatives.
The abolition of marriage without other radical changes in their position
would have left women even more exposed, resulting not in greater
freedom but in the loss of financial security and status in the eyes of the
community. *La Voz*, though a spirited intervention into an important
terrain, had limited appeal, primarily because it lacked a deeper concern
for the needs and beliefs of the women it sought to influence.

2
Mobilisation without Emancipation? Women's Interests, the State and Revolution in Nicaragua

> In Nicaragua, we cannot conduct a struggle of a Western feminist kind. This is alien to our reality. It doesn't make sense to separate the women's struggle from that of overcoming poverty, exploitation and reaction. We want to promote women's interests within the context of that wider struggle.
>
> Nora Astorga, *Comandante Guerrillera*[1]

The fall of Nicaraguan dictator Anastasio Somoza in July 1979 could not have been achieved without the mass urban insurrections which brought the capital, Managua, and other key cities under the increasing control of the revolutionary forces. This was the culmination of a process of growing popular opposition characterised by the incorporation of a wide cross-section of the population into political activity.

Large numbers of women from all social classes joined the youth and the urban poor who entered the realm of politics in the 1970s, many for the first time. Women's participation in the Nicaraguan Revolution was probably greater than in any other recent revolution with the exception of Vietnam. Women made up approximately 25 per cent of the Frente Sandinista de Liberación Nacional (FSLN) combat forces and, at its peak in 1979, the latter's women's organisation, the Association of Women Confronting the National Problem, or AMPRONAC, claimed over 8000 members.[2] Many more women who were not involved in organised politics provided vital logistical and back-up support to the revolutionary forces, and still others gave their support silently by refusing to denounce their revolutionary neighbours, or by hiding a fleeing combatant.[3]

The extent of women's participation in the struggle against Somoza has been regarded by many authors as an obvious enough response to the widespread repression and brutality of the regime on the one hand, and the appeal of the FSLN's vision and strategy, on the other.[4] The specific ways in which women became political subjects have not been the object of rigorous analysis, partly because women's extensive revolutionary activism is seen as the effect of the universalising character of the opposition to Somoza. In the words of one author, this process dissolved the specificity of political subjects in the generalised struggle against the dictatorship.[5] Put simply, all were united against the dictatorship, and differences of class, age and gender were transcended. It was this unity that accounted for the strength and ultimate success of the opposition movement.

However, much depends upon what is implied by subjects 'losing their specificity' and goals being universalised. For the universalisation of the goals of revolutionary subjects does not necessarily entail a loss of their specific identities, and it is certainly doubtful whether this can be said to have happened in the case of Nicaraguan women. As far as women were concerned, it would be difficult to argue that a loss of their gender identities occurred, except perhaps to a limited extent among the front line *guerrilleras* where a degree of masculinisation and a blurring of gender differences took place.[6] Rather, representations of women acquired new connotations, ones that *politicised* the social roles with which women are conventionally associated, but did not dissolve them.

The participation of women in political activity was certainly part of the wider process of popular mobilisation, but it was entered into from a distinctive social position to men, one crucially shaped by the sexual division of labour. Moreover, for different classes and groups of women, the meaning of political participation also differed, whether in the case of students, young middle-class women, or the women in the *barrios*.[7] For many poor women, entry into political life began with the earth-quake of 1972, when in the aftermath neighbourhood committees were organised to care for the victims, feed the dispossessed and tend the wounded. The anger that followed Somoza's misappropriation of the relief funds intensified as the brutal methods used to contain opposition escalated. Many women experienced their transition from relief workers to participants in the revolution as a natural extension, albeit in combative form, of their protective role in the family as providers and, crucially, as mothers. This transition to 'combative motherhood' was assisted by the political and ideological work of the radical clergy, the Sandinistas and by AMPRONAC, which linked these traditional identities to more general strategic objectives and celebrated women's role in the creation of a more just and humanitarian social order. The revolutionary appropriation of the symbol of motherhood was later institutionalised in the FSLN's canonisation of the 'Mothers of Heroes and Martyrs', a support group which became an active part of the Sandinistas' political base.[8]

However, if the revolution did not demand the dissolution of women's *identities,* it did require the subordination of their specific interests to the broader goals of overthrowing Somoza and establishing a new social order. This raises an important question, which lies at the heart of debates about the relationship between socialist revolution and women's emancipation. For if women surrender their specific interests in the universal struggle for a different society, at what point are these interests rehabilitated, legitimated and responded to by the revolutionary forces or by the new socialist state? Some feminist writing implies that they are never adequately reestablished and that this is why socialism failed to fulfil its promise to emancipate women. Such critics point out that not only did gender inequality still persist in these states, but also in some ways women could be considered to be worse off than they were under capitalism. Far from having been 'emancipated' as the official rhetoric sometimes claimed, women's workload increased in the absence of any redefinition of the relations between the sexes. To the traditional roles of housewife and mother were added those of full-time wage worker and political activist, in the absence of adequate childcare facilities. As one Soviet woman summed it up, 'If this is emancipation, then I'm against it.'[9]

The conventional explanations of these and other shortcomings – at least in the poorer states – in terms of resource scarcity, international pressure, underdevelopment or the 'weight of tradition', were therefore greeted with scepticism. A feminist writer expressed an emerging consensus when she wrote: 'if a country can eliminate the tsetse fly, it can get an equal number of men and women on its politburo'.[10] An even more negative view of the record of socialist states sees them as representing merely another form of patriarchal domination. It suggests that the 'revolutionary equality' commonly claimed as the experience of women and men freedom fighters in battle is replaced in the post-revolutionary period by the *status quo ante* with men in the positions of power. As the all-male leadership grows increasingly unconcerned about advancing women's interests, it appears that women's sacrifices in the struggle for a better society have gone unrewarded by those whom they helped to bring to power. Women, like the working class in another conception, appear to have been 'sold out' – only in this case not by a 'new bureaucratic bourgeoisie', but by a more pervasive and at the same time analytically elusive entity, 'the patriarchy'.

This chapter focuses on the Nicaraguan revolution and its progress after the seizure of state power by the Sandinistas in July 1979, in order to consider the proposition that women's interests are not served by socialist revolutions. It examines how women are affected by government policies in the aftermath of a successful revolutionary seizure of power in which they participated on a mass scale. The first part of the discussion reviews some of the theoretical questions raised by this debate, particularly the concept of 'women's interests'. The second section describes and interprets the policies that the revolutionary government adopted in relation to women in order to determine how women's interests were represented within the Sandinista state.[11] Women in Nicaragua certainly did not achieve equality, let alone emancipation. But the argument set forth here takes issue with the view that women's interests were denied representation or were deliberately marginalised through the operations of 'patriarchy'.[12]

Women's Interests

The concept of women's interests is central to feminist evaluations of socialist societies and, indeed, to social policies in general. Most feminist critiques of socialist regimes rest on an implicit or explicit assumption that there is a given entity, women's interests, that is ignored or overridden by policy-makers. However, the question of these interests is far more complex than is frequently assumed. As the problems of deploying any theory of interest in the analysis of post-revolutionary situations are considerable, the following discussion must be considered as an attempt to open up debate rather than to attain closure.

The political pertinence of the issue of whether states, revolutionary or otherwise, are successful in securing the interests of social groups and classes is generally considered to be twofold. First, it is supposed to enable prediction or at least political calculation about a given government's capacity to maintain the support of the groups it claims to represent. Second, it is assumed that the nature of the state can be deduced from the interests it is seen to be advancing.[13] Thus, the proposition that a state is a 'worker's state', a capitalist state or even a 'patriarchal state' is commonly tested by investigating how a particular class or group has fared under the government in question.

However, when we try to deploy similar criteria in the case of women a number of problems arise. If, for example, we conclude that because the Sandinistas seem to have done relatively little to remove the means by which gender subordination is reproduced, that women's interests have not been represented in the state and hence women are likely to turn against it, we are making a number of assumptions: that gender interests are the equivalent of women's interests, that gender is the principal determinant of women's interests and that women's subjectivity, real or potential, is structured uniquely through gender effects. It is, by extension, also supposed that women have certain common interests by virtue of their gender and that these interests are primary for women. It follows then that transclass unity among women is to some degree given by this commonality of interests.[14]

Although at a certain level of abstraction it can be said that women have some interests in common, there is no consensus over what these interests are or how they are to be formulated. This is in part because there is no theoretically adequate and universally applicable causal explanation of women's subordination from which a general account of women's interests can be derived. Women's oppression is recognised as being multicausal in origin and mediated through a variety of different structures, mechanisms and practices, which may vary considerably across space and time. There is, therefore, continuing debate over the appropriate site of feminist struggle and over whether it is more important to focus attempts at change on objective or subjective elements, 'men' or 'structures', laws, institutions or interpersonal power relations – or all of them simultaneously. Because a general conception of interests (one which has political validity) must be derived from a theory of how the subordination of a determinate social category is secured, it is difficult to see how it would overcome the two most salient and intractable features of women's oppression – its multicausal nature and the extreme variability of its forms of existence across class and nation. These factors vitiate attempts to speak without qualification of a unitary category 'women' with a set of already constituted interests common to it. A theory of interests that has an application to the debate about women's capacity to struggle for and benefit from social change must begin by recognising difference rather than by assuming homogeneity.

It is clear from the extensive feminist literature on women's oppression that a number of different conceptions prevail as to what women's interests are, and that these in turn rest, implicitly or explicitly, upon different theories of the causes of gender inequality. For the purpose of clarifying the issues discussed here, three conceptions of women's interests, which are frequently conflated, will be delineated. These are women's interests, strategic gender interests and practical gender interests.

Women's Interests

Although present in much political and theoretical discourse, the concept of women's interests is, for the reasons given earlier, a highly contentious one. Because women are positioned within their societies through a variety of different means – among them, class, ethnicity and gender – the interests they have as a group are similarly shaped in complex, and sometimes conflicting, ways. It is therefore difficult, if not impossible, to generalise about the 'interests of women'. Instead, we need to specify how the various categories of women might be affected differently and act differently on account of the particularities of their social positioning and their chosen identities. However, this is not to deny that women may have certain general interests in common. These can be called 'gender interests' to differentiate them from the false homogeneity imposed by the notion of women's interests.

Strategic Gender Interests

Gender interests are those that women (or men, for that matter) may develop by virtue of their social positioning through gender attributes. Gender interests can be either strategic or practical, each being derived in a different way and each involving differing implications for women's subjectivity. Strategic interests are derived in the first instance deductively, that is, from the analysis of women's subordination and from the formulation of an alternative, more satisfactory, set of arrangements to those which exist. These ethical and theoretical criteria assist in the formulation of strategic objectives to overcome women's subordination, such as the abolition of the sexual division of labour, the alleviation of the burden of domestic labour and childcare, the removal of institutionalised forms of discrimination, the attainment of political equality, the establishment of freedom of choice over childbearing and the adoption of adequate measures against male violence and control over women. These constitute what might be called strategic gender interests, and they are the ones most frequently considered by feminists to be women's 'real' interests. The demands that are formulated on this basis are usually termed 'feminist', as is the level of consciousness required to struggle effectively for them.[15]

Practical Gender Interests

Practical gender interests are given inductively and arise from the concrete conditions of women's positioning within the gender division of labour. In contrast to strategic gender interests, these are formulated by the women who are themselves within these positions rather than through external interventions. Practical interests are usually a response to an immediate perceived need, and they do not generally entail a strategic goal such as women's emancipation or gender equality. Analyses of female collective action frequently deploy this conception of interests to explain the dynamic and goals of women's participation in social action. For example, it has been argued that by virtue of their place within the sexual division of labour as those primarily responsible for their household's daily welfare, women have a special interest in domestic provision and public welfare.[16] When governments fail to provide these basic needs, women withdraw their support; when the livelihood of their families – especially their children – is threatened, it is women who form the phalanxes of bread rioters, demonstrators and petitioners. It is clear, however, from this example that gender and class are closely intertwined; it is, for obvious reasons, usually poor women who are so readily mobilised by economic necessity. Practical interests, therefore, cannot be assumed to be innocent of class effects. Moreover, these practical interests do not in themselves challenge the prevailing forms of gender subordination, even though they arise directly out of them. This is vital in understanding the policies of states or organisations and their capacity or failure to win the loyalty and support of women.

The pertinence of these ways of conceptualising interests for an understanding of what Kaplan calls 'women's consciousness' is a complex matter, but three initial points can be made. First, the relationship between what I have called strategic gender interests and women's recognition of them and desire to realise them cannot be assumed. Even the lowest common denominator of interests, which might seem uncontentious and of universal applicability (such as complete equality with men, control over reproduction and greater personal autonomy and independence from men), are not readily accepted by all women. This is not just because of 'false consciousness' as is frequently supposed – although this can be a factor – but because such changes realised in a piecemeal fashion could threaten the short-term practical interests of some women or entail a cost in the loss of forms of protection which are not then compensated for in some way. Thus, the formulation of strategic interests can only be effective as a form of intervention when full account is taken of these practical interests. Indeed, it is the politicisation of these practical interests and their transformation into strategic interests *that women can identify with and support* which constitutes a central aspect of feminist political practice.

Second, the way in which interests are formulated – whether by women or political organisations – will vary considerably across space and time and may be shaped in different ways by prevailing political and discursive influences. This is important to bear in mind when considering the limits and possibilities of cross-cultural solidarity. Finally, because women's interests are significantly broader than gender interests, and are shaped to a considerable degree by class factors, women's unity on gender issues cannot be assumed. Such unity has to be constructed, it is never given. Moreover, even when a consensus may exist, it is always conditional. The historical record suggests that unity is threatened by acute class conflict. It is also threatened by differences of race, ethnicity and nationality. It is, therefore, difficult to argue, as some feminists have done, that gender issues are primary for women, at all times.

This general problem of the conditionality of women's unity and the fact that gender issues are not necessarily primary is nowhere more clearly illustrated than by the example of revolutionary upheaval. In such situations, gender issues are frequently displaced by class conflict, principally because although women may suffer discrimination on the basis of gender and may be aware that they do, they nonetheless suffer differentially according to their social class. These differences crucially affect attitudes toward revolutionary change. This does not mean that because gender interests are an insufficient basis for unity among women in the context of class polarisation, they disappear. Rather, they become more specifically attached to, and defined by, social class.

An awareness of the complex issues involved serves to guard against any simple treatment of the question of whether a state is, or is not, acting in the interests of women, that is, whether all or any of these interests are represented within the state. Before any analysis can be attempted it is necessary to specify in what sense the term 'interest' is being deployed. A state may gain the support of women by satisfying either their immediate practical demands or certain class interests, or both. It may do this without advancing their strategic interests at all. However, the claims of such a state to be supporting women's emanci-pation could not be substantiated merely on the evidence that it maintained women's support on the basis of representing some of their more practical or class interests. With these distinctions in mind, I shall turn now to the Nicaraguan Revolution and consider how the Sandinistas have formulated women's interests, and how women fared under their rule.

The Nicaraguan Revolution

The Nicaraguan Revolution represents an extreme case of the problems of constructing a socialist society in the face of poverty and under-development, counterrevolution and external intervention. It could therefore be seen as an exceptional case and its usefulness as an example consequently limited. Yet while the Sandinistas faced a particularly severe constellation of negative circumstances, most socialist revolutions have encountered difficulties of a similar kind and even degree. One has only to think of the encirclement and internal disruption by enemy forces which the Bolsheviks faced after 1917; the conditions of dire scarcity which prevailed in post-revolutionary Mozambique, China or South Yemen; the blockade of poor nations such as Cuba; or the devastation through war wreaked on Vietnam, to realise that such conditions were more common than not in the attempts to build socialist societies.

Yet the fact that the Nicaraguan revolution shared certain circum-stances with the states referred to above does not imply that it belongs to the category of revolutions that these countries represent. They were, or became, for the most part avowedly communist in their political ideology and anti-capitalist in their economic practice, moving rapidly to place their main resources under state control. Most, too, aligned themselves directly with the Soviet Union or at least maintained a distance from the North Atlantic Treaty Organisation bloc of countries in their foreign affairs. All of them were one-party states in which dissent was allowed little, if any, free expression.

By contrast, the forces which overthrew Anastasio Somoza in July 1979 distinguished themselves by their commitment to a socialism based on the principles of mixed economy, non-alignment and political pluralism. An opposition was allowed to operate within certain clearly defined limits, and more than 60 per cent of the economy remained in private hands, despite the nationalisation of assets belonging to Somoza and his associates. 'Sandinismo' promised to produce a different kind of socialism, one that consolidated the revolutionary overthrow of the old regime through the creation of a new army and its control of other organs of state power, but was more democratic, independent and moderate than many other state socialisms had been. Through its triumph and its commitment to 'socialist pluralism', Nicaragua became a symbol of hope to socialists, not only in Latin America but around the world. It was, perhaps, this, as much as its 'communism', that accounted for the ferocity and determination of the Reagan administration's efforts to bring the process to an end.

The Nicaraguan Revolution also gave hope to those who supported women's liberation, for here too, the Sandinistas were full of promise. The revolution occurred in the period after the upsurge of the 'new feminism' of the late 1960s, at a time when Latin American women were mobilising around feminist demands in countries like Mexico, Peru and Brazil. The Sandinistas' awareness of the limitations of orthodox Marxism encouraged some to believe that a space would be allowed for the development of social movements such as feminism.

Some members of the leadership seemed aware of the importance of women's liberation and of the need for it in Nicaragua. Unlike many of its counterparts elsewhere, the FSLN, the revolutionary party, did not denounce feminism as a 'counter-revolutionary diversion', and some women officials had even gone on record expressing enthusiasm for its ideals. The early issues of *Somos AMNLAE*, one of two newspapers of the women's organisation, contained articles about feminist issues and addressed some of the ongoing debates within Western feminism.

In practical terms, too, there was promise. The FSLN had shown itself capable of mobilising many thousands of women in support of its struggle. It had done this partly through AMPRONAC, its women's organisation that combined a commitment to overthrow the Somoza regime with that of struggling for women's equality. Feminist observers noted the high level of participation of women in the ranks of the combat forces, epitomised in Dora María Tellez's role as Commander Two in the seizure of the Presidential Palace by the guerrillas in 1978, and they debated how the Sandinista commitment to women's equality would be realised if they triumphed.

Once they were in power, these hopes were not disappointed. Only weeks after the triumph, Article 30 of Decree no. 48 banned the media's exploitation of women as 'sex objects' and women FSLN cadres found themselves in senior positions in the newly established state as ministers, vice-ministers and regional coordinators of the party. In September, AMPRONAC was transformed into the Luisa Amanda Espinosa Association of Nicaraguan Women (AMNLAE) to advance the cause of women's emancipation and carry through the programme of revolutionary transformation. Public meetings were adorned with the slogan 'No revolution without women's emancipation: No emancipation without revolution'. The scene seemed to be set for an imaginative and distinctive strategy for women's emancipation in Nicaragua.

But after the first few years in power, the FSLN's image abroad began to lose some of its distinctive appeal. The combined pressures of economic scarcity, counter-revolution and military threat were taking their toll on the Sandinista experiment in economic and political pluralism, placing at risk the ideals it sought to defend. In the face of mounting pressure from US-backed counter-revolutionaries in 1982, a further casualty of these difficulties appeared to be the Sandinista commitment to the emancipation of women. AMNLAE, the women's union, reduced its public identification with 'feminism' and spoke increasingly of the need to promote women's interests in the context of the wider struggle. Already, at its Constitutive Assembly at the end of 1981, it had defined its role as enabling women to integrate themselves as a decisive force in the revolution. AMNLAE's first priority was given as 'defence of the revolution'. But it was only in 1982, as the crisis deepened and the country went on to a war footing, that the priority really did become (as it had to) the revolution's survival, with all efforts directed to military defence. AMNLAE became actively involved in recruiting women to the army and militia.

Under such circumstances it is hardly surprising that the efforts to promote women's emancipation were scaled down or redefined. Emancipation was to come about as a by-product of making and defending the revolution. Yet, even before the crisis deepened, little had been achieved to tangibly improve the position of women, and FSLN cadres considered that progress in this area was necessarily limited. In the first major speech on women's status since the overthrow, the minister of defence, Tomás Borge, acknowledged that although certain important advances had been made, 'all of us have to honestly admit that we haven't confronted the struggle for women's liberation with the same courage and decisiveness [as shown in the liberation struggle] ... From the point of view of daily exertion, women remain fundamentally in the same conditions as in the past.'[17] Was it the case then that women's specific interests had not been adequately represented in Sandinista policies?

Sandinista Policy

As a socialist organisation, the FSLN recognised women's oppression as something that had to be eliminated in the creation of a new society. The 1969 programme of the FSLN promised that 'the Sandinista people's

Revolution will abolish the odious discrimination that women have been subjected to compared with men' and 'will establish economic, political and cultural equality between women and men'. This commitment was enshrined a decade later within the *Estatuto Fundamental*, the embryonic constitution that proclaimed 'the unconditional equality of all Nicaraguans without distinction of race, nationality, creed or sex'. It went further in pledging the state to 'remove by all means available ... the obstacles to achieving it'. This provided the juridical context for future legislative and policy measures aimed at securing some of the conditions enabling this equality to be achieved.

Most modern states have enshrined within their constitutions or equivalents, some phrase which opposes discrimination on the grounds of race, sex or creed. As discussed further in Chapter 5, what distinguished socialist states such as Nicaragua was their recognition of the specificity of women's oppression and their support for measures that combined a concern to promote equality with a desire to remove some of the obstacles to achieving it. Some of the strategic interests of women were therefore recognised and, in theory, advanced as part of the process of socialist transformation. In its essentials, the FSLN's theoretical and practical approach to women's emancipation was influenced by Marxism and bears some resemblance to that found in the communist states. Its official literature linked gender oppression to class oppression and advanced the view that women's emancipation could only be achieved with the creation of a new socialist society and with the further development of the productive capacity of the economy. In the meantime, however, measures could be taken to alleviate the considerable inequalities between the sexes and begin the task of what the FSLN termed 'humanising life and improving the quality and content of human relations'.[18] This involved implementing the principles of the classic socialist guidelines for the emancipation of women.

Some of these principles were incorporated into AMNLAE's official programme, which listed its main goals as:

1. defending the revolution
2. promoting women's political and ideological awareness and advancing their social, political and economic participation in the revolution
3. combating legal and other institutional inequalities
4. encouraging women's cultural and technical advancement and entry into areas of employment traditionally reserved for men, combined with opposing discrimination in employment

5. fostering respect for domestic labour and organising childcare services for working women

6. creating and sustaining links of international solidarity

The 1969 programme of the FSLN also made special mention of eliminating prostitution and other 'social vices', helping the 'abandon-ed' working mother and protecting the illegitimate child. Each of these issues was addressed in subsequent legislation and social policy. As will be discussed in Chapter 3, there was also official concern for allowing greater freedom of choice to women in the matter of childbearing, by making contraceptives more widely available and by not prosecuting those who performed abortions, except in a few cases.

Although these goals, if realised, would be insufficient to achieve the complete 'emancipation of women', based as they are on a somewhat narrow definition of gender interests, they did embody some strategic concerns, in that they were directed toward eliminating some funda-mental sex inequalities. However, progress in Nicaragua was uneven. Despite official endorsement of the full programme, only some of the principles were translated into policy, and then only with limited effect. Employment opportunities in the formal sector were slightly expanded but remained restricted both in number and scope. Most Nicaraguan women continued to eke out a living as small traders, informal workers or domestic servants, remaining at the bottom of the income structure.[19] The socialisation of childcare and domestic labour affected only a minority of women: by mid-1984, 43 childcare centres were able to absorb around 4000 children, and further expansion was not envisaged because of mounting financial difficulties caused by the Contra War.[20] The reformed Provision Law, the *Ley de Alimentos*, passed by the Council of State at the end of 1982, aimed to establish a more democratic, egalitarian and mutually responsible family, but it was never ratified, and public discussion of the issues it raised all but ceased in 1983. The greatest benefits that women received were from the welfare programmes and from certain areas of legal reform. Women also felt the impact of change in the realm of political mobilisation in which they played an increasingly active part. Despite these advances it was evident that the gap between intention and realisation was considerable.

Beyond the fact that broader changes take time, there are three other considerations to be examined. The first concerns the practical limita-tions, which restricted the state's capacity for social transformation; the second involves factors of a general political kind; and the third concerns the nature of the policies themselves and the way in which the

Sandinistas' commitment to women's emancipation was formulated. All these issues have to be taken into account when assessing the position of women in post-revolutionary Nicaragua, for they help to explain why the social policy initiatives of the Sandinistas to improve the position of women were diluted and why the government on occasion adopted different priorities – which were sometimes at variance with the proclaimed goal of emancipating women.

The problems of material scarcity in an underdeveloped economy or the tolls of military threat do not require extensive discussion here. Details can be found elsewhere of the parlous state of the Nicaraguan economy, the ravages of war and natural disasters, the effect of the *contras* and US pressure and the size of the external debt. Most striking in all of this was the government's success in shielding the population from the effects of these difficulties throughout 1982 and much of 1983. However, the combined effects of material scarcity and the destabilisation efforts of internal and external forces limited the resources available, ones which had to satisfy not only the military requirements of the war, but which were also crucial for investment in long-term economic programmes, meeting short-term consumer needs and fulfilling popular expectations of expanded social services. It is not difficult to see how these factors reduced the scope of planning objectives, channelling scarce resources of both a financial and technical kind, as well as human potential, away from social programmes into national defence and economic development. By 1984 more than one-third of the national budget was being channelled into defence.

These two factors, scarcity and threat, partly explain the restrictions placed on the funding available for such projects as building and staffing nurseries and expanding female employment, and they go some way toward explaining why the 'emancipation of women', except within a rather narrow interpretation, was not considered a priority.

Even where the resource base existed, the government still faced problems of implementation in the form of political opposition to some of the proposed reforms. The Nicaraguan Revolution is a clear illustration of the truism that the acquisition of state power does not confer on governments absolute power either in formulation or implementation of policies, even when they might have widespread popular support. The overthrow of Salvador Allende in 1973 was a dramatic demonstration of the ever-present threat of counter-revolution and of the diversity of sites within the state and civil society through which it can be organised. The Sandinistas were in a stronger position internally than the government of Popular Unity in Chile, even if they faced a more determined threat from the United States and its allies in the region. They dismantled Somoza's repressive apparatus, replacing it with their own military and police forces, and established control over a number of state and government institutions. In the five years following the fall of Somoza, the revolutionary government also succeeded in consolidating its power base through the establishment of the 'mass organisations', the popular defence committees, the militia and the FSLN itself. Moreover, the opposition – both civilian and military – was unable to offer a credible alternative, in part because of its links to the United States and to the *Somocistas*.

Despite the strategic and political advantages that accrued to the Sandinistas as a result of these transformations of the state and of its institutions, they did not include the elimination of the opposition. The constitutional commitment to the principles of economic and political pluralism allowed a space, albeit a restricted one, from which opposition-al forces could operate. The FSLN attempted to maintain, as far as the situation permitted, a broad multiclass base of support. It tried to win over a sector of the capitalist class, and on the whole it also sought to maintain a conciliatory attitude toward its opponents, sometimes in the face of considerable provocation. The opposition therefore had the right to make its views heard and could organise to protect its interests, providing these did not jeopardise the government's overall survival or place the interests of the majority at risk. When these were considered threatened, the Sandinistas intervened. The state of emergency, declared in 1982, allowed the state to curb some of the opposition's activities and imposed censorship on the main opposition paper, *La Prensa*. By inter-national standards, these moves were moderate, especially given the conditions of war that increasingly prevailed after 1983. Moreover, the government lifted the state of emergency to allow for the preparations for the late 1984 elections, and the opposition was encouraged to contest them.

The commitment to allow dissent and opposition parties and press represents an important principle of socialist democracy. Too many socialist countries have interpreted socialism as merely the socialisation of the economy and failed to implement the other side of the equation – the democratisation of political power. In this, the Sandinistas tried harder than most. However, as with most attempts at compromise, there was a price. The commitment to 'pluralism' and to maintaining the support or at least neutrality of the capitalist class had as one of its necessary effects the imposition of certain limits on the transformative capacity of the state in some areas of policy. This was especially clear with regard to the government's programme to improve the position of women.

The maintenance of a sizeable private sector (78 per cent of industry, 60 per cent of commerce, 76 per cent of agriculture) and the granting of a measure of autonomy to it allowed some employers, especially in the smaller non-unionised enterprises, to evade legislation designed to protect and improve the working conditions of women, as well as to pursue discriminatory employment policies. There are many other examples of this kind. But perhaps the most powerful ideological force and that which offered the most sustained resistance to Sandinista reforms was the conservative wing of the Catholic Church. Its extensive institutional presence, forms of organisation, access to the media (it had its own radio station) and base within a substantial section of the population made it a formidable opponent. Its impact on slowing reform in the areas directly concerned with women was considerable. Conservative clergy actively opposed educational and family reforms, enforced bans on weekend work (which made it difficult for voluntary labour schemes to achieve much), opposed the conscription of women and were strong advocates of traditional family life and the division of labour which characterises it.[21] The conservative Church also opposed divorce reform and urged adherence to the papal encyclical stating that it is sinful to employ 'unnatural' methods of birth control. As will be discussed in the following chapter, it also opposed the legalisation of abortion.

What was therefore a positive feature of the Sandinista Revolution – its active civil society – did have the effect of diluting policy measures and weakening the government's capacity for implementation. It is therefore erroneous to imagine that just because a state might have a coherent set of policies and a unifying ideology that it has the capacity to be fully effective in social policy terms. It should be clear that the most favoured solution historically is problematic to say the least: the subjugation of the opposition and the strengthening of the state.

A second and related political factor, crucial to the success or failure of government policies, was that of the population's degree of support for, or resistance to, the policies. As far as changes in the position of women were concerned, the Sandinistas were limited in what they could do both by the conservative influence of the Catholic Church and by the relatively small social base of support for feminism. There was no history of an effective, popular and militant feminism in Nicaragua (as there had been in Cuba, for example), with the result that the Sandinistas had to contend with deeply entrenched *machista* attitudes and considerable hostility among much of the population to the idea of women's emancipation.

Nevertheless, the revolutionary war provided the initial context for the weakening of the traditional stereotypes and conventions, and it was on this basis that the Sandinistas began to build popular support for AMNLAE's campaigns. These tended to be successful when sufficient time and energy was devoted to explaining the objectives and learning from the women's responses – that is, creating and reproducing an organic link between the organisation and the people it was representing, a process which amounted to synthesising the practical and strategic aspects of women's interests. Yet, as we shall see shortly, the campaigns suffered from a number of limitations, including the fact that they were directed mostly at women and did not seek to make radical changes in men's attitudes and behaviour. As the pressure of the war mounted, AMNLAE was forced to abandon some of its more feminist campaigns for fear that they would alienate popular support.

It is in this context that discussion of the third factor that accounts for the limitations of the Sandinista record on women is relevant – that of their conception of the place of women's emancipation within the overall context of their priorities. Chapter 5 discusses some of the broader issues of socialist policies aimed at women and much of that analysis helps to explain Sandinista thinking on this issue. It is clear that the FSLN was able to implement only those parts of the programme for women's emancipation that coincided with its general goals, enjoyed popular support and could be realised without arousing strong opposition. The policies from which women derived some benefit were pursued principally because they fulfilled some wider goal or goals, whether these were social welfare, development, social equality or political mobilisation in defence of the revolution. At the same time the political mobilisation of women supposed some attempt to persuade them that their interests, as well as more universal concerns (national, humanitarian and so on), were represented by the state and did not require autonomous representation from below.[22] This is, in effect, what the Sandinistas meant by the need to locate women's emancipation within the overall struggle for social reform and survival against intensifying external pressure.

Although these considerations were shared by most socialist states, the peculiar circumstances of the Nicaraguan Revolution determined the relative emphasis placed on these policy objectives as well as the state's capacity to implement them. For example, in Nicaragua there was no absolute shortage of labour, nor was production greatly expanded. There was, therefore, no urgent requirement for women to enter employment despite some expansion in state sector demand. Initially, women were called upon to supply a considerable amount of voluntary labour as health workers and teachers in the popular campaigns (health in 1981, literacy in 1982). But there was no strong material incentive to provide childcare while the economy did not depend upon a mass influx of female labour. Moreover, because most women worked in the informal sector it was assumed that these jobs were compatible with their domestic responsibilities. This situation would only change in the event of a significant escalation of military activities, necessitating the entry of women into jobs vacated by men serving in the armed forces.[23]

As noted earlier, the emphasis of the government was on two other strategies, that of political mobilisation and legal reform. The new laws regarding the family were designed to strengthen the institution, promote greater family cohesion and remove the gender inequalities that prevailed. The high rate of male desertion, migrancy and serial polygamy left large numbers of women as the sole providers for their children: 34 per cent of Nicaraguan households were female headed – in Managua, it was 60 per cent – a factor which contributed directly to the high incidence of female poverty.[24] The new Provision Law made all adult members of the family, on a three-generation basis, legally liable for maintaining the family unit which included taking a share in the household tasks. In addition to these changes, the health and safety provisions for women workers were improved while new legislation gave rural women workers an entitlement to their own wages to redress a situation in which a family wage was usually paid to the male head of the household.[25]

As far as the political mobilisation of women was concerned, by 1984 there were more women mobilised than at any time since the months leading up to the overthrow. AMNLAE claimed a card-carrying membership of 85 000, and women made up 22 per cent of FSLN membership and more than one-third, or 37 per cent, of the leadership.[26] Women's participation in the other mass organisations and in the organs of popular defence also expanded with the deepening of the crisis. Approximately half of the members of the Sandinista Defence Committees, a type of neighbourhood association, were women, and women made up a similar proportion of the militia. These, then, were the areas in which the greatest advances were registered in relation to achieving policy objectives which concerned women. Yet more women benefited, and benefited more, from the implementation of measures designed to secure general objectives. Chief among these was welfare.

A detailed analysis of the impact of Sandinista social policies is beyond the scope of this chapter.[27] Instead, I will briefly summarise some of the relevant conclusions by considering the effects of the reforms in terms of the three categories of interest referred to earlier. If we disaggregate women's interests and consider how different categories of women fared in the first five years of the revolution, it is clear that the majority of women in Nicaragua were positively affected by the government's redistribution policies. This is so even though fundamental structures of gender inequality were not dismantled. In keeping with the socialist character of the government, policies were targeted in favour of the poorest sections of the population and focused on basic needs provision in the areas of health, housing, education and food subsidies. In the short span of just five years, the Sandinistas reduced the illiteracy rate from over 50 per cent to 13 per cent, doubled the number of educational establishments, increased school enrolment, eradicated a number of mortal diseases, provided the population with basic health-care services, and achieved more in their housing programme than Somoza had in his entire period of rule. In addition, the Land Reform cancelled peasants' debts and gave thousands of rural workers their own parcels of land or secured them stable jobs on the state farms and cooperatives.[28]

These policies were important in gaining the support of poor women. According to government statistics, women formed more than 60 per cent of the poorest Nicaraguans; in the poorest category in Managua (incomes of less than 600 cordobas per month), there were 354 women for each 100 men.[29] It was these women, by virtue of their *class* position, who were the direct beneficiaries of Sandinista redistributive efforts, along with their male counterparts. Of course, not all women were to benefit from these programmes; women whose economic interests lay in areas adversely affected by Sandinista economic policies (imports, luxury goods, and so on) suffered financial loss, as did most women from the privileged classes as a result of higher taxation. It was also the case that while poor women benefited from the welfare provisions, they were also the most vulnerable to the pressures of economic constraints and especially to shortages in basic provisions.[30]

In terms of *practical* gender interests, these redistributive policies also had gender, as well as class, effects. By virtue of their place within the sexual division of labour, women were disproportionately responsible for childcare and family health, and they were particularly concerned with housing and food provision. The policy measures directed at alleviating the situation in these areas had, not surprisingly, elicited a positive response from the women affected by them, as borne out by the available research into the popularity of the government. Many of the campaigns mounted by AMNLAE were directed at resolving some of the practical problems women faced, as exemplified by its mother and child health-care programme or by its campaign aimed at encouraging women to conserve domestic resources to make the family income stretch further and thus avoid pressure building up over wage demands or shortages.[31] A feature of this kind of campaign was its recognition of women's practical interests, but, in accepting the division of labour and women's subordination within it, it could entail a denial of their strategic interests.

With respect to strategic interests, the acid test of whether 'women's emancipation' *was* on the political agenda or not, modest but significant progress was made. Legal reform, especially in the area of the family, confronted the issues of relations between the sexes and of male privilege by attempting to end a situation in which most men were able to evade responsibility for the welfare of their families, and make them liable for a contribution paid in cash, in kind or in the form of services. This also enabled the issue of domestic labour to be politicised in the discussions of the need to share this work equally among all members of the family. The Land Reform encouraged women's participation and leadership in cooperatives and gave women wages for their work and titles to land. There was also an effort to establish childcare agencies such as nurseries and preschool services. Some attempts were made to challenge female stereotypes, not just by outlawing the exploitation of women in the media but also by promoting some women to senior positions and emphasising the importance of women in the militia and reserve battalions.[32] And finally, there was a sustained effort to mobilise women around their own needs through the women's organisation, AMNLAE, along with discussion of some of the questions of strategic interest, although this was sporadic and controversial.

To sum up, it is difficult to discuss socialist revolutions in terms of an undifferentiated conception of women's interests and even more dif-ficult to conclude that these interests were not represented in state policy-making. The Sandinista record on women was certainly uneven. Nonetheless, it is clear that the Sandinistas went further than most Latin American governments in recognising both the strategic and practical interests of women and sought to bring about substantial improvements in the lives of many of the most deprived. When AMNLAE stated that its priority was 'defence of the Revolution', because the latter provided the necessary conditions for realising a programme for women's emancipation, it was, in certain respects and with some qualifications, correct.

Yet these qualifications nonetheless remain important and have a significance which goes beyond the Sandinista Revolution to the wider question of the historic relationship between socialism and feminism. Three of these issues can be listed here in summary form. The first is that what we have called strategic gender interests – although recognised in the official theory and programme of women's emancipation – remained narrowly defined, based on the privileging of economic criteria. Feminist theories of sexual oppression or the critique of the family or of male power had little impact on official thinking and, indeed, were sometimes suppressed as being too radical and too threatening to popular solidarity.[33] Yet Nicaraguan activists recognised that there was a need for greater discussion and debate around these questions both among the people and within the organs of political power, so that the issue of what would constitute the conditions for women's emancipation could remain alive and open, and did not become entombed within official doctrine.

The second issue concerns the relationship established by planners between the goal of women's emancipation and other goals, such as economic development, which had priority. It is not the linkage itself that constitutes the problem – principles like social equality and women's emancipation can only be realised within determinate conditions of existence. So linking the policies on women to these wider goals need not necessarily be a cause for concern, because these wider goals may indeed constitute the preconditions for realising the principles. The question is, rather, the nature of the link. Are gender interests *articulated into* a wider strategy of economic development (for example), or are they irretrievably *subordinated to it?* In the first case we would expect gender interests to be recognised as being specific and irreducible, and requiring something more for their realisation than is generally provided for in the pursuit of the wider goals. Thus, when it is not possible to pursue a full programme for women's emancipation this can be explained and debated. The goal can be left on the agenda, and every effort made to pursue it within the existing constraints. In the latter case, the specificity of gender interests is likely to be denied or its overall importance minimised. The issues are trivialised or buried; the policies on women are conceived in terms of how functional they are for achieving the wider goals of the state.

And this raises the third general issue, which is that of political guarantees. For if gender interests are to be realised only within the context of wider considerations, it is essential that the political institutions charged with representing these interests have the means to prevent their being submerged altogether, and action on them being indefinitely postponed. Women's organisations, the official representatives of women's interests, cannot conform to Lenin's conception of mass organisations as mere transmission belts of the party. Rather, they must have independence and exercise power and influence over party policy, albeit within certain constraints. In other words, the issue of gender interests and their means of representation cannot be resolved in the absence of a discussion of socialist democracy; it is a question therefore not just of *what* interests are represented in the state, but ultimately and critically of *how* they are represented.

3

The Politics of Abortion in Nicaragua: Revolutionary Pragmatism – or Feminism in the Realm of Necessity?

Abortion is an incredibly complex subject here. This is a Catholic country, and we all know the position of the Church on abortion. It has always been condemned here as a criminal act except where the woman is clearly at risk. Most abortions are illegal and are done by unqualified people. The result is often haemorrhage and infection ... Peasant women have a historical role and that's having children. They see abortion as murder. For them, God sends children and you have to have them – seven, eight or ten children. City women are different: they're more involved in defence and production and see that a lot of children can be 'a problem' for them, a limitation. So they use contraception and, if necessary, abortion ... But it's being discussed all over the place – it's a big issue now.

Susana Veraquas, Natural Childbirth Centre, Esteli, 1987.[1]

One way of depleting our youth is to promote the sterilisation of women in Nicaragua ... or to promote a policy of abortion.

President Daniel Ortega, 1987.[2]

Nicaragua was an anomaly among socialist states.[3] Its comparatively advanced record on general political issues – pluralism, democracy, abolition of the death penalty – contrasted with a surprisingly conservative position on reproductive rights.[4] After coming to power in 1979 Nicaragua's revolutionary government pledged itself to women's emancipation and implemented a range of policies and legal reforms designed to establish greater equality between the sexes. However, it did not legalise abortion, and nor did it amend the pre-revolutionary *Somocista* codes. Abortion was declared illegal under the Criminal Code of 1974, and, while 'therapeutic' terminations could be obtained, the grounds had to be of a strictly medical nature. Worse still, under this legislation the woman herself could not request permission: the request had to originate from her spouse or next of kin, who was in addition required to give formal permission. Requests for abortion had to be considered by a three-member medical panel: its members were, in the normal course of events, men.

In 1988, nearly a decade after the triumph of the revolution, the options open to the majority of Nicaraguan women who wanted an abortion were the same as they had been under the Somoza dictatorship: these were limited to self-abortion or to seeking out illegal practitioners. Both courses of action were dangerous and the latter was expensive, costing the equivalent of five months' wages for an average (urban) woman worker. Most backstreet abortions were performed in squalid and dangerous conditions; but even for those women who could afford a safer termination, the risks were high. Illegal practitioners have inadequate facilities and cannot usually maintain the necessary standards of hygiene. Nicaragua's acute shortage of medical goods – equipment, drugs and sterilising fluids – compounded the risks. Even in hospitals, due to acute resource scarcity, operations such as caesareans and hysterectomies were on occasion performed without anaesthesia.[5]

The social and medical costs of such legislation were high, to say nothing of the toll in human misery. Nicaragua had a high maternal death rate, 3 per 1000 compared with 0.5 per 1000 in most developed countries. Many of these deaths were due to improperly performed abortions. These were estimated to account for some 60 per cent of admissions into the main women's hospital in Managua. Research carried out between March 1983 and June 1985 found that 8752 women were admitted to this hospital with complications arising from abortions, equivalent to an average of ten women every day. In the sample group 10 per cent died and 26 per cent required hysterectomies, of whom 16 per cent had not yet had children. According to one doctor, it was likely for a variety of economic, social and demographic reasons that the abortion rate had gone up since the revolution rather than down.[6]

How, then, did the Sandinistas reconcile their support for women's emancipation with facts such as these? An answer to this question, inevitably tentative as it must be, can help illuminate not only some of the paradoxes of the Nicaraguan Revolution, but also some of the political difficulties encountered by a certain radical feminist position on reproductive rights. Some feminists have argued, for example, that abortion is '*the* feminist issue of our times' and have proceeded to judge both women's movements in certain countries and government legislation in terms of this criterion. Yet the Nicaraguan case allowed for no easy conclusions in this regard and may be said to have sensitised those who followed the fortunes of its revolution to the complexities of the issue. Precisely because of the central place of the abortion issue in relations of gender power, campaigns in support of it have met deeply entrenched resistance. An abstract proclamation of women's rights had to be matched by a concrete attainment of the conditions, both political and subjective, for the implementation and vigilant defence of those rights. This proved as true in Europe and the United States as in Nicaragua.

Sandinista Policy

In the years following the overthrow of the Somoza dictatorship, the Sandinistas made a considerable effort to promote improvements in women's socioeconomic position: as noted in Chapter 2, women saw an extension of their rights within the family and in the workplace through legal reform; they became more involved in the political life of the country than ever before; and they were encouraged to participate in the defence and development efforts, entering various kinds of economic activity in large numbers.[7] Despite these advances, however, the majority of women still lacked the means to control their fertility safely, and the termination of unwanted pregnancies was always regarded as a problem for which there existed no clear policy solution.

From 1979 there were a variety of shifts in official thinking about the related issues of abortion and women's rights. Each change in legislation directed at improving the social and legal position of women aroused considerable, sometimes stormy, public debate. Over these years, the FSLN devoted an increasing amount of time and energy to debating women's issues within the party itself. This was despite the parlous economic situation and the ever present and deepening effects of the Contra War. Yet, as far as abortion was concerned, the party had yet to clarify its position, even though it appeared to be broadly in favour of some change in the law and in health provisions.

Some members of the leadership at times publicly acknowledged support for women's right to reproductive self-determination. In 1982 the then Minister of Health, Lea Guido (subsequently head of the women's organisation AMNLAE),[8] explained the FSLN position thus: 'While we don't have a problem of over-population (far from it), abortion and contraception are a human right. We want to make these available, but since there is opposition to it, we must be careful how we proceed.'[9] Doris Tijerino, who won the status of *comandante* through her role in the struggle against Somoza, and was acting Chief of Police, adopted a similar position:

> I am for abortion – not just as a woman, but also as a police officer. The current law restricts the civil rights of the woman by denying her the right to freely determine maternity. But this law should not just be changed by decree. Discussion and education must first take place among the broad masses of women.[10]

At the same time, however, research carried out into the abortion issue by the Women's Office of the National Directorate concluded: 'The studies show quite clearly that penalising abortion has negative effects on women's health, raises maternal mortality and hospital costs and contradicts state policies aimed at improving health conditions.'[11]

The organised opposition to legalising abortion came largely from the hierarchy of the Catholic Church and from the political parties and groups to the right of the FSLN. However, many Catholic supporters of the Sandinistas and some members of the party were themselves reluctant on religious grounds to endorse abortion, and some opposed it. Many radical priests and nuns, adherents of the 'theology of liberation', even found contraception a difficult issue, advocating at most the 'scientific rhythm method', that is, the use of charts in an effort to identify the so-called 'safe' period.[12] Popular attitudes among both men and women towards abortion show the influence of Catholicism, which retains considerable institutionalised power within Nicaragua. The situation in Nicaragua was not analogous to that in socialist Cuba, a Caribbean island, where for a variety of historical reasons Catholicism did not have a significant hold over the population at the time of the revolution. Abortion is legal there, and available virtually on demand and at negligible cost. Cuba shares with the United States and Uruguay the most liberal position in the Americas on abortion. Nicaragua remained, by contrast, even less liberal than that of a number of other Latin American states, including neighbouring Honduras and Costa Rica, as well as Bolivia and Venezuela, all of which allowed abortion on social as well as medical grounds.

The FSLN, itself divided over the issue and fearful of a political backlash organised on religious grounds, therefore chose to pursue a cautious policy with respect to women's reproductive rights. This entailed leaving the old law intact for the time being, while trying to alleviate its effects in three main ways. First, the FSLN ensured that nobody was prosecuted for having or performing illegal abortions, unless gross violations of medical practice were brought to the attention of the authorities. Second, efforts were made to ensure that contraceptives were more widely available than hitherto – both through medical and market outlets. Third, a sex education programme was set in train to increase public awareness of the 'facts of life' and, in theory, to prevent unwanted pregnancies. This policy was adopted in 1985, when a commission funded by the United Nations agreed to promote a national programme of sex education aimed largely at teachers and young people as a means of curbing the high female drop-out rates in schools. Despite the good intentions behind them, such measures did little to increase the realm of real freedom available to Nicaraguan women. An anomalous situation of semi-legality with regard to abortion may be preferable to repressive controls in the absence of any alternative, but at the same time it hinders controls of genuine abuses and stalls the adoption of state-led initiatives to provide safe methods of terminating pregnancies (among them the vacuum method).

As far as reducing the necessity for terminations through more widespread use of fertility control is concerned, this too met with limited success. Nicaragua had a very low rate of contraceptive usage and availability. In 1983 only 9 per cent of the relevant section of the population was estimated to be using prophylactics – chiefly IUDs and the contraceptive pill.[13] Contraception was regarded as almost exclusively women's responsibility and there was very little uptake of condoms, which Latin American men tend to see as emasculating. Overall, the availability of contraceptives remained too restricted to constitute a reliable form of fertility control, and supplies (all of which had to be imported) became even scarcer from 1985 as a result of growing economic difficulties. There existed, in addition to these practical questions of supply, the problems of widespread ignorance of how to use contraceptive methods, real and imagined fears about their effects and, especially important in Nicaragua, men's resistance to fertility control of any kind. The cults of machismo and *hombría* (manliness) place considerable store on being able to father large numbers of children, biologically if not socially. At the same time, women who use contraceptives are suspected of infidelity, and often have to resort to secrecy. The Church, too, weighs in with its admonitions against contraceptives, which are frequently equated with immoral behaviour. Zealous clerics have not been above refusing confession to women if they have had IUDs fitted or are on the pill. Sex and reproduction thus remained bound together by belief and necessity. Contraceptive use and fertility control were thus indissolubly linked to power relations between the sexes and to the ideological control of religion, neither of which could be addressed if the problem was defined simply as one of supply.

The Sandinistas placed their hopes on sex education to change the attitudes and behaviour of men and women. While it was a welcome initiative in that it addressed at least some of the problems, it proved to be a highly charged issue. One example will suffice: a biweekly series called *Sex and Youth,* which was shown on national television. The twelve programmes took up a wide range of sensitive issues including sexually transmitted diseases, birth control, homosexuality (male and female), abortion and masturbation. The series caused something of a furore. Criticism came from a variety of quarters, with the material being accused among other things of being 'too realistic'. As a result, a three-man review committee was established and some of the programmes were duly censored. Among these was a discussion of female masturbation and a scene showing childbirth – one of the censors apparently fainted at the showing of the latter. The programme was eventually rescheduled from a daytime slot to late at night, when few people would be able to watch it. As these responses showed, Catholic attitudes helped to keep Nicaragua a socially conservative country and the government would have had to allocate substantial resources, time and energy to fund and sustain such campaigns directed at altering public attitudes.

Inadequate though these measures were, they at least responded to some of the problems and represented some inroads into a difficult area of reform. Doubtless too, they would have been more effective in a country which had not had its economy destroyed and its human resources depleted by the US-backed Contra War. They also have to be seen in their internal political context. In essence, they represented a compromise on the part of the Sandinista government not only with Catholic sensibilities but also with members of the growing feminist lobby,[14] which developed within and around the women's organisation, AMNLAE. This latter comprised legal advisers, educationalists, health workers, journalists and activists among others, whose position gathered strength in 1984. This was an important year, one in which the popularity of the Sandinista government was put to the test in the free elections of November. The preparation for this event, and analysis of its aftermath, made party activists more aware of, and take more seriously, the hopes and aspirations of different sections of the population.

Where did all this leave abortion? The situation had apparently not worsened, but nor had it improved. At the official level there continued to be concern about the problem, with no clear commitment to reform even on the part of the reorganised women's movement. In July 1987 Silvia McEwan, one of the members of AMNLAE's new National Directorate, explained where things stood:

> Abortion is a serious social problem and merits a profound analysis to help formulate a law which will both benefit woman and respect her dignity as a mother. AMNLAE has not taken a position with respect to abortion, but it considers that there now exist the conditions to have a wide discussion about it.[22]

In September 1987 at a 'face the people' meeting called to mark the tenth anniversary of the founding of AMNLAE, more than a thousand women gathered to meet President Ortega and the Minister of Health, Dora María Téllez. Among the issues that were raised from the floor were sterilisation, birth control and abortion. A worker at a shoe factory reminded the leadership that for many women workers sterilisation was just as important an issue as abortion. She complained that not only were sterilisations very difficult to get, but that they even required the husband's permission. To prolonged applause from the meeting she asked, 'Are we our husband's property?', and went on to propose that women with three or more children should have an automatic right to sterilisation without 'consulting anybody'. The Minister of Health promised to do something immediately about the requirement of husbands' authorisation. Another delegate said she wanted to raise a problem that was regarded as a 'touchy issue' and one which was often labelled as a 'petty bourgeois concern', namely abortion. She noted that the government was prepared to take on *other* 'difficult issues' such as confiscating property through land reform; as for the supposed class character of the issue, abortion was in fact a more serious problem for the poor because they suffered most from the consequences of illegality.

In their concluding speeches to the gathering, the President and the Minister of Health indicated that they saw the issues in rather different terms. Téllez said she thought the solution was 'not to defend the right to abortion, but to prevent abortions'. This was being tackled by simultaneously improving the availability of birth control devices and by maintaining public education campaigns. For his part, President Ortega reportedly caused concern in the audience with his remarks on sterilisation and abortion. These issues, he said, had to be seen in the context of US government policy towards colonial and semi-colonial countries. Rather than carry out a just distribution of wealth, US policy had been to 'freeze the population growth in these countries, to avoid the risk of an increase in the population that could threaten a revolutionary change'. Nicaragua, he argued, had a small population and was subject 'to a policy of genocide' through the US-sponsored Contra War: 'The ones fighting in the front lines against this aggression are grown men': 'One way of depleting our youth is to promote the sterilisation of women in Nicaragua ... or to promote a policy of abortion ... the problem is that the woman is the one who reproduces. The man can't play that role.' He said that some women, 'aspiring to be liberated', decide not to bear children. Such a woman 'negates her own continuity, the continuity of the human species'.[23]

Whether or not this was representative of FSLN opinion, Ortega's speech nonetheless sent a wave of disapproval through feminist circles in both Nicaragua and beyond. Ortega was a man who lived the war every day, and his remarks reflected a pragmatic, political attitude towards what he saw, above all, as an issue of national interest. Yet there was a suggestion of moralism in his formulations in the implication that women were passive bystanders in the revolutionary process and must therefore discharge their debt to the nation by having babies. The implicit denial of women's place in the world of men, a common cultural trope in Latin America, was at odds with Nicaragua's policies promoting gender equality, and women's public roles in the defence of the nation and in employment. What annoyed many women was the fact that Ortega saw fit to use the authority and discourse of the revolution and the war against the *contras* to attack and demobilise the campaigners and supporters of women's reproductive choice.

Inconsistencies in the speech were also noted: in particular that it was delivered in happier times, when peace not war seemed to be on the agenda, amidst the autumn euphoria of the Central American Peace Accord. This was seen by FSLN leaders and newspapers as heralding the ebbing, if not the ending, of the war. However, many in the FSLN viewed the problems of peace as possibly even more insuperable than the problems of war. Bayardo Arce, a member of the National Directorate, expressed the disquiet thus: 'Peace may have other costs. We are facing an emotional and provocative mood on the right in this country ... We must prepare for the political struggle, which will become more intense when we achieve peace.'[24] Such fears were well-founded with respect to the political fortunes of the FSLN; and peace, although deeply desired, could have certain negative implications for the women of Nicaragua.

The advent of peace to the region would entail two immediate consequences for women. First, an estimated 70 000 soldiers would return from the armed forces and expect jobs – in many cases ones which women in their thousands had occupied for the duration of the Contra War. Second, the sense of social and political solidarity that typifies nations at war would be prone to weakening during peacetime, with an attendant rise in social and political tensions. In such circumstances governments are forced to compromise with the opposition, and in Nicaragua the Catholic hierarchy was a powerful, cynical and intransigent force to bargain with. It might be considered that peace, in the short term at least, could adversely affect the prospects for progress in the more difficult areas of reproductive rights such as abortion or sterilisation.

Sandinista Reservations

The case against establishing full reproductive rights from within the FSLN drew on three main arguments: that, as Ortega expressed it, Nicaragua was underpopulated and suffered from a labour shortage; that 'the people' were against any change on religious grounds; and that the issue was itself so explosive that to tackle it would lend support to the opposition. There was some validity to each of these arguments but the issues were far from clear-cut and nor did they necessarily justify the legal *status quo*.

The population issue was an especially sensitive one within developing countries, many of whose governments felt that the problem of underdevelopment was largely externally generated by imperialism and that the issue of population growth was merely a diversion, something confected by the advanced capitalist countries to obscure the underlying causes of global power imbalances. This view changed over subsequent years, and many developing countries – China, most notably – saw the benefits of lower rates of population growth and changed their policies accordingly. However, intervention by foreign agencies through population control measures especially directed at indigenous people has a long and bitter history in Latin America and Ortega's emotive remarks on 'genocide' would have been well-understood by his audience.[25] From a Latin American feminist perspective these are difficult questions to deal with, but the issue becomes less one of why fertility control should be encouraged than how, and by what means, and with what degree of choice, this control can come about.

As far as the population issue was concerned, Nicaragua did have a lower population density than its neighbouring states. This was compounded by the heavy losses it suffered both in the struggle to overthrow Somoza and in the US-backed Contra War. An estimated 50 000 died in the former and 40 000 from both sides in the latter, in a country with a population of around only 3 million. However, whether there was, as a result, a shortage of labour and of population was a matter best decided by economists and demographers and, even then, these matters remained open to interpretation. If shortages existed, they had to be dealt with by adopting a variety of different strategies. Within the range of planning options available, limiting women's access to safe abortions, or even to voluntary sterilisations, came rather low on the list and certainly could not remedy the immediate problem of labour shortages.

At least two factors were seen as mitigating any scarcity in the short term. Peace, or a significant reduction in *contra* forces, would release many of the people in the army for other work, while at the same time, Nicaragua would regain access to labour reserves elsewhere in the region, from which the country had drawn in the past, especially for its seasonal labour. In the longer term, leaving aside the question of change in Nicaragua's demand for labour through technological innovations, the problem of labour shortages could be offset by its high rates of natural reproduction. Nicaragua had one of the highest birth rates in the world, with a total fertility rate of 6.3 and a natural rate of population growth of 3 per cent per annum.[26] It could, therefore, be expected over time to make up such absolute deficiencies as may have existed. Indeed, if the population issue was paramount then it could reasonably be argued that the unsafe abortions carried out, leading to involuntary sterility, premature subsequent births and spontaneous abortions, illness and death, were themselves a brake on Nicaragua's natural birth rate.

If, as Ortega argued, the military threat continued and pro-natalist policies were indeed the only answer to the problem of labour supply, this could not constitute an argument against extending the realm of women's choice in matters concerning reproduction. As many FSLN members themselves believed, it was not as if the moral claims of labour supply planning should, even if valid, have prevailed over those of women's health. Pro-natalist policies could, in any case, be pursued with some degree of sensitivity to women's needs and preferences. As some other developing countries had found, pro-natalist policies could coincide with extending reproductive rights to women. The adoption of spaced birth policies, which aim to maintain high birth rates but make it possible for women to plan their fertility by leaving a few years between pregnancies, had been shown to have positive health effects for both women and children, reducing maternal and child morbidity and mortality. Such programmes depend upon an acceptance of the principle of providing access to fertility control including, if necessary, abortion for social as well as medical reasons. It was evident that if reform in the law was to occur at all, health arguments such as these would occupy a critical place in the debate.

The second and third arguments concerning 'popular' opposition and the threat of a political backlash carried more weight, although they were less amenable to empirical investigation, let alone practical resolution. They were of course linked; if the people were against any change on religious grounds, then the issue was likely to be explosive and any substantial change to the laws would be used to political advantage by the opposition. In Nicaragua as in Ireland, long a redoubt of conservative clergy, the organised power and cultural hegemony of Catholicism was an effective opponent of reform because of its resonance within the population. In Ireland, unlike Nicaragua, the Constitution specifically outlawed abortion (as it did divorce), thus making any attempt at legal reform a complicated process.[27] However, even in such resilient contexts, some progress could be made through public campaigns directed at mobilising support for realistic goals, that is, those that would be framed within the cultural context of what is acceptable and can be treated as a first step in a longer campaign. Reproductive rights and especially abortion have never been 'popular issues' anywhere in the world, let alone in societies that are deeply religious or socially conservative in character. With the exception of state socialist societies, in every case where the reform or repeal of abortion laws occurred, this did not occur without struggles carried out by feminists and their supporters. In Nicaragua a public campaign around reproductive rights was not organised by the FSLN or by AMNLAE, and nor were feminists encouraged to form a movement in support of the reform. Without gaining some measure of public popular support and neutralising the opposition, any radical legal reform would entail clear political risks. At the same time the FSLN feared the consequences of allowing such a campaign to take place. It is not clear how much research was undertaken in Nicaragua to canvass views on the matter; certainly not enough information existed to justify the view that 'the people' as a whole uniformly opposed reform of any kind. In this, as in every case, the people were likely to be divided along lines of sex, class and age, politics and belief. Abortion is no simple matter even, or especially, for women; in Catholic countries where women's identification with motherhood is positive and particularly strong, many women may oppose it on principle despite the fact that they may have had recourse to it.[28] Moreover, as one Nicaraguan feminist explained:

> The losses of the war have strengthened rather than diminished the emotional significance of motherhood. There are 11 000 women in Managua alone who are mothers of soldiers who have died in the fighting. Abortion in such a context is associated with more death; for some women it's unthinkable.[29]

Abortion on demand was therefore a remote prospect in Nicaragua, as was its full legalisation. It was, moreover, important to recognise that even if legality were to have been achieved by some miracle, it would have made little difference to women's range of choice on its own. The scarcity of facilities, equipment and qualified personnel to perform abortions would continue and the backstreet operator would therefore still thrive. For the state to meet existing demand, far-reaching changes in the health system would have been required, involving training, resource allocation and new equipment. In the straitened circumstances of Nicaragua very strong arguments would have had to be made to convince the authorities that abortion had priority over other areas of health provision. It is for these reasons, both political and practical, that more moderate reforms, such as the decriminalisation of the law, allowing social reasons for terminations and removing the legal sanctions over women's fertility practised by spouses, were more likely to be on the agenda.

Conclusions

This difficult and unresolved problem of reproductive rights encapsulates the tension between feminist visions of women's emancipation and the practical realities and policies of governments. Two points should, however, be clear from the foregoing discussion and can help to guard against any simple attribution of the causes of slow progress on women's rights primarily to acts of bad faith by men in position of power, anxious to retain the privileges of their sex. The first is that the FSLN itself was not of one mind on this question, let alone on how it defined its support for women's emancipation. While few were against some form of women's emancipation, the conceptions of what constituted this emancipation varied considerably, from a limited, traditional 'protection' of women, and mobilisation of them behind certain national campaigns (employment, defence of the revolution, mass education and health), to policies informed by feminism, which saw an alteration of gender relations and the full implementation of reproductive rights as the goal towards which the revolution should have been moving. The debate was, therefore, not only about whether or not the FSLN supported its commitment to women's emancipation, but what the definition of that emancipation was, and how much of a priority it represented, given other demands on resources.

The second point which the Nicaraguan case underlined is that all campaigns for women's rights have to take account of the objective as well as the subjective conditions for their implementation. The point is illustrated if reform of women's position is compared with other social reforms of a kind that post-revolutionary regimes carried out – land reform, or nationality rights, or workplace democracy. These, as much as the emancipation of women and the guaranteeing of reproductive rights, were part of the programme of post-revolutionary regimes, but all equally required certain conditions to be met before they could be successfully implemented. Precisely because they challenged existing power relations and widely held ideologies, including ones introjected by the social category subordinated within oppressive power relations, they could only be successful if the ground for contest were adequately prepared. A land reform decreed against a landowning class that still retained widespread power in the countryside, and in the name of a peasantry that was not adequately mobilised, organised and supported to assume the rights given to it by the reform, could end in disaster – landlord sabotage and revolts, widespread harvest failures and shortages and counter-revolutionary mobilisations of the peasantry.

For all the differences that exist, some parallels with the position of women can also apply; the very deep-rootedness of the oppression of women, its tenacious and at times violent defence by men and the often ingrained acquiescence in it by some women, make it something that cannot simply be abolished by decree, but must also be prepared for. Women's emancipation requires a determined challenge to the structures of power – with specific emphasis on gender relations and the Catholic Church, a programme of education amongst women and their mobilisation and organisation in support of reform, and decisive and united action by the revolutionary state.

It is, therefore, to underestimate the entrenched nature of women's subordination to suggest that a programme of emancipation can be decreed and implemented by fiat in any society. Revolutions accelerate the rate of change and strike at established practices. They involve struggle, but they still take place within the constraints of opposition and support existing in their societies. The course of other revolutions indicates that Nicaragua was not alone in facing this problem. If Cuba is not a suitable point of comparison, because of the different conditions prevailing there, a more appropriate comparison may be that of Mexico, a revolution that did, in the 1930s under Cárdenas, confront the Catholic Church head on. Yet it is significant that even in Mexico, where Cárdenas tried to mobilise women, the issue of reproductive freedom was not raised and that, later, the feminist component within the revolution was suppressed. Women did not get the vote in Mexico until 1953, two years before Nicaragua, and the legal position on abortion and its consequences was similar to that in Nicaragua.

The abortion issue in Nicaragua therefore summed up many of the tensions that existed between socialism and feminism, ones which were accentuated in the conditions of extreme precariousness, both political and economic, which were a particular feature of this revolution. It was clear that to do nothing entailed the continuation of the catalogue of injustice and misery which the situation inflicted upon women; yet to do anything substantial entailed political risks, on the one hand, and considerable economic outlay, on the other. Ultimately such measures as needed to be taken could only be arrived at with the political will to address the problem with solutions appropriate to the political, social and economic constraints which Nicaragua faced. That political will, however, could only emerge with sufficient conviction when there were enough voices within the leadership, or positions of influence within the society more generally, that were prepared to press the case and come up with workable answers.

Those answers depended upon the overall course of the Nicaraguan revolution in the difficult months and years ahead and on the specific outcome of the debate between different schools of thought on women's emancipation within the FSLN and outside it. If there were reasons for accepting that an immediate policy of full reproductive rights was neither prudent nor capable of implementation, it was equally evident that the FSLN could have done more than it had hitherto achieved in this area. The outcome was to depend to a considerable extent on what Nicaraguan women themselves, including those who had suffered under the existing legislation, could demand and enforce.

4

State, Gender and Institutional Change: The Federación de Mujeres Cubanas*

We have gone through three periods since the revolution. In the first we looked to the state to solve all our problems and we managed more or less OK. In the second, from 1988, we found the state couldn't meet our needs, and we were unable to meet them ourselves. Since 1993 we no longer rely on the state because we know that it cannot deliver what we need. But at least now we can begin to provide for ourselves.

Former FMC functionary, then working for an NGO.[1]

The 1990s were a time of particular uncertainty in Cuba – a crisis associated, on the one hand, with the collapse of the Soviet system and, on the other, with the emergency associated with the 'special period'.[2] When, in 1990, Cuba was officially declared to be in the 'special period in peacetime', it was a signal that the campaign of *rectificación*,[3] begun in 1986, had ended and that a new era of even greater austerity was at hand. As subsidies and trade with the Eastern bloc plummeted after 1989, the Cuban economy, already faltering throughout the latter part of the 1980s, suffered a severe if anticipated shock. The years 1989–93 registered the lowest growth rates since the revolution in 1959 – a near 50 per cent fall in global social product (GSP).[4] The crisis was reflected not only in the sharp contraction of the economy, but also in the acute shortage of basic goods and energy supplies that hit the Cuban population hard.[5]

While government policies, foreign investment and tourism had brought some alleviation of the worst hardships from the middle of 1994 onward, there could be little doubt that the political and economic

*All interviewees have been anonymised and all the translations, except where otherwise indicated, are by the author.

76

model espoused for nearly four decades was in crisis. Among the population there was a widespread recognition that the system had to yield to the forces of change, while the political leadership was preoccupied with controlling the pace and direction of such change. That this process had accelerated beyond what was initially foreseen was evident in the legalisation of the dollar in 1993, followed in 1995 by the passing of a revised property law, the licensing of small businesses and the introduction of new taxation measures in January 1996. The spread of markets throughout the island and of informal sector activities – most notable in Havana in the rapid expansion of the *paladares,* or semi-private eating houses, and in the omnipresent *jineteras* in the tourist areas, were evidence of the multifaceted nature of the move toward a greater role for the market, signalling major changes in state–society relations.[6]

For any society, the removal of its ideological and strategic patron and a collapse in national output over a five-year period would be challenge enough. Combined as these problems were with an unrelenting and vengeful pressure from the United States and with an apparent inability of the regime itself to take any political initiatives, the situation was especially acute.[7] Yet in this situation of protracted crisis, in which the dangers of a violent upheaval and of the loss of the considerable social gains of the revolutionary period were ever present, a debate opened up on the future of the Cuban political system in which, for the first time since the triumph of 1959, the possibility of political reform was creatively explored. Both in Havana and in Miami, voices were raised that sought to chart a course for Cuba that would navigate the worst dangers facing it. Such a course would avoid the imposition on Cuba of 'shock therapy', compounded by the revanchist proclivities of returning exiles, but would also demand from the regime a political change consonant with the economic reforms it was introducing.[8]

Examples of such views can be found in material produced within Cuba during the 1990s by semi-official and independent groups, and in analyses attuned to such changes produced abroad.[9] One Cuban contribution, written from a position that stressed the achievements of the revolution, argued that political liberalisation was both urgent and possible in contemporary Cuba.[10] The author, Haroldo Dilla, had little time for the argument that political change should be postponed until the economy had recovered, or for the view that democratic and constitutional politics were not 'appropriate' to Cuba. While critical of US hostility, he also dismissed the claim that the confrontation with Washington made such a democratisation impossible.

Dilla's argument was instead that economic change of the kind associated with the 'special period' could not be disassociated from political reform, that is, democratisation. The crisis of the Cuban system was not just a result of events in the USSR or of US pressure: it was a result of the changes brought about by the revolution itself:

> Civil society has changed. In the first place, its popular sectors are today more educated, with better political formation and greater ability to participate. New generations have entered political life carrying a message of political commitment, but demanding new spaces and renovated forms in which to exercise it. Half of the population, women, is hoping for greater opportunities to express its aspirations in an autonomous manner against a patriarchal order weakened, but not destroyed, by more than 30 years of revolutionary life.[11]

The crisis of the Cuban Revolution had, therefore, occurred at the time when Cuban society was best able to respond creatively to it.

The discussion that follows is a reflection on the changes under way in Cuba, ones which placed the Cuban system of state socialism under pressure to reform. I focus in particular on one of the mass organisations, the Federación de Mujeres Cubanas (FMC – Federation of Cuban Women) and on the changing place of gender issues within the Cuban Revolution.[12] I seek to locate the discussion of the FMC in the context of the arguments summarised above, linking the issue of political change and liberalisation to the impact of social and economic change, by examining the degree to which the FMC has been able to adapt to the new realities it has faced.

'The Woman Question' and the Revolutionary State

The FMC in 1990 was one of the largest of the mass organisations in Cuba, claiming a membership of 3.2 million, or 80 per cent of the adult female population.[13] An analysis of the Federation is of interest for three main reasons. The first is that in membership terms it is not only the largest mass organisation in Cuba, but the largest women's organisation ever seen in Latin America.[14] Second, its record raises questions about the nature of the regime and its legitimacy in the eyes of its constituency.[15] The record of the Cuban Revolution in regard to 'women's emancipation' is an achievement celebrated both internally and to some degree externally as evidence of socialism's superiority over capitalism. The

FMC and the Communist Party are jointly credited with achieving above average levels of progress for the Latin American region on key indicators such as female mortality, educational levels, legal rights, healthcare and employment. This progress is argued to have provided the regime with legitimacy and considerable support among the female population. If this latter claim were to be substantiated, then the Cuban case differs from the experience of Eastern Europe and suggests a greater degree of support for government institutions than prevailed there; it also suggests that the FMC may enjoy a correspondingly greater degree of effectiveness in responding to the needs of its constituency.

A third reason for focusing on the FMC is that its membership and constituency contain a high proportion of those who are most likely to be adversely affected in the short to medium run by any process of adjustment that eventuates from attempts to resolve Cuba's economic crisis. As studies of the social effects of adjustment have shown, the move toward a greater role for the market can be expected to exacerbate social inequalities and to deepen gender divisions. In Cuba's transition, too, there is already evidence that women suffer a disproportionate burden of the costs of economic crisis, and this trend is likely to accelerate. If the current regime is to avoid the fate of the Sandinistas in the Nicaraguan elections of 1990, when 'the largest block of sentiment' against them was composed of women,[16] it will have to address the fact of the gendered nature of economic restructuring and be seen to be taking adequate measures to offset them. Much depends, then, on the character of the FMC.

The FMC: Origins and Evolution

The official account of the FMC attributes its origins, in a predictable but by no means inaccurate manner, to socialist principle combined with what must in rather more critical terms be characterised as paternalism. According to these accounts, 'Fidel himself' set up the revolution's women's organisation, the Federation of Cuban Women, in 1960, and appointed his sister-in-law Vilma Espín as its head, a position she has enjoyed ever since.[17]

The FMC was set up to organise and mobilise women for the defence and consolidation of the revolution. In function as well as in structure, it followed the pattern established in other socialist states, operating as a 'mass organisation' under the general direction of the party and acting in Lenin's terms as 'a transmission belt'. Its leadership was drawn from the handful of women who were close to the guerrilla command in the 1950s

soon became embroiled in the confrontation between East and West in the missile crisis of 1962. The tense international situation helped to lock Cuba into a path, as an ally and showcase of the Soviet Union, which had profound effects on its population as a whole, ones that were clearly gendered in character. Although enjoying considerable popular support, which continued for some time after the initial confrontation with the United States, the Cuban leadership had nonetheless set in place by the mid-1970s a system that, modelled on the USSR, was premised on centralised, bureaucratic control and, without Soviet subsidies, was economically unsustainable. The Cuban Communist Party (CCP), founded in 1965, was a highly centralised body, modelled on the Communist Party of the Soviet Union. The Cuban press was as controlled as any in the socialist bloc. The party bureaucracy, dominated by men, sought to direct all social and political life; if the secret police were less evident than in the USSR and its allies, other bodies – notably the CCP itself and the Committees for the Defence of the Revolution (CDRs) – performed analogous functions. Despite a greater use of mass meetings, the charismatic power of its leader, the system of *poder popular*,[22] and a more sustained commitment to participation through voluntary labour in the development efforts of the state, the political process was broadly similar. If this was true of the party and state in general, it was also true of policy on what, in conventional socialist terminology, was referred to as 'the woman question' and of the ideological and organisational forms this policy took.

The FMC in the 1980s: Adaptation and Resistance

The combined effects of Cuba's insertion into the Soviet bloc, the re-formulation of Cuban political and cultural activity along Eastern bloc lines, US-enforced international isolation, and the regime's own controls over intellectual life all but succeeded in insulating the revolution from the major international currents of social and political thought until the early 1980s. It was then that in response to a variety of related circumstances – some internal, some international – a measure of opening up began to occur. The exodus of 125 000 Cubans from Mariel in 1980 was followed by a loosening of some control over economic and social life, with a small private sector being allowed to develop in the service and agricultural domains, and a greater – if still limited – measure of contact being permitted with the Western world. The FMC was perhaps more exposed to these processes than were some of the other mass organisations, if only because the United Nations Decade for Women of 1976–85, along with the Latin American presence within it, became an important and new focus of its international activity.[23]

By the late 1970s, it had become evident that the FMC was no longer operating within the official socialist policy universe and that it existed in tension with two complementary forces – one coming from outside, from a self-confident international women's movement that had strong regional counterparts in Latin America,[24] the other generated internally by women's increasing expectations and self-assertiveness. In retrospect, it can be said that the UN Decade for Women was a defining moment for the debate on women's place in society in the communist states.[25] As these states saw it, they had a 'superior record' on women's rights and social indicators preferable to most of the capitalist states. The events associated with this initiative presented them with an opportunity to make a bid for a share of the resources that became available during the decade. Many an official women's organisation declared itself to be a non-governmental organisation for the purpose of this exercise and the FMC, too, duly followed suit. It was in the context of regional meetings for Latin America that the Cuban delegates encountered the diverse currents of activism within the women's movements of Latin America, including one current for which they hitherto had little but contempt – feminism.[26]

Since its inception the FMC had maintained an attitude of open hostility to feminism,[27] and this attitude remained unchanged throughout the 1970s. The official position of the FMC, in keeping with the standard Soviet line, attributed women's subordination to capitalist imperialism, a system against which both men and women should unite. Feminism was seen as 'bourgeois' and divisive, and in its insistence on autonomous organisational forms, it was considered at variance with the FMC's acceptance of 'democratic centralism' under overall party control. Feminist writings were therefore banned and there was never any serious engagement with feminist theory within the FMC or beyond it. Vilma Espín insisted that the FMC was a 'feminine rather than a feminist' organisation and clarified the difference on the eve of the UN Decade for Women, explaining that, 'We never fought for partial demands; we were always conscious that the problem of women is a part of the whole society and integrally related to the struggle of all the people for their liberation, to men and women together sweeping aside the very foundations of capitalist society to build a new life.'[28]

In 1977, however, rather than offering a blanket denunciation of feminism, Espín was careful to identify the main enemy as its North American variety – that is, liberal, non-socialist and 'radical' feminism:

'We have never had a feminist movement. We hate that. We hate the feminist movement in the United States. We consider what we are doing is part of the struggle. We see these movements in the USA which have conceived struggles for equality of women against men! That is absurd! For these feminists to say they are revolutionaries is ridiculous!'[29]

The FMC was, however, unable to sustain this negative stance. As feminism began to attain greater support within the Latin American left and even to acquire a popular following in the region, official policy shifted to one of cooptation. The policy process gradually began to absorb feminist issues, urged on by women's advocacy within the UN. A handful of younger women sympathetic to feminism began to work within the FMC, and later a few were even sent to Europe, some to the UK, to study gender issues. At the same time, pressure from within the island had been mounting. By the mid-1970s, it was evident that the Cuban record on 'women's emancipation' was, in its own terms, in need of improvement. Women's participation in the organs of institutionalised power, particularly in those positions with any real authority, remained at strikingly low levels.[30] Moreover, daily life for women in shortage economies was hard, all the more so where there was reliance on a considerable degree of mass participation and voluntary work. These problems had become all too apparent from within as well as from outside because of the growing international scrutiny to which Cuba was subjected in feminist fora in Latin America and in the activities of the UN Decade.

In contrast to several countries of the Soviet bloc, no dissident feminist groups or writing emerged in Cuba itself, but the leadership was prompted into a growing awareness of the problems women faced every day in work and in political life. As the seventies progressed, public disillusion set in, although the US embargo took much of the blame, and scepticism about the FMC's role in regard to women grew. The party had counted on the substantial involvement of women at the base of the political pyramid – in the institutions of popular power and in the CDRs. Here, women carried out the tasks of community management and *vigilancia* (neighbourhood watch), and those who were *integradas* (activists in one of the mass organisations or in the party) helped to mobilise women to participate in national campaigns. These women, too, voiced their grievances against the system, making persistent demands for improved childcare, housing and transport, and for longer opening hours for shops. These issues, neglected in what was in many other respects an exemplary record of public provision, had been far from the central concerns of the FMC.

From the mid-1970s, galvanised perhaps by participation in the UN Decade, there occurred some shift in party policy toward the achievement of greater sexual equality and enhancing women's political participation. The Family Code of 1975, modelled on the East German legislation passed a year before, initiated a campaign to increase male responsibilities within the household. This phase of greater awareness of the need to address the problems women faced – dubbed the 'revolution within the revolution' by one analyst[31] – saw a greater emphasis on improving women's situation overall, an emerging critique of gender divisions in everyday life and a revised FMC agenda showing more sensitivity to the kinds of issues that had been raised within women's movements. In 1984, Cuba hosted a preparatory regional meeting for the women's conference marking the end of the UN Decade. Many Latin American feminists attended the conference, some of international repute; a few, known to have a position of critical support with regard to Cuba, were granted an audience with Castro himself. One participant recalled that this meeting seemed 'indicative of some kind of reconciliation with feminism, yet how much this was a genuine accommodation and how much window-dressing is hard to say'.[32] In any event, the FMC Congress in 1985 seemed to many observers to show signs of a greater sensitivity in its handling of gender issues than had been evident in the past.

None of these events, however, was accompanied by significant changes in the style of work performed by the FMC or in the internal character of the organisation, which continued much as before. The 1980 Congress had noted that local-level work in the delegations and blocks was unsatisfactory and that attendance was falling in the study circles.[33] This decline continued throughout the 1980s; in 1985, Espín had to defend the very existence of the organisation in the face of harsh attacks on its performance, exciting speculation that it might cease to function. There appeared to be a disjuncture between the revitalisation taking place within official discourse and the practice of the organisation itself.

The character and priorities of the FMC could not, however, be detached from general trends in society as a whole. In the mid-1980s, the limited process of economic liberalisation was halted. In one of those sharp counter-moves characteristic of socialist states, Castro turned against the farmers' markets and closed them down, arguing that they had led to the emergence of social inequalities and worse, a corrupt, parasitic sector that was undermining the revolution. This move did not at first have a great impact on the FMC's agenda, and the organisation appeared to maintain a commitment to the tenor of the 1985 Congress. Yet in response to pressures of a quite different kind, it was called upon to undergo a revitalising transformation that came from dramatic changes in the policies of the Cuban state as a whole: just as the Soviet Union was embarking on its reforms, and indeed to some extent perhaps because of this very fact, Cuba took a very different path – a 'rectification of errors' campaign marked by a return to earlier policies and to slogans designed to fortify the revolution against its internal weaknesses.

Rectificación occasioned much affirmative rhetoric from within and was greeted by at least some writers abroad as proof of the vitality of the Cuban Revolution. It gained some popular support because of its attack on bureaucratic inertia, privilege and corruption, and because of the opportunity it afforded for greater public discussion about the social problems Cubans faced. On the other hand, the suppression of the nascent private sector was accompanied by a political clampdown designed, in part, to preempt contagion from the growing mood of reform in the USSR. The hidden agenda of the *rectificación* period was evident in the critical manner with which the Cuban press reported, or often failed to report, events in the USSR and Eastern Europe – one which contrasted with the regime's support for the Chinese Party in its suppression of the Tien An Men demonstrations in June 1989. Signs of political unease within the regime were also evident in the trial and subsequent execution of senior military officers and close allies of Castro.[34]

If judged by economic indicators, *rectificación* was a failure in that the general orientation of the economy did not change substantially in this period and the policies pursued did little to halt the coming crisis. At best, the campaign merely staved off, in the name of a return to an unattainable socialist purity, the reforms that Cuban society needed; at worst, it fostered political discontent and postponed economic reform. Trade and other links with the Soviet Union and Eastern Europe were maintained until 1990, while the economy as a whole returned to the more centralised, unresponsive but still functioning, mode of the 1970s.

As far as women were concerned, there was evidence of a continuing commitment to address some of their needs and some of the social problems that they faced: following demands made at the 1985 Congress, measures were taken to increase childcare provision and a greater stress was placed on the need to share housework in line with the 1975 Family Code. There were increased provisions of contraception and renewed efforts at sex education in attempts to reduce the high rate of teenage pregnancies. At the same time, more efforts were made to incorporate women into economic activity, with the result that their participation in the labour force grew.[35] In terms of policy, it could be argued that the FMC and the Cuban state in general maintained a gender-aware policy stance in the *rectificación* period,[36] and its rhetoric reflected some of the concerns of its constituency. But against this positive interpretation, other considerations should be registered: the overall aim of the *rectificación* period was to improve the productivity of the labour force and to mobilise large numbers of 'voluntary' workers. This mass mobilisation was not without its social costs, specifically what Cubans call 'a crisis in time management' as people struggled to fulfil the multiple demands made upon them. 'Participation' there was, but to what extent it could be taken as a sign of support for the regime is difficult to say. Volunteering for such work was often the only way to gain a promotion at work, housing points or access to scarce goods. Arguably, it was, above all, considerations of regime survival, that determined the policy of the FMC in this period as in others. The increase in the number of childcare centres and women in work, and the efforts regarding teenage pregnancies and abortion reflected the concerns of a state worried about the deepening economic and social crisis it was facing.[37]

This social crisis was reflected most tellingly in the increasing desire of many Cubans, particularly the young, to flee the country by any means, legal or illegal.[38] This was the context in the second half of the 1980s, with the FMC reputedly the most unpopular mass organisation on the island, unable to halt declining attendance at meetings or to address the growing dissatisfaction arising from a deteriorating economic performance. Despite its evident efforts to assimilate some of the debates about women's place in society and the resultant modernisation of its rhetoric and improved policies on some issues, the Federation had failed to achieve a strong political profile. For some analysts, this failure was because it did not seek to mobilise around issues of a feminist or controversial kind and rarely contested official policy. Its main periodical, *Mujeres*, avoided difficult (that is, interesting and relevant) questions, preferring 'to stick to recipes'. Certainly, it was widely acknowledged to have failed to attract younger women into its ranks, and its own cadres responded to this problem by denouncing the increasingly depoliticised youth as morally bankrupt and frivolous. By the end of the decade, the organisation was seen as having lost momentum and there were again calls for it to be closed down.[39]

This contradictory evolution was evident by the time of its Fifth Congress, held in 1990. A random survey of 100 women taken a week before the Congress revealed a striking indifference to the FMC's activities. Of the total respondents, 70 per cent did not know that the Congress was taking place, and only 6 per cent had great hopes regarding its outcome. An ambitious agenda had been promulgated and discussed prior to the Congress itself, but at the Congress it was overruled by a more traditional stress on mobilising women in defence of the revolution (under the old patriotic slogan 'socialism or death') and was as a consequence never realised. The Congress ended with a unanimous vote of confidence for Castro, described as 'the Father of all Cubans and guide to all Cuban Women'.[40] In the words of one Latin American feminist in Cuba for the preparatory regional meeting of the Cairo Population Conference, 'the atmosphere had changed, the old guard were back, the ones who were sympathetic to feminism seemed to have disappeared'.[41]

In the period that followed the Congress, the main determinant of women's position was not any shift in FMC attitudes to feminism, but the crisis that engulfed the whole Cuban regime and society as a result of events in the Soviet Union and Eastern Europe. The precipitate decline in the economy exposed the population to extremes of deprivation they had never dreamt of, and while women struggled to cope as best they could, the FMC was unable to protest publicly about official policies or offer much in the way of support to its membership. Instead, women were once again called upon to defend the revolution by redoubling their efforts. Thousands entered the microbrigades to build houses, or volunteered to work in the agricultural sector.

The FMC in the 1990s

The 1990s held out the prospect of even greater challenges to the FMC that threatened further to detach it from its remaining supporters. The consultative efforts prior to the 1990 Congress had led the organisation to develop what its officials described as a somewhat more 'feminist' approach and to seek a more visible role among its constituency.[42] These imperatives, however, came at a time when the demands placed both on the organisation and on its members were acknowledged to be particularly severe. The FMC had faced a difficult situation during the years of *rectificación* and the 'Special Period' placed under renewed strain its dual function as a promoter of women's equality and arm of the party. Partly in response to this new situation, the FMC renewed its attempts to refashion itself as an NGO, a status few outsiders were prepared to credit, given its ties to the party, and one that it did little to confirm in its rhetoric.[43] The Sixth Congress in 1995 re-emphasised the principal role of the organisation as 'defence of the revolution', and the general secretary's speech once again invoked the heroic, militant and nationalist past of Cuban women, placing the *federadas*[44] at Fidel's right hand in resisting the imperialist blockade and defending the gains of the revolution. The rearticulation of the themes of revolutionary national-ism, *lealtad* (loyalty) and identification of the party with Cuba's national history, together with the invocation of a militant Cuban womanhood, underscored the political character of the FMC in a frank restatement of its priorities.

The combination of economic crisis and the policies adopted to deal with it nonetheless placed the FMC under pressure to justify its existence in somewhat different terms: to its functions it added renewed fund-raising efforts in the international arena for its projects, ranging from healthcare delivery and social work to publishing programmes. Yet, although it claimed to defend the cause of sex equality through govern-mental and policy channels, it acted less as a vehicle for advancing women's interests than as a means for managing female discontent and mobilising increasing numbers of *federadas* into voluntary work.

On paper the organisation maintained and even increased its organisational strength. In 1994, more than 3.5 million women paid their dues as a result of special efforts to increase membership and to collect the money on which the FMC depended for a substantial portion of its funds. In the same year, it claimed representation in 72 874 *delegaciones* and 12 114 *bloques*; it had a paid staff of 1327 and 242 008 voluntary leaders at the base of the organisation.[45] Despite these impressive figures, FMC activity at neighbourhood level was patchy, sometimes minimal, and as the CDRs declined in importance, so too did the FMC. Although the CDRs were to revive in some areas, by 1996 the FMC was widely regarded as 'irrelevant' to the needs of Cuban women. Some acknowledgement was given to the fact that good people worked within the organisation, but one woman expressed a common view that 'the top layer is too rigid, everyone says that as an organisation it has to change'.[46] It had, therefore, not succeeded in acquiring a more positive image in the eyes of the Cuban public, a problem exacerbated by the fact that for the previous two years, as a result of a paper shortage, it had been unable to publish its periodicals, *Mujeres* and *Muchachas*. The general contraction of resources associated with the Special Period inevitably affected the overall organisational capacity of the Federation. It also sapped the morale of its permanent staff on their dwindling real incomes and that of the large voluntary workforce of *federadas*, whose time was already under considerable pressure from the demands of surviving in increasingly difficult circumstances.

From its own organisational perspective and from the vantage point of what were seen as the recovery years of 1995–6, the FMC had not only survived the worst years, but saw itself as well-placed to play a key role in the changing policy environment. In early 1996 it was preparing to engage in an island-wide 'consultation' process for feedback on the resolutions of the Sixth Congress and it had already held a number of, in its view, successful sessions. With the easing of the paper shortage, *Mujeres* and *Muchachas* were to be revived and a new periodical was planned for diffusion abroad, largely for fundraising purposes. The Federation's magazines were to be aimed at a broader and younger readership, but with editorial control remaining in the hands of senior members of the revolutionary generation.

The organisation counted among its successes the Casas de Orientación de la Mujer y la Familia (also known as Casas de la Mujer, or Casas), an idea loosely based on the 'Women's Houses' supported by women's movements in Latin America and elsewhere that offered a variety of services such as refuges from domestic violence and centres of advice and support. Following demands made at the previous Congress in 1990, it had also expanded the number of childcare centres to a total of 1156. Its activity in the field of health was given prominence and a new project, assisted by UN funds, was underway in which the FMC organised volunteer health workers for an extensive screening for cervical cancer.

The mobilisation of women into voluntary work was an important aspect of the Federation's response to the crisis, continuing in some measure the policy of the *rectificación* period. However, if voluntary programmes were important in themselves and could provide the organisation with a civic role in the transition, they also revealed some of the ambiguity of the FMC's dual function as a women's organisation and as an instrument of state policy. This ambiguity was particularly evident in the FMC's social work programme, which involved some 53 000 volunteers. In keeping with its growing concern regarding what it saw as a crisis in the family, the Federation directed considerable energy and resources towards 'family support' initiatives, many of which aimed to help more than 10 000 single mothers and 36 000 children in need. The FMC's volunteers assisted in locating absconding fathers for purposes of legal recognition of children and financial support, and in arranging subsidies and care for abandoned, abused or distressed children.

Much of this work was channelled through the Casas de Orientación de la Mujer y la Familia, which by 1994 numbered 155 throughout the island. These Casas served as a vehicle for FMC initiatives at the local level: as such, they differed radically in conception from those programmes established by women's movements in other countries. They were, as their name suggested, designed principally to 'guide' (*orientar*) women; they offered a drop-in service of social, psychological and legal advice, and organised a range of courses, some of which aimed to help women to acquire a trade and set up their own small businesses. In 1996, the most important of these Casas, in the Municipio Plaza de la Revolución, located in Havana and serving a population of 171 000, offered courses in repairing bicycles, sewing and hairdressing.[47]

However useful such services might have been, the manner in which they were delivered said much about the character of the FMC. The offer by the Casa de la Mujer of free advice from social workers and legal experts, for example, should have served as a useful resource for women, but because the FMC was perceived by its clientele as an arm of the government, its advice was not considered disinterested. Nor could those women visiting the Casa expect to find redress from the actions of the state itself. Those seeking help in handling difficult issues – such as drug dealing and abuse in their family, a *jinetera* daughter, a suspected AIDS infection, an alcoholic or violent husband, or a son considering the option of becoming a *balsero* (rafter emigrant) – knew that they would receive an official response that exposed the person seeking advice to a political lecture or, worse, to the possible involvement of the law, whether they wished it or not.[48] It is not surprising, therefore, that the rates of take-up among the population for the services on offer at the main Casa in Havana were strikingly low, with only 181 visits recorded for 1995.

In part it was the very multifunctionality of the FMC as well as its lack of autonomy from the state that prevented it from effectively serving the needs of its constituency in this type of work. As an organisation, it had always suffered from overloading, a problem that continued because it felt itself unable to disperse some of its activities to non-state agencies. The FMC had both too much power and too little; as far as its role in the delivery of social welfare was concerned, it might have had more success if it had redefined its status, acting either as part of the welfare ministry – that is, as an acknowledged and adequately funded department of the state – or as an autonomous body, a genuine NGO. As the only permitted women's organisation, and encumbered by its function as a party organisation, it was constrained in developing an independent response to the changes that Cuba was undergoing and that would only accelerate in the future. Such was the view expressed by several former *federadas* and confirmed to some degree by the FMC's initial response to the new economic conditions;[49] this was to play down their effects on women and to join in the party leadership's condemnation of those who were 'enchanted by capitalism'. It did, however, acknowledge the extra strains endured by women in the Special Period; Vilma Espín made a point of praising the efforts of Cuban women in her speech to the Sixth Congress. Later studies by the FMC detailed some of the negative effects on women of the economic crisis. But, again, many of the most serious problems women faced – housing, poverty, job loss, sexual abuse, rape or rising violence against women resulting from the overall crisis – were ones that the organisation felt unable either to acknowledge publicly or to discuss except in familiar rhetorical terms. This inability resulted in part from the continuing role the FMC played in disseminating party propaganda both at home and in the international arena. In short, the Federation was able to offer little in an epoch that called for remedial policies rather than slogans.

This failure was particularly evident with regard to female employment. The government announced its intention of reducing employment by half a million, and the number was expected to rise to a million over the course of 1996–7.[50] The FMC, however, painted an optimistic picture of the situation of female workers in the Special Period, arguing on the basis of 1994 data that no decline in female participation rates had occurred. A full 44 per cent of Cuban women were in employment in 1993, constituting a female labour force of 3 203 904. One FMC study argued that far from falling, women's participation in the areas designated 'priority sectors' (tourism, agroscience, technology and health) made them 'a respectable force'. Overall, whereas men's employment in the civilian state sector declined from 62.5 per cent of the total in 1985 to 59.3 per cent in 1994, women's employment rose from 37.5 per cent to 40.6 per cent. The authors of the analysis were able to conclude that 'Cuban women have become a vital force in the country's economy', that they have been and continue to be 'a vital factor in development'.[51] If sustained, this status could cushion other trends that affected women's employment adversely. But the analysis presented a partial picture of female employment trends and avoided confronting the issue of the future role of women in the economy. It took little account of inconsistencies in the way employment and unemployment were defined and ignored the fact that many women registered as employed were on extended 'leave' from work to devote themselves to the daily tasks of survival for their families. In Havana in 1996, there was considerable evidence of female unemployment and underemployment. More than one stallholder in the craft market in Vedado was a young woman professional either out of work or unable to manage on what she earned: one nurse was supplementing her wage which she could no longer live on; another 23-year-old engineer reported that she had been sacked from her job and could find no other. Half a dozen women interviewed in Havana complained that they had been made redundant and then offered inappropriate or distant alternatives, which they declined – the latter typically for 'family reasons'. Young professionals expressed considerable discontent at a situation where they could not find jobs commensurate with their skills and expectations. Significantly, the FMC was not seen as able to offer any solution, useful training or valuable advice to these women beyond referring them to voluntary work and putting them on a register, an option that was regarded with scepticism and that few seemed willing to try.

It is clear that under such circumstances state agencies could not be counted on, as in the past, to provide the solution either to unemployment or to the declining standards of living that many already faced or would face in the near future. Other means of support and of satisfying expectations of social mobility had to be found: chief among these ranked the opportunities afforded by the market, specifically the expansion of the informal sector and petty trade.[52] Although many women entered this sector, whether as producers of goods or providers of services, this move in many cases entailed a deprofessionalisation and consequent loss of earlier skills as architects, doctors, nurses, teachers and other professionals, unable to live on their earnings in the state sector and unable to sell their skills abroad, turned to the tourist sector for work and dollars. One recourse for women that reveals the less benign face of informal sector activity is prostitution, which, with the onset of the crisis, became a strategy for many women (and some men) in the tourist areas of the island. Although not illegal *per se*, prostitution has always been discouraged. In the conditions of the Special Period it was officially tolerated as 'the social price we pay for development'[53] and subject to regulation by the authorities ostensibly for reasons of public health. For the women involved, it represented not only a means of obtaining dollars but, for some, the hope that it would provide a husband and a life abroad. For the older revolutionary generation, prostitution represented a return to a shameful past, and the unsound attitudes of 'the youth' were routinely invoked to explain it. Yet for many *habaneros* (residents of the capital), it was seen as resulting from economic necessity and gained a degree of tacit support from family members who were themselves dependent on the income generated.

Some FMC functionaries acknowledged the complexity of the issue of prostitution, but explained it as an inevitable effect of the blockade and consequent economic difficulties faced by Cuba. At the same time, they deplored the practice, insisting that many *jineteras* were not pushed into it by poverty but by bad attitudes and sometimes greed, and they successfully lobbied the government at the end of 1995 to pass legislation banning sex workers from hotels. They also went to hoteliers, 'explaining to them why this had to be'.[54] Although such legislation might have reassured the promoters of family tourism in Cuba, it did little to address the problems of prostitution – let alone of the women engaged in it.

The mixed results of these various government policies notwithstanding, there was evidence from early 1996 of some improvement in the overall economic situation as well as in that of the average household. The state maintained its commitment to social expenditure, so the population enjoyed some protection from destitution,[55] but there could be little doubt that, overall, considerable hardship and insecurity continued. In such conditions, women's invisible and unpaid labour on behalf of the household tends to expand. Their responsibilities in the domain of reproductive work involve an extension of their work time in the home, either preparing food or performing services of various kinds (cleaning, caring for the elderly and children, washing clothes and gardening) that might previously have been paid for or were provided by the state.[56] With prices high for scarce goods, time must be spent hunting out bargains, and as numerous studies attest, it is generally women who are involved in negotiating exchanges of goods and services and short-term loans through local networks and kin ties. Cuban surveys show that the traditional sexual division of labour in domestic work remained virtually unchallenged by years of FMC efforts to raise awareness of the problem or by the 1975 Family Code. Women bear the main burden, whether or not they are in employment.[57] The declining quality and accessibility of public services creates a redefinition of the boundaries between the public and private realms with greater responsibility being devolved from state to family. In a context where the availability of good quality childcare is threatened and where there is a growing population of elderly whose overall security is diminishing, female kin step in to fill the gaps in public provision. The granting of special leave to women workers for 'family reasons' is one indicator that they are already doing so; their earnings and career patterns are on the line, however, and will be affected by such practices in the short as well as in the longer run. These issues are given little consideration in the current context: indeed, the absence of public debate and public policy on these issues was striking.

These are some of the ways in which gender asymmetries acquired a new salience in Cuba's Special Period. At the broadest level, this novelty is given by the gradual redefinition of state–society relations which began to create new social divisions, new economic agents and new vulnerabilities for much of the female population. The processes set in train in the move toward marketisation have contradictory effects on women – acting to the detriment of many of those in employment and especially those who constitute the working poor, but providing others with the means to become new economic agents. It will be some time before the long-term trends are more clearly visible, but in the meantime the issue is whether the significance of these gender asymmetries has been absorbed into public policy arenas – and responded to with appropriate policies that succeed in reaching the most vulnerable groups. The FMC has so far shown that it has been slow to offer an adequate response to these processes. As a government organisation, its capacity to operate as an effective advocate of particular group interests has been constrained, and its work is not supported by other, independent NGOs. The FMC remained the only women's organisation legally permitted on the island and, particularly pertinent here, the only NGO licensed to deal specifically with women's issues.[58] The one independent feminist organisation to emerge in post-revolutionary Cuba, MAGÍN was founded in November 1994 but closed down after a brief flowering.[59] NGO activists who wanted to work with women tended to do so as a part of larger non gender-specific projects. One Cuban woman said: 'If we want to work with women, we avoid the FMC. It is better to work without them. They are still stuck in old ways of "macro-thinking", they need a new perspective.'[60]

Gender, State and Revolution: Conclusions

After more than three decades of socialist policies, the Cuban population before 1989 had achieved greater access to health and education, and the poorest sectors of society had seen a marked improvement in their standard of living. With regard to women, Cuban socialism had presided over their mobilisation into considerable activity at all levels of public life, but had imposed a toll on daily life, one common to shortage economies, and the social division of labour retained its essential inequalities as far as the gender order was concerned. Thus the decades of communist rule, for all that they did bring changes in social relations, had only a limited effect on the balance of power between the sexes in the home and in the public realm.

The role played by the FMC in this process was in many ways a contradictory one: it was an authoritarian organisation that took its orders from above and allowed little internal dissent, let alone public debate of policy issues. Its senior members were never – any more than any other officials of the party or state elite – subject to a genuine electoral process. Its input into policy, even as a mild form of pressure group on behalf of women, was hampered by its primary allegiance to the party and by the latter's control over budget allocation and overall policy. It had relatively few resources to undertake research on issues relating to women; the result was that even if it had wished to, it had limited means of arguing for or against policies on the basis of their popularity, effectiveness or likely impact on women's lives beyond what its officials reported.

Yet the FMC was supposed to represent more than just a mouthpiece of the party, and it did provide a space, albeit one within determined limits, for activities and discussion on issues of gender equality. Any attempt to assess its significance is bound by larger considerations about the meaning of the revolution and the socialist project itself. For those who see the entry of women into the public sphere – their education and employment – as a good in itself, the Federation clearly assisted in achieving this entry. For those who stress the negative terms of that involvement, placing the emphasis on the Federation's lack of autonomy and authoritarian character, the gains are diminished as an effect of instrumentalist policies or the inevitable processes of modernisation.

Within the prevailing political context, there can be little doubt that the FMC played an important role in helping to realise government goals in relation to women. Women's emancipation constituted one of the ideological platforms of state communism and the women's union had a legitimate role in promoting these principles. Advancing the project of women's emancipation and hence improving the lot of its female constituency were achievements of which the regime was particularly proud. It certainly made available abundant evidence of the benefits that Cuban women enjoyed under the patronage of the state in terms of education, health and expanding employment opportunities. But there is another reading of this history of progress that is not captured by the statistics and that places these gains in a more negative light.[61]

Ultimately, such judgements in the case of Cuba will have to wait until the emergence of an internal feminist critique and until this critique is, in turn, put into perspective by history. It is often said by

Cubans themselves that the FMC did play a useful role in the early period of the revolution and enjoyed support by virtue of its positive association with a popular revolution. The latter brought tangible benefits to many who had suffered under the previous system, bringing them a measure of upward mobility. As a women's organisation dedicated to sexual equality, the FMC may even have benefited from Cuba's long and distinguished history of activism by women's movements,[62] although it chose to distance itself from that past, preferring to attribute to the Revolution of 1959 the key role in women's struggle for emancipation.

Whatever its failings, Cuban socialism created a distinctive kind of women's movement, albeit one that was a creature of the state. The FMC represented a sustained, and in some ways successful, attempt to legitimate an institutionalised women's movement, just as populist regimes in Latin America had played an innovative role in shaping an institutionalised labour movement. The Cuban Communist Party sought to construct new gender–state relations and the women's movement it created was authorised to represent and pursue women's interests, as officially defined. In myriad ways – by mobilising women, creating a female constituency, funding a women's organisation and diffusing an official discourse of women's rights and sexual equality – the leadership effectively legitimated women's claims on the state and against certain structures of authority and discrimination. But in return for policy initiatives supporting women, the state expected complete loyalty to the party line and brooked no rivals.

The successes as much as the failings of the FMC as a women's organisation cannot be understood, therefore, without taking due account of its relation to the state and that state's evolution in Cuba over the 40 years of its existence. After the excitement of the first decade and despite some enlargement of its agenda, the FMC became, as many observers have indicated, increasingly ossified: along with other mass organisations, it was criticised by its membership for its bureaucratic character, which had placed evident limits on its pretensions to act on behalf of that membership. Much feminist criticism of the FMC and of the Cuban record with regard to its policies on women has focused on the resilience of patriarchal privilege, sexual inequality and machismo and the social and gendered divisions of labour, with the implication that the Women's Union and the state could and should have devoted more efforts to 'transforming society'. Although it is undoubtedly true that the organisation could have done more to address these issues, the problem may have been the reverse, namely, that *too much* or the *wrong kind* of intervention occurred, that too much energy was expended in attempts to force a diverse population into conformity with the party line. The FMC's lack of autonomy and its instrumentalism may have enhanced its effective capacity to bring about change in some areas, but it seems also to have generated some resistance to conformity. This resistance was evident in declining support for the FMC, in the falling proportion of women in most political institutions and in young people's boredom with the old rhetoric – all of which may have symbolised a more general dissatisfaction and retreat from an increasingly exhausting public domain.

In the 1990s, extra strains were placed on women and on the state institutions that were charged with their protection. As Cuban socialism faced increasing pressures for democratic reform, the leadership set its face against it.[63] Many on the island wanted change but feared its consequences: the market promised opportunity, but it could not provide protection against the risks it brings. The evolution toward a regime that is politically democratic and socially just and that embodies the positive legacy of the revolution depends on many factors, both external and internal. Among the former, a change in the policies of the United States predominates; among the latter can be instanced the development of civil society to complement the space occupied by other institutions and practices intrinsic to democracy. As a site of female activism, civil society is particularly important, be it in the form of NGOs, publishing initiatives, neighbourhood associations or other unofficial groupings. In regard to both social preconditions – and what people within the island are themselves aware of and willing to encourage – the opportunity for a move toward democratisation, consonant with a preservation of Cuba's independence and the social values of the revolution, is in the realm of the possible. It remains to be seen what role Cuban women choose to play in such a process. Women have historically been in the forefront of struggles for social rights and have looked to the state for their delivery. Whether Cuban women perceive their interests as dependent upon not just the development of civil society but also the creation of a transformed, democratic state in which they can achieve much greater and more independent articulation, is a question that their experience of socialism and of its crisis has posed in especially acute form.

5

State Socialism and Women's Emancipation: A Continuing Retrospective

> Utopias do exert enormous influence over the actual course of historical events. Sometimes they are so promptly incorporated into political practice ... that there is hardly time for the glue to dry under their utopian label; sometimes they are deemed to have been brought into reality and then they imperceptibly merge into conservative ideologies.
>
> Zygmunt Bauman, 1976

> Cuban housewives are no longer the women who traditionally lived only to take care of individual or family matters. Today they contribute their labour, their initiative and their enthusiasm to the work of the revolution.
>
> Communist Party of Cuba, First Congress, 1975[1]

In 1991, during the final months of Soviet communism, demonstrators paraded in Moscow with a banner proclaiming 'Seventy Years – On the Road to Nowhere'. An implicit denunciation of official proclamations of the achievements of socialism, indeed of any vision of socialism as a road to a better future, this banner highlighted the claim that, in the end, Communist Party rule had achieved nothing. Yet state socialism was a system that above all justified itself in terms of historical progress and the gains and advances it brought about. Communism, once reached, was to represent the realisation of a historical potential, one for which capitalism may have prepared the ground, but which it could not itself attain.

The crisis and collapse of communism overturned – arguably destroyed – this progessivist perspective. Not only had communist revolution been shown, contrary to the rhetoric, to be reversible, but in the

99

aftermath of the fall it became conventional to stress how little was achieved, how wide the gap was between rhetoric and reality and how impermanent the apparent 'transformations' turned out to be.[2] Paralleling a broader scepticism concerning ideas of progress and development, the communist states and their policies were represented as a disastrous experiment in pursuit of the unattainable: social equality. Perhaps nowhere was this gap between socialist aspiration and reality felt to be greater than in regard to women's emancipation: communist parties had claimed to solve 'the woman question', and, in so doing, to have achieved what capitalism could not – real sexual equality. In retrospect it appeared that this, too, was an empty claim, a 'false emancipation'.[3] Such a view was sustained by evidence of the gender gap in communist states – women's pay was around two-thirds that of men's, women still performed the bulk of the housework and childcare and were largely absent from the centres of political power. This was as true in Third World revolutionary states as in the USSR and Eastern Europe. Communism had, therefore, not represented the supercession of capitalism, but a dead end, for men and women alike; capitalism with a human and consumerist face came instead to represent a more desirable goal the world over.

But in focusing on the failures, post-communist assessments present only a partial account of a more complex and challenging reality. State socialism was certainly marked by a high degree of make-believe, what Vaclav Havel called the 'Great Lie'. Its economic model was inefficient and unsustainable. It was characterised by a pervasive system of authoritarian rule which prevailed even in the comparatively less repressive states such as Cuba or Yugoslavia. Yet if state socialism was a failure in terms of its goals, the claims its rulers made about the changes it had wrought were more than mere rhetoric: communist parties presided over some of the most dramatic and widespread attempts at social change in modern times. Throughout much of the twentieth century, communist parties worldwide embarked on an ambitious and comprehensive programme of social reform with the proclaimed goal of eradicating social inequality and injustice. Previously oppressed groups, whether peasants, workers or women, were to be set free and endowed with new rights and status. As a result of the policies adopted by communist states, women's socio-economic position was radically transformed: under Communist Party rule women acquired new rights and obligations; they entered the public realm in substantial numbers, as workers and political actors; they attained similar, if not superior, levels of education to men; and the family was modernised and placed on a foundation of legal equality between the sexes. On any conventional definition of progress, let alone one based on feminist criteria, as far as the situation of women was concerned, the communist states merit some recognition.

This commitment to altering the position of women was not incidental. State socialism, as one of the inheritors of the socialist tradition, was associated from its origins with the idea of women's emancipation, an emancipation conceived as liberation from the constraints of premodern patriarchal authority, from the 'bourgeois' family and from the exploitation of capitalism itself. In terms of these three goals and the standards that were set by the rulers of state socialism, these regimes achieved much of what they set out to do. Whether what was achieved can be considered 'emancipation' in any sense is questionable, but the fact remains that many of the ideas and policies that communist parties put into effect from 1917 onwards had much in common with those that originated with feminism. This was partly because of the latter's influence on the socialist tradition and partly because of a shared radical commitment. Feminist aspirations were certainly annexed to the communist project, an annexation that occurred via the common ground shared by socialism and feminism, indeed shared by liberalism and nationalism too, in which women's emancipation was part of a broader project of modernisation and economic development.

Some writers have taken this convergence as proof that feminism's project and vision was misconceived, or that it constituted a strategy so collusive with power that it negated its emancipatory vision. The collapse of state socialism challenged not just the communist claim to have emancipated women but the very goal of emancipation itself, along with the entire project of modernist, egalitarian social change.[4] Yet such totalising judgements fail to grasp the contradictory, ambivalent and complex character of this process, just as they do not distinguish between the different elements of their critique. Such a precipitous abandonment of the feminist programme and aspirations of radical social change fails, too, to take account of the conditions of human misery that led to the adoption and endorsement of these policies, especially in many parts of the less developed world. The argument advanced here is that the failure of state socialism and its programme for women's emancipation lay less in its goals of social equality, development and progress, than in the manner in which it sought to realise them, through its association with an authoritarian, centralised state and economy. For all the invocations of revolution from below, state socialism was a project that relied on a coercive radicalism imposed from above.

The aim of this chapter is to locate the communist approach to 'the woman question' within this context. It begins by considering the affinities and tensions between feminism and socialism and examines how Communist Party programmes on 'the woman question' evolved. It then discusses the ideas of modernity and progress within the Marxist tradition and how these implicated gender relations. The last section offers a gendered reading of state socialism and concludes with a discussion of some implications of the communist record for contemporary debates.

Women's Emancipation

Though associated most evidently with radical social movements of the nineteenth and early twentieth centuries, the idea of 'women's emancipation' had many tributary currents. In Roman law, 'emancipation' referred to freedom from the patriarchal authority enshrined in the *patria potestas*. It retained this meaning over time: in the eighteenth and nineteenth centuries 'emancipation' appears in the work of legal theorists such as Maine who, also referring to emancipation from patriarchal authority, identifies it as freedom from civil disabilities. Emancipation entered the language of modern politics through the movement for the abolition of slavery as it developed in the eighteenth and nineteenth centuries. In this usage, it rested on liberal humanist conceptions of the individual's entitlement to dignity, freedom and rights. Those who lived in a state that deprived them of such rights were denied basic humanity. Such arguments were extended to all states of servitude, and liberals such as Mill, and later socialists and feminists of different political sympathies, likened women's situation within marriage and their deprivation of civil rights to the state of slavery. As Mill expressed it in *The Subjection of Women*, a text that was first published in 1861, the year of the outbreak of the American Civil War, 'no slave is a slave to the same lengths, and in so full a sense of the word, as a wife is'.[5] This analogy was frequently made in the writings on 'the woman question' that circulated in the socialist movement, notably in August Bebel's *Women in the Past, Present and Future* and Friedrich Engels' *Origin of the Family, Private Property and the State*. Engels wrote that 'woman was a slave before the slave existed', and in his denunciation of the family as a site of female oppression, he spoke of the 'open or disguised enslavement of the women' that it condoned.[6]

Against this state of subjection, and counterposed to it, was the idea of the free, sovereign individual, encapsulated in the concept of citizenship, a status which combined freedom with equality, dignity and rights. Freedom from servitude and the acquisition of rights were bound up with ideas of progress and modernity shared by liberals and Marxists alike. States of subjection and servitude were an abhorrent feature of the Old World, out of tune with the values of the modern enlightened order. However, while the laws of history had begun the process of delivering freedom and justice to men, women remained subjects and outside the calculus of citizenship, 'slaves of injustice', as Wollstonecraft expressed it. Reformers like Mill saw women's oppression as a 'relic of the past ... discordant with the future and which must necessarily disappear'.[7] Such views were enthusiastically endorsed within the growing movements for women's rights and against the double standards in social life that prevailed.

The promise of autonomy, variously defined as freedom from patriarchal servitude, from the oppression of pre-modern society and from religious authority, drew many women into the ranks of radical modernist movements in the nineteenth century, not only in the conditions of industrialisation and revolution in Europe and America, but also in Latin America, Asia and the Middle East.[8] From the particularities of their experience, women poets and writers, educationalists and workers, protested at the injustice they suffered in a system which placed them under the control of men and subjected them to humiliation and suffering. For all their differences with regard to what they identified as the causes of their misery and the solutions to it, women joined in a denunciation of the social order that prevailed in their countries. They dreamed of an alternative in which 'new women', that is, free, modern women, could forge a destiny for themselves.

The idea of women's emancipation contained within it both modern aspirations for rights and citizenship and earlier meanings of freedom from patriarchal authority. This implied freedom from the despotic authority and injustice of the old social order, and freedom for women to realise their true potential in the modern world. Feminists, whether socialist, liberal or nationalist, embraced modernity. They too linked their achievement of autonomy to the development of a modern society. Modernity signified equality and general social progress. The economic changes which capitalism brought transformed the character of society, and loosened the ties of kinship, community and religion that bound women into servitude, while offering them an escape through economic independence. The achievement of women's emancipation would come about both through the efforts of women's movements but also as part of a broader process of human emancipation that would accompany scientific advance and economic development. Liberal feminists envisaged this occurring within a humanised capitalism, socialists through revolutionary transformation and nationalists through the birth of the sovereign nation liberated from imperialism. In all cases a specific form of modernity and of development would provide the structural, political and social basis for a more egalitarian, more just and humane society.

Within feminism more broadly, this politics comprised three elements which were not seen as in contradiction: the emancipation and liberation of the individual woman from patriarchal subordination; collective social and political action by women; and reforming state intervention to secure the rights and conditions necessary to achieve equality. Feminism generated its own visions of modernity, variously promoting ideas of full equality, free love, a state welfare system, scientific advance in health and reproductive matters, freedom from domestic servitude, socialised childcare, marital equality and equal participation in the public spheres, especially in education and employment. Thus, if the nineteenth century was widely epitomised by images of the worker or peasant throwing off his shackles, the early twentieth century was represented by that of the emancipated woman freeing herself from the patriarchal bonds of the old society.

Some of these feminist demands received support from broader currents of reform. To nineteenth- and twentieth-century radicals and reformers alike, women's subordination or servitude within marriage and the family was both an evil in itself and a symbol of backwardness, an obstacle to progress. Within the prevailing evolutionary perspective, what was not modern, where modern meant Western, was by definition redundant and backward, to be rejected. When nationalists in China called for the abolition of footbinding and the education of women, in India, for the end of child marriage and *suttee* (a Hindu woman's act of devotion to her husband, in which she sacrifices herself on her husband's funeral pyre); or in Turkey, for the end of veiling and for women's civil and political rights, they saw this as necessary for the development of their country.[9] The entry of women into public life, the education of women, the reform of the family, so passionately advocated by feminists, were all in turn seen as requirements of modernisation.

The spread of such ideas took place in a context dominated by the impact of imperialism, direct and indirect. As a result, the belief in the need to embrace modernity, and to promote modernisation, was common currency in the nineteenth and twentieth centuries, not just in Europe but also in the less developed nations threatened by the rapid growth of their industrialised rivals in the West. Responses to imperialism nonetheless varied. As a consequence, in Asia, Latin America and the Middle East there arose a bitter debate – one which continued for the duration of the twentieth century – over how to confront the challenge of the industrialised world. On one side, conservatives argued for closing the frontiers, both economically, via protectionism, and culturally, through resistance to Western influence, especially on matters of women's rights and deportment. On the other side, modernisers denounced traditional society as doomed, and argued that progressive change was necessary and inevitable. Such change could only be achieved through the modernisation of social institutions and values, along with political and social reform. From both perspectives the family and the status of women were key signifiers of, in the first case, a cultural authenticity to be left unchanged and, in the second, a backwardness which required reform. Gender relations were therefore a subject of concern to oppositional social movements and states alike, something which remained the case throughout the twentieth century. As we shall see, they also became central to the communist project of modernity.

Socialism and Women's Emancipation

The idea of an egalitarian modernity, in which all forms of oppression were abolished, (including that based on gender) expressed both the optimistic evolutionism of the nineteenth century and the founding principle of socialism. The goals of early feminism – women's emancipation from servitude and their attainment of full personhood, autonomy and equality – were ones that were also promised by liberalism and by the socialist movements of the nineteenth century. To socialists, women were doubly oppressed – they were exploited as wage slaves and oppressed within the family. 'The woman question' was of concern to the leaders and theorists of socialist movements, many of whom addressed the subject in speeches, pamphlets and books and sought to mobilise women into their cause. Some of the theories that became important to feminist movements, notably Engels' materialist explanation of women's subordination, originated within the socialist tradition, and socialists, both in and out of power, were often among the most influential advocates of reforms that would secure women's emancipation.

In Russia as elsewhere, the pre-1914 workers' movement was closely associated with the campaign for women's suffrage. When the Bolsheviks came to power in 1917 they drew up a programme which remained the basis for subsequent Communist Party policy across the world. This combined a general support for the principle of women's emancipation with a range of policies that reflected many of the demands that feminists had been calling for. The programme that they drew up aimed to end legal inequality, exploitation in the workplace and 'domestic servitude'. The 'historically oppressed female sex' would be educated and employed; communal services would alleviate domestic work and childcare; women would acquire equal opportunities and would be mobilised into political work and into government administration. Protective legislation would 'safeguard women's childbearing capacities'.[10] The essential difference from liberal and social democratic or reformist socialism, lay in the claim that only through *revolutionary* change that destroyed class society could women's emancipation be attained.

As a current within radical thought, and as a social movement, feminism had a close association with socialism, but it was one that was often antagonistic and became more so with time. In practice the political links forged between these two traditions constituted what was often a fraught and conditional alliance. For all that they were both descendants of the Enlightenment and of its evolution through the French Revolution and the radical traditions of the nineteenth century, a clear, analytic and political, distinction divided them. This was evident as much in their analysis of inequality and exploitation as in the measures needed to overcome them. While socialism allocated primacy to the class relations arising out of the economic system and its property relations, feminism emphasised the importance of tackling oppressive gender relations, masculine power and privilege materialised in the family, in the society at large and in the organisation of the socialist movement itself. This difference was all the greater in regard to the revolutionary variants of socialism that came to power in the wake of Soviet consolidation.

When in power, communist parties more often than not deployed the power of the state to convert their distrust of 'bourgeois feminism' into the suppression of any independent expression of feminist dissent, while selectively instrumentalising feminist aspirations and subordinating them to other priorities. Of these, the consolidation of state power and the radical restructuring of the economy in the name of the freeing of the proletariat from capitalist exploitation were superordinate. The party would emancipate women through its top-down programme. If this did not achieve the promised results, then these would occur at some indeterminate point in the future and would follow from the broader programme of revolutionary change.

The tension between socialism and its feminist critics was all the greater because of the overlapping of analysis and commitment, taking the form of feminist currents within socialism and of socialist currents within feminism. Throughout the history of the socialist movement there has, therefore, been a strand of feminist critique from within. Many feminists shared in the vision of a just society, but criticised the ways in which communist parties sought to bring it about. Amongst the Bolsheviks, Inessa Armand (1874–1920) and Alexandra Kollontai (1872–1952) were early critics of their party's policies and practice, and they, along with anarchist feminists such as Emma Goldman, laid some of the early groundwork in identifying socialism's failures. They outlined what they saw as the indispensable components of an alternative socialist commitment to women's emancipation, one which depended not only upon the incorporation of women into the labour force and equality in political life but also on a transformation of the domestic sphere and the realisation of sexual freedom.[11] While Armand and Kollontai shared the view that the transformation of the domestic sphere and of sexual relations were closely linked to political revolution, they envisaged difficulties: 'the path to this emancipation is long and thorny', Armand declared.[12] They did, therefore, lay much greater emphasis than Lenin and the majority of his male associates on the need to promote change in the domestic and sexual domains and they argued eloquently, but unsuccessfully, for separate associations for women.

In the end, a conservative recomposition of Soviet 'morality' combined with the character of economic policy meant that both the domestic sphere and sexuality were annexed to the state in ways that incorporated, but at the same time erased the radical import of the feminist critique. Decades later, the elements of this critique were reworked and added to by feminists of different persuasions as communism's failures *vis-à-vis* its emancipatory agenda became increasingly evident. Both within and outside communist and socialist parties in Europe and elsewhere, feminists developed their own criticisms of the USSR and its allies and of Marxist theory itself. The theoretical and philosophical contribution of Simone de Beauvoir, writing in the 1940s in a context of general political identification with the communist movement, interrogated the 'monist' (that is, reductive) premises of Marxism and inaugurated a theoretical debate over its adequacy for the understanding of female subordination.[13] This critical attitude to socialist orthodoxy in the communist world coexisted, however, with a substantial interest in the West in developing a Marxist or Marxisant theoretical approach within feminism, and it was this endeavour that was to prevail amidst much of the writing that emerged with the revival of feminism in Western Europe and the USA in the late 1960s and onwards. Yet even within this theoretical project there was little attention paid to state socialism as such or to the policies these states adopted in relation to women. The Eastern European and Soviet cases were criticised in general terms for their authoritarianism but otherwise ignored, while Third World revolutions received a considerable measure of general sympathy from socialist and liberal feminists alike.

In the very different contexts of Third World revolution there were also some critical female voices. In the 1940s the feminist writer Ting Ling was condemned by the Chinese Communist Party for criticising its narrow and instrumental view of women's emancipation in the areas under its control in Yenan province.[14] In Vietnam and Mozambique, feminist dissent was voiced in relation to the neglect of women's needs; and as we have seen (Chapter 2), the later revolution of the Sandinistas in Nicaragua saw the emergence of what is perhaps the most thoroughgoing socialist feminist critique of patriarchal power and elite practice from within the developing countries as a whole.[15] In the countries of Eastern Europe as well as in Russia itself, feminist currents had re-emerged by the later 1970s and were adding their own contribution to the debate over state socialism's failures. This critique emphasised more than any other the continuing hardship and exhaustion experienced by women in these modern, industrial nation-states where the barriers to formal equality had been removed. In all this evolution, while reworked in different ways, the central and common elements of feminist critique were strikingly consistent: they revolved round the failure of the party adequately to represent women's interests, the need for an independent expression of these, the attitudes of communist parties towards issues of sexuality and the family, the difficulties experienced by women in combining work with childcare, and the continuing expressions of masculine power and privilege within society, party and state.

In the analyses that ensued from this critical engagement, however, little agreement was reached on how to theorise or explain the persistence of women's subordination in a context where so many of the formal obstacles to equality had, on the face of it, been removed.[16] Some approaches placed the emphasis on untransformed family relations, others stressed the absence of feminist debate, others still the exploitation of women's unpaid labour in subsistence agriculture and in the home. But two elements were consistently identified as particularly important in explaining the continuing subordination of women: the inadequacies of Marxist theory – seen as the formative influence on state attitudes and policy concerning women – and the existence of various institutionalised forms of male dominance in the state and society as a whole – in a word, 'patriarchy'. The two forms of explanation were not mutually exclusive, in that it could be (and often was) argued that it was precisely because of the 'gender blindness' or 'androcentrism' of Marxism, in particular in the work of Engels, that it did not identify and seek to overcome those social relations that the category of 'patriarchy' subsumed. At the same time, the difference in emphasis of the two approaches is such that they merit separate, if convergent, examination. The one can be seen as locating a specific 'patriarchal' element within Marxist theory itself from which all policy (errors and oversights) flowed, the other as ascribing the position of women in these societies to the workings of more generalised patriarchal practices, ones which it was argued could operate at least as much in socialist states as in feudal or capitalist ones. As we will see, it was more than Marxist theory, whatever its critical limitations, that would be necessary to account for the gender regime that prevailed at the heart of the revolutionary project.

Socialist Revolution and 'Progress': Two Steps Forward?

If feminist theorists sought their explanation of communism's failures in Marxist theory and the tenacity of patriarchy, the fact remained that the communist states were the earliest to apply egalitarian principles in matters of law and policy. For much of the twentieth century they had the most explicit commitment to promoting women's emancipation. The guiding principles behind their policies claimed inspiration from the work of Marx, Engels and Lenin, and had their origins in an official codification of their ideas by the Bolsheviks. The latter's proclamations on women's emancipation, agreed at the Second Congress of the Comintern in 1920, laid out a programme which remained the basis of policy on women for the duration of the communist system. This included bringing women out of the home and into the economy, reorganising peasant households that 'kept women in subservient positions', developing communal services to alleviate domestic work and childcare to relieve them from 'domestic slavery', providing equal opportunities for women, mobilising women into political work and into government administration, and providing protective legislation 'to safeguard women's reproductive activities'.[17] In addition, legislation was passed which provided for maternity leave, social insurance, civil marriage, consensual divorce and, in time, abortion on demand. As a consequence not just of legal reforms, but of these combined with a range of supportive policies, it could be said that, with the exception of Scandinavian social democracy, the states which made the most efforts to improve the social position of women and to remove formal inequalities between the sexes were those which officially endorsed orthodox Marxism and which drew on the classic texts for their theoretical and ethical justification of state policy. In comparative terms they seemed to have achieved more, and to have done so earlier, than most of the Western liberal democracies, which they charged with having 'failed' women.[18] Well before most governments of Western Europe or the United States gave women equal rights, equal pay and the vote, or began to introduce state-provided nurseries and paid maternity leave, the ruling communist parties were able to claim that many of these policies had either already been implemented or were in the process of being so.

Communist states were also able to assert with apparent pride until the mid-1980s that in such areas as education and employment, women had attained greater equality with men than under capitalism. Public education programmes were indeed a priority for most communist governments. The female sex, which everywhere lagged behind in terms of access to education at all levels, benefited disproportionately from the literacy campaigns and the expansion of education which followed the accession of communist parties to power. It is a striking testimony to Bolshevik policy that in the USSR as early as 1923 half of all university students were female, well before the first female students were routinely admitted to university colleges in Britain and the USA. From the perspective of the Bolsheviks, bourgeois democracy, for all its promise of gender equality, had failed to deliver on it: under capitalism, they wrote 'woman has remained a being without rights, a domestic animal, part of the furniture of the marital couch'.[19]

With regard to employment, a similar picture emerges. In 1980 half of the labour force of Eastern European countries consisted of women, compared with 32 per cent for Western Europe; even as the capitalist states began to catch up, by the middle of that decade, only Sweden, Denmark and Finland had higher rates of female participation than East Germany (77.5 per cent) and the USSR (70 per cent). The less developed regions under communist rule also showed significant increases over their capitalist counterparts. 1980 figures for the Muslim Central Asian republics of the USSR showed that a full 40 per cent of the labour force was female; in Vietnam, 45 per cent; and North Korea, 46 per cent. By contrast, the average for the Middle East at that time was 20 per cent; for Latin America, 22 per cent; and for the Far East (the second highest average after the centrally planned economies), 35 per cent. Finally, in terms of health indicators, the communist states were able to show improvements in the general health of their populations with rising life expectancy and declining rates of morbidity and mortality.

This apparently more advanced programme was not, however, either sustained or comprehensive. As in other respects, notably economic growth and welfare provision, communist aspiration after 1917 was increasingly rivalled, and in some cases overtaken, by capitalism, at least in some of the developed Western states. In the legislative sphere, for example, for reasons as diverse as East–West rivalry and the pressure exerted by women's movements, some of the advanced capitalist countries subsequently caught up, and in some respects overtook, their socialist counterparts. By the end of the 1980s the achievements of liberal democracy in the domain of women's legal rights and social status were becoming increasingly evident.

On the other hand, the contrast in certain areas of social provision remained. Most capitalist states in the 1980s could not rival the CPEs in maternity support and nursery provision. Their record on employment in general was one which failed to check rising unemployment, while their expansion of women's employment opportunities was far slower, and often skewed towards part time and casual work. If in the more developed Western states this difference between capitalism and 'real socialism' narrowed, the same could not be said of the poorer countries of the South. Here a far greater gulf with respect to women's overall social and economic position separated capitalist from communist states. In these less developed countries ruled by communist governments, the female population obtained greater legal equality, access to health, education at all levels and practical support for entry into employment. An even more striking contrast was the commitment which these states made to discouraging customary practices which were harmful to women, such as footbinding in China, compulsory veiling and *purdah* (seclusion of Muslim women) in Central Asia and female genital mutilation in South Yemen. Women's organisations, controlled by the ruling party, were given some scope for furthering the policy aims of the party with respect to women and provided 'women's issues' with some visibility and legitimacy. As a consequence, it could be claimed with some accuracy that in such developing communist states, women suffered less publicly sanctioned discrimination on the basis of sex than did those in comparable capitalist states.

This history was, however, only in part a consequence of the historic socialist commitment to women's emancipation. Communist parties did not deliver, and did not seek to establish, full sexual equality, yet they sought to alter the socioeconomic position of women in profound ways. The major changes in gender relations that they introduced, and the policies which gave rise to them, as well as their failings, can only be understood as resulting from a combination of ideological commitment with three other elements of the socialist programme: the emphasis on rapid economic development, a radical interpretation of modernity, and a belief in the need for a strong central state.

Socialism and Development: Conceptual Origins and Subsequent Materialisation

Comparative indicators of the kind noted above suggest that the substantial changes in women's socioeconomic position in the CPEs were not merely a by-product of modernisation and economic development.[20] The relatively higher rates of women's participation in education and in the national economies of these states were brought about as the result of deliberate policy interventions, ones which were supported by an overall context of greater state control over economy and society, itself a product of the distinctive strategic goals of communist states.

The goal that communist parties claimed to be moving towards, though in the distant future, was a new form of society, 'advanced communism'. Yet this was not the course that these societies took: behind the claims of communist teleology, encapsulated in the term 'transitional states', other objectives predominated. In retrospect, the trajectory of these societies should not be understood as a move, a 'transition', to a new socialist and supposedly emancipatory socio-political order. Rather, this project combined broad ideological goals relating to the building of a new order with two much more immediate concerns: the consolidation of state power in a post-revolutionary situation and the mobilisation of domestic resources for the task of development. The commitment to development was itself ambivalent: if it was seen as a way of achieving 'socialism' and establishing an alternative to capitalism, it was also a means of competing with, catching up and overtaking the capitalist world. This link between socialism and development was already clear to the early Bolsheviks: the revolution was to solve the problem of Russia's backwardness. Kollontai, in a letter of 1921, wrote: 'I believe we, sooner than any capitalist country, will enter into a period of prosperity.'[21] Stalin was to convert this dream of prosperity into a series of five-year plans, while Khrushchev, renouncing the inevitability of war with capitalism, was to announce, in 1961, that the USSR would 'catch up with and overtake' the capitalist world within a generation. Mao Tse-tung, too, echoing the same aspiration in the Great Leap Forward, announced that China was set to overtake the West. Hence, any assessment of what these states did, or tried to do, has to look both at their proclaimed goals and at the same time at their impact. It has to examine the 'construction' of socialism on the one hand, and at the dominant realities of state consolidation and mobilisation for economic development, on the other.

Socialist Development Goals

If communist governments prioritised economic development, this was in no small measure due to the fact that, with the exception of East Germany and the Central European states (Hungary, Czechoslovakia and Poland), most had come to power in the poorer, less developed regions of the world. Revolutionary leaderships promised to eradicate poverty and to set in place the social and economic programmes that they believed would succeed in developing their countries and bring about greater social justice. Long present in the Marxist classics, the themes of economic development and the social progress that it could bring, if harnessed to the specific form in which it was to be achieved under socialism, were taken up and elaborated upon by their followers. Ideas of social justice, national independence, equality and progress were combined with a commitment to development, the latter seen as a transformation of existing social relations and as a means to compete with the West.

The history of socialism is therefore inextricably bound up with developmentalism.[22] Economic development became the ultimate measure and goal of progress, and socialist theorists and economists drew their lessons from capitalism with regard to industrialisation and the organisation of work. Yet their development strategy was to destroy the dynamic force of the capitalist market, replacing it with a powerful state, which they believed was capable of achieving the desired results 'at a stroke'. Development was to be achieved through the revolutionary transformation of the entire society, in the process of which the traditional obstacles to such progress would be swept away and a new foundation would be laid. The abolition of 'want and scarcity' could only be achieved through economic growth and an integrated, modern society. If 'bourgeois freedoms' were to be sacrificed, this was but a small price to pay.

This pursuit of an accelerated process of development and modernity had major consequences for the female sex. Women's emancipation, as noted earlier, had constituted an integral part of the overall socialist revolutionary project; it was an ethical commitment, but one with practical implications. Women were to be delivered from servitude as part of the pursuit of greater equality, while at the same time their emancipation would assist in the efforts to bring about social modernisation and economic development. It was, therefore, the articulation of the idea of women's emancipation with development concerns, but combined with a radical, state-directed programme of social transformation, that underlay the policies of communist states and gave them their distinctive character.

Marx and Modernity

This perspective on the emancipation of women, indeed on social transformation as a whole, had its roots in socialist thought. It was contained within the overall Marxist commitment to modernity and its recognition and realisation of the potential contained within the ongoing development of modern society. The division between men and women, like that between classes, and between nations, would be gradually, or not so gradually, subsumed into a broader unification of all humanity into a new social order. Modernity was both a recognition of a reality, something that was already underway, and a programme of change. Marx abhorred the backwardness and stagnation of the old societies of Europe and Asia and their 'barbaric' customs – among the chief victims of which were women. In *The Holy Family,* he quoted with approval the observation of the utopian radical Charles Fourier on the relation between social development and the status of women: 'The change in a historical epoch can always be determined by the progress of women towards freedom, because in the relation of women to man, of the weak to the strong, the victory of human nature over brutality is most in evidence. The degree of emancipation of women is the natural measure of general emancipation.'[23] Like other nineteenth-century progressivists, whether liberal or socialist, he saw the struggle for modernity as necessitating the end of traditional patriarchal societies. As Engels argued in his *The Origin of the Family, Private Property and the State,* in undermining patriarchal power and bourgeois marriage and by drawing women into employment, capitalism could begin the process of liberating women from the shackles of tradition, but socialism would complete it.[24] While women's emancipation was part of a historically determined process of modernisation, its full realisation was to be assured under socialism, by the ending of the patriarchal family, by the incorporation of women into the labour force and by the socialisation of childcare.

In his debate with the Utopian Socialists, Marx stressed that socialism could not be built on the basis of want and scarcity, that economic development was necessary to provide the material foundation on which a new type of society was to be erected. While Marx's originality lay in his emphasis on class struggle as the motor of progress and on the contradictory character of capitalist development – its progressive aspects vitiated by the profound injustices inscribed within its economic system – he embraced the idea of modernisation and development with enthusiasm, seeing the superiority of a future socialist society as lying in its ability to create greater wealth and to realise full human freedom. Marx wrote in the *Manifesto*, 'The constrictions of bourgeois (class) society would be stripped away so that the full potentiality of the modern epoch could be fulfilled', thereby enabling the wounds of modernity to be healed through what Marshall Berman called 'a fuller and deeper modernity'.[25] Socialism was seen as part of an inevitable historical evolution. History was moving forward and was on the side of the working class struggle for socialism. Within this broad historical process, the development of the economy, and in particular of industry, played a central part, both in preparing the ground for its successor, socialism, and in building the material basis for socialism itself.[26]

Marx and Engels were notoriously brief about what form the new society would take, but even the summary points made in the *Manifesto* testify to the way their materialist conception of modernity shaped their view of a future society: the communist revolution was to be 'the most radical rupture with traditional property relations; no wonder that its development involves the most radical rupture with traditional ideas'.[27] In order to accomplish this task, the victorious proletariat had to 'centralise all instruments of production in the hands of the state' and 'increase the total productive forces as rapidly as possible'.[28] Thus, the classical Marxist view was, in essence, a radical reworking of the prevailing belief in modernity: the transformation of the world by scientific and technical progress was to be welcomed; large-scale industry was leading to a new form of society, accelerated by class struggle; and, once the revolution had come, it would continue this process, transforming not just property relations but the whole political, social and cultural system as well. It was only under 'advanced communism' that humanity would be able to tap the full richness created by production, as the realm of necessity would be replaced by the realm of freedom and plenitude and the conditions for the 'free development of each for all' would finally be established.

In order to reach this ideal end-state, it was necessary to prepare the way in what was envisaged as a transitional stage, one in which the material base of the new society would be forged. Harding has argued that this transitional stage, not yet communism, but socialism, laid the theoretical basis for the foundation of what became the Soviet state.[29] This stage was characterised by a centralising state that would mobilise labour and develop a modern industrial sector, and increase the social surplus.[30] Marx counterposed to the capitalist state – which he condemned as irresponsible, anarchic and unjust – the socialist state, which would establish a rational, planned and just social order based on state control of production and distribution of the surplus product. In addition to these economic roles, Marx acknowledged that in the transitional period the state would continue to have a repressive function. The term 'dictatorship of the proletariat' described the coercive power that would be wielded against the enemies of the proletarian revolution; this dictatorship would preside over a centralised administrative structure and effect the tasks of revolutionary transformation.

This vision of socialism as a necessary, if painful, stage on the road to freedom and plenty retained its appeal among sympathetic quarters throughout the history of the twentieth century and was to be reinforced by the outbreak of revolution in comparatively less developed societies. Its sweeping vision of change under the firm direction of the ruling party would bring the desired progress and transform the whole society, eliminating oppression and backwardness and drawing the entire population into the course of an inevitable historical advance. Marx and Engels envisaged development in nineteenth-century evolutionary idiom as a movement of supercession in which the 'old society' would be erased and replaced by a higher stage of life. In this process all previous patriarchal, traditional 'feudal' and 'barbaric' pre-capitalist relations would be swept into the dustbin of history. Peasants, slaves, serfs and women would be emancipated and delivered from their oppressors, to be made full participants, through their entry into the labour force, in a collective effort to secure the basis of the new social order. It was these concerns, above all those of realising the tasks of development, which later theorists and Communist Party rulers elaborated upon in their attempt to fashion a workable alternative and rival to capitalism.

These progressivist elements, present in Marx's thought, coalesced in Russian Marxism. Here the general vision of historical advance was given added urgency by Russia's poverty and relative underdevelopment at the turn of the twentieth century. They were systemised by Lenin into a vision of socialism which was distinct from the humanist conceptions of cooperation, individual self-fulfilment and social equality that had animated parts of the socialist movement. In the years after 1917, socialism came increasingly to be identified with state control over production, discipline and the maximisation of socially useful work.[31] The ideas of thinkers like Proudhon that socialism should be built on the basis of spontaneous, bottom-up and local initiatives of men and women freed from dependency and submission, were seen to offer no solution to the pressing problem of development. The society of self-governing individuals was an image of socialism remote from the statist model that was soon to evolve.

The Bolsheviks: The Founding Model of State Socialism

Within their own historical perspective, the Bolsheviks were enthusiastically committed to catching up and overtaking the capitalist world. They identified themselves with the project of social modernisation and economic development and applied a modified Marxist developmentalism to this end. The need to overcome Russia's backwardness was something that reformers of various persuasions had perceived since the eighteenth century. The increasing social tensions generated by the failure of successive rulers in the nineteenth century to deliver economic and social reform was a decisive impetus to the revolutionary upheaval which swept the Bolsheviks to power.

Lenin confronted the problem of turning Russia into a modern nation-state with characteristic determination. He opposed the agrarian populists' vision of a community-based socialism growing out of the communal property form, the *mir*, because it could not sustain the required levels of economic growth. In defiance of Marx's view that socialism could only be created on the basis of the productive forces developed by capitalism, Lenin set about constructing socialism in a society where capitalism was unevenly and superficially rooted. The immanence of the world proletarian revolution would guarantee the survival and strengthening of socialism in the more weakly developed states.[32] The sheer force of revolutionary will would triumph over capitalism, and a powerful central state would help to overcome underdevelopment and the devastation of the war. The chief party theorists, Lenin, Bukharin and Trotsky, were all agreed by 1920 on the need to establish centralised control and to expand the state's coercive capacity and control over the economy.[33] The market-oriented character of the New Economic Policy (NEP) – adopted as a short-term expedient – was phased out and by 1923 centralisation was well under way. Although the transformation of property relations proceeded unevenly, political control over the population was increasingly established entailing the suppression or neutralisation of opposition, presented as a necessary response to the conditions of crisis and social disorder. A parallel development was the establishment of labour discipline in the workplace and an institutionalised system of tame trade unions and other mass organisations, which would act as 'transmission belts' of the party. In the face of a diminished social base, and in the midst of national disaster, the model of Soviet socialism as the dictatorship of the proletariat was acquiring material form.

The elements already in place under Lenin coalesced under Stalin into the centralised system of economic management and political authority that came to be known as state socialism. Its principal elements were to constitute the central programme of subsequent communist parties everywhere: the abolition of private property in the means of production; centralised directive planning over the economy; the expansion of the state's role and authority within society; the establishment of the party as uncontested authority and consequent suppression of autonomous institutions; the establishment of a system of free public education and welfare; the mobilisation, control and disciplining of labour.[34] Socialism, therefore, evolved not into a system based on worker's control and democratic accountability, as Lenin had momentarily suggested in 1917, but into an authoritarian state, one whose chief goals were increased productivity, economic efficiency and social control.

Under Stalin, these ideas were applied in a particularly brutal way under a highly centralised power structure, which sought to extinguish all dissent, real or imagined. The state took over or eliminated all independent institutions – in the areas of education, political life, religious practice and in the economy. The forced collectivisation of agriculture, along with massive construction and industrialisation projects, were the goals of the planned economy, and from 1928 onwards, successive five-year plans were implemented by means of the growing power and reach of the state.

The Soviet state achieved control over the economy and at immense social and human cost, a heavy industrial infrastructure was built up and the class and property relations of the society were transformed. Estimates vary, but between 20 and 50 million people were the victims of labour camps, starvation and the widespread system of repression. The

Soviet Union in the 1930s began to rival the depression-gripped West in its rate of economic growth, industrial output and arms production, and from the late 1950s claimed growth rates not dissimilar to those of its capitalist antagonists. An underdeveloped society, it seemed, had been able to modernise and achieve its social and economic objectives of catching up with the West.

Modernising Intimacy: Transforming Women

[T]hose who fight most energetically and persistently for the new are those who suffer most from the old. And in the present family situation the one that suffers most is the woman – the wife and the mother.

Trotsky, 1970

The efforts to transform the economy were paralleled by the setting in place of an extensive and ambitious programme of social modernisation. Schools were built, mass health and literacy programmes were launched and an assault on 'old attitudes' was led by party activists. The con-struction of a modern society was seen to depend upon the top-down transformation of all that was backward; archaic social institutions, relations and practices were to be modernised or abolished outright. In a grandiose foreshortening of history, the pre-existing social system, with its power relations, property forms and ruling classes, was to be dismantled and replaced with a new economic, social and cultural order. Religious and cultural institutions were either abolished or were to be brought under the control of the party-state.[35]

Efforts to effect this process of accelerated modernistation and transformation of society inevitably involved women as part of the populations affected by these policies, but women also became the targets of reforming policies in more direct ways. They were seen as the chief victims of tradition in 'feudal' societies and of exploitation in capitalist ones. Moreover, as those most trapped in obscurantism they not only needed liberating but enlightening, as their backwardness, 'lack of culture', conservatism, religiosity and ignorance was something that stood in the way of progress. Once delivered, as part of the oppressed masses, women could be mobilised as political actors in the service of revolution.

Such were the ideas behind the policies applied throughout the USSR in its modernising efforts. But the link between the emancipation of women and the assault on backwardness was most clearly demonstrated in the confrontation in the 1920s between the modernising Bolshevik state and the rulers of Central Asia. In a continuation of the Tsarist policy of Russification, and to consolidate their control over the 'East', the Bolsheviks sought to 'civilise', revolutionise and modernise the societies they found there. Like Marx and Engels before him, Lenin, speaking of the 'East' had a reaction which was 'an amalgam of shock, frustration and disgust'.[36] Trotsky too denounced the 'most backward of the backward' and the 'barbarity of patriarchal life' which prevailed there.[37] Massel has argued that the approach adopted in the East by the Bolsheviks rested on two linked assumptions: that the key to undermining the traditional social order was the destruction of traditional family structures and that the breakdown of the kinship system itself could most speedily be achieved through the mobilisation of women.[38] Women, therefore, came to be percieved by the party leadership as a structural 'weak point' in the traditional order. Because they were so downtrodden in the old order they were considered to have revolutionary potential and could even substitute for the absent proletariat. In extending land rights to women through the Land Code of the 1920s and rights within the family enshrined within the new Family Code, the Bolsheviks attempted to 'stimulate and exploit ... sexual and generational tensions designed to induce upheaval in a traditional system of values, customs, relationships and roles, beginning with the primary cell of that system, the extended patriarchal family'.[39]

Mobilising women and emancipating them from tradition were, as noted earlier, not ideas unique to the Bolsheviks. Not only were they present in socialist and nationalist thought well before the Russian Revolution, but in the 1920s the Bolsheviks were not the only government that sought to mobilise women in the service of the developing nation. Their most notable contemporary, Turkey's Kemal 'Ataturk', abolished the *Shariah* Law (the sacred law of Islam, prescribing religious and other duties) in 1926, replacing it with a form of the Swiss Civil Code as part of his efforts at secularisation. He made sweeping changes in women's status, discouraged veiling and gave women the vote in order to bring Turkey into the modern world. Indeed Ataturk's reforms probably inspired the wave of Bolshevik radicalism which swept through Central Asia in the 'attack' (*Kuzum*) on the 'feudal patriarchal mode of life' of 1926–8.[40]

Other nationalist modernisers pursued similar objectives in the course of the twentieth century: the Mexican revolutionary state deployed legal reform to destabilise and then modernise the rural family in the 1920s as a way to advance its agrarian development programme.[41] In the 1930s the modernising Reza Shah of Iran brought in measures reforming women's legal, educational and social position which echoed those of Turkey. Family reform, secularisation and women's incorporation into public life increasingly came to be seen by modern statesmen as a fundamental component of social modernisation for the developing nations of the world. Such top-down modernising projects involving women had sometimes also formed part of the strategy of rule of European colonialism at various times in its history.[42]

But the rulers of the Soviet Union entertained a far more radical vision than the modernising secular nationalisms of the early twentieth century, even though the latter shared their impatient iconoclasm and contempt for the old society. While in their different ways these modernising states embraced Enlightenment ideas of secularism and rationalism as essential in the creation of a modern developed society,[43] what distinguished the Bolshevik vision even from the extremity of the Turkish case was its more thoroughgoing efforts at social change. Such efforts were premised on the complete overthrow of the old order and backed up by an array of interventionist policies. These were designed to incorporate women into the labour force and to provide them with rights that would promote the dissolution of the structural basis of the patriarchal family. Even the most radical of nationalist projects did not match the scale of the transformations attempted by the communist states.

Beyond the USSR: State Socialism and Women's Emancipation in the Socialist Periphery

On Decree No. 7 pertaining to Afghan women's rights:

> This decree ... [ensures] ... equal rights of women with men ... in the field of civil law ... [it] removes unjust patriarchal feudalistic relations between husband and wife and consolidates sincere family ties.[44]

The basic institutional features of the state and economy that evolved in the Soviet Union were transposed to those countries where Party rule was imposed after World War II – Czechoslovakia, Poland, Hungary and East Germany. Elsewhere, as communist parties came to power they voluntarily imitated a model they saw as promising to solve their development problems, meet the welfare needs of their populations, achieve independence from the Western powers and build up a viable economy. Mongolia led in 1921, and in the 1940s Albania and China opted to establish Soviet-type institutions of power, with a form of centrally planned economy. Other post-revolutionary Third World states followed, emulating the less brutal Soviet system that emerged after the death of Stalin. For all their diversity in origin and trajectory, each of these new states modelled their official rhetoric, constitutions, institutions and forms of state on the USSR.[45] Thus, despite its national and historical variations, its internal rivalry and territorial disputes, the communist movement had a common ideological programme. This homogeneity reflected three formative factors: a shared orthodoxy, 'Marxism-Leninism', originally codified within the Second International; the authority which, after 1917, the Bolshevik Revolution exerted over other communist parties, even those which later broke with it (Yugoslavia, China); and the creation of an alternative economic, military and political community, which in the conditions of the Cold War offered a temporary refuge to aspiring nations from an imperialist and hostile capitalist world. This affinity was reflected in their adoption of a common programme for women's emancipation, similar institutions of state and cognate social and economic policies.

While these state socialist systems differed in important ways, not least because some were imposed by the USSR, and others came into existence as a result of popular revolutions, these commonalities place their evolution within a common historical project, one that allows, indeed requires, comparative consideration. It is not that China or Cuba became societies identical to the USSR, but that their respective leaderships shared a conception of the social order they wanted to bring into being. In many areas they adopted policies influenced by a similar theoretical and ideological language and way of thinking. Marxism-Leninism was itself a universalising 'scientific' theory and its policy prescriptions were held to apply, with modifications, within very different contexts. The programme, policies and laws pertaining to women's emancipation were as a consequence remarkably consistent across the divide of history and culture. Engels' classic work became the authoritative text and required reading for party cadres and school-children alike, while party leaders from Enver Hoxha and Ceauşescu to Mao and Castro repeated its lessons in their own discourses on 'the woman question'. Naturally, the results of these efforts differed as did, to a variable extent, the manner of their realisation, but even within the diversity of outcome, some common patterns can be discerned with respect to gender relations.

Gender and Communist Policy and Practice

These various factors combined to create both a distinctive and a common approach to women's emancipation within state socialism. A discourse linking women's emancipation to socialist development had been forged in the early years of the Bolshevik Revolution. For their own reasons and in acknowledged contrast to liberal capitalism, the Bolsheviks and their successors clearly recognised women as a specific interest group and placed them squarely within their social project. There evolved a clear strategy and programme aimed at incorporating women into the epic post-revolutionary development efforts. This linking of women's emancipation to development gave a particular significance to the meaning of emancipation itself. Within Soviet Marxism emancipation was linked to the idea of liberating women from the constraints of the traditional (patriarchal) social order and from the exploitation of capitalism; in practice it had little to do with more libertarian ideas of freedom and self-fulfilment or with 'bourgeois' notions of rights. It was an emancipation *from* servitude and exploitation, one judged necessary to achieve the full human and individual emancipation which Marx had originally envisaged in his *Economic and Philosophical Manuscripts* of 1844,[46] but which later came to mean not free development so much as the freedom to enter into the service of the state.

The heirs to the communist movement continued the policies of the Bolsheviks and shared in their general objectives. They, too, adopted the language of historical progress and of the need to destroy the old in order to build the new. They, too, sought rapidly to dismantle pre-existing social relations and replace them with a new economic, social and cultural order. The 'emancipated woman' portrayed in socialist iconography came to symbolise everywhere the modernist and progressivist goals of these states as she beamed from posters, spanner, hoe or stethoscope in hand. Millions were mobilised across more than half a century in this project. Although subject to variations given by the policy priorities of revolutionary elites and the specific socioeconomic and cultural formations of different regions, women were drawn into these efforts in much the same way as they had been under the Bolsheviks. Women were brought into public view, sometimes by force – as in Central Asia in the 1920s, so too in Afghanistan in 1980 – and made the object of measures aimed at social reform. The idea that women could be important participants in the development of their national economy and of the nation-state was nowhere applied with more determination and consistency than in the Soviet Union and in the countries which emulated it. As a result of this general model and of accompanying mobilisations, women were absorbed into employment and public life in massive numbers. This was no mere response to the special demands of war economies; this was a permanent structural feature of the economies and societies of the socialist bloc.

In the countries where pre-capitalist social relations prevailed, such as China, Albania, Yemen and Afghanistan, the freeing of women from customary kin and sociocultural controls became central to the overall revolutionary process, given the household's importance in sustaining the pre-existing order, especially in the rural areas. In such national and regional contexts, reforming women's status was envisaged by communist parties as having a society-wide impact. Within the pre-modern household, women were more often than not directly subjected to patriarchal authority, but their subjection formed an important component of the social system as a whole and of its property systems in which they were exchanged in marriage and denied landholding rights. The emancipation of women from these controls could serve both to release women and, in modernising marriage and family relations, could remove one of the underpinnings of the whole productive and class system. Furthermore, the efforts aimed at destroying traditional allegiances, whether based on kinship (tribes, clans) or religion, in removing the basis of earlier solidarities, served to consolidate state control over society.[47]

Thus, family reform was often linked to land reform, because in pre-capitalist formations the family, especially the rural family, was a productive unit. Whether its forms of property were based on collective (tribes/lineages) or private property (peasant households/feudal estates), socialist governments sought to eliminate or drastically reduce this activity by expropriating the land in order to establish state property with more or less egalitarian rights of usufruct for the (male) producers. These transformations could be on a massive scale; under the first Chinese Land Reform of 1950, and as a prelude to collectivisation, over 100 million acres of farmland were taken from four million landlords and given to 50 million landless peasants within the first three years of the Communist Party's administration. The Chinese Marriage Law, which came into being at almost exactly the same time, attacked the pre-existing system of ownership (identified as based on the 'feudal family') and thus sought to make the transformations even more difficult to reverse.[48] Free choice, monogamous marriage was seen as evidence not only of the Communist Party's commitment to women's emancipation,

but as a way to enable women to challenge the gender hierarchy on which patriarchal authority and the previous systems of power and production were premised.[49] This corresponded both to political requirements – the need to strengthen state and party control – and to economic ones – the maximisation of labour supply as part of the state-centred development model. Modernisation and development depended upon increased production and upon the extensive mobilisation of workers. Women were perceived as a valuable reserve of labour, which had to be utilised in conditions of low technological levels and an extensive programme of social reform.

In a very direct sense, then, freeing women from the constraints of the previous social order conferred on the concept of women's emancipation a particular meaning in the pre-modern societies under communist rule, one that gave to it, as far as communist governments were concerned, a *practical policy* significance. Through liberating women from the old society and its constraints, and drawing them into socialised labour, it helped to promote some of the conditions necessary for achieving economic development and social change – and thus served as a prerequisite for socialist construction. Simply put, women's emancipation was seen to converge with the development goals set by communist parties. Policies on women as much as on other areas such as land reform, or industrialisation, were to a considerable degree the reflection of the macroeconomic policies these parties pursued to compete at the international economic level.

The wider international arena, both politically and economically, provided a range of initial conditioning factors which directly affected state policy, including the five-year plans, great leaps forward and the like. All these policies implied major accelerated social transformation, which impacted on the populations under communist rule. Formulated as responses to the perceived need to realise the potential of modernity and to pursue and win an international rivalry against the antagonistic capitalist world beyond, such states sought to mobilise women and transform their social position as part of the planned reorganisation of society. Women's emancipation from traditional servitude and entry into modern life could assist in the realisation of several related objectives: it could modernise social relations; extend political support for the regime through the mobilisation of women into the party; it could assist in the creation of a larger workforce; and through education and training, the quality, skill and discipline of labour could be enhanced.

In this way, Engels' classic text *The Origin of the Family* evolved into a theoretical and ethical justification of Communist Party policy with respect to women: for all the changes within the USSR itself and the different national contexts of other post-revolutionary societies, this theoretical inheritance of the Bolsheviks continued to play a significant part in the presentation of state policy throughout the period of communism and across five continents. Engels' work came to play a double role; while formulations and quotations from his work appeared in official texts as the orthodox discourse on women's emancipation, their more practical significance for socialist planners was the role they came to play in legitimising their development strategies and in mobilising women's support for, and integration into, this project. Official Communist Party discourses therefore emphasised two aspects of Engels' theory: women's entry into productive, socialised labour in order to liberate them from privatised, domestic entrapments, and the abolition of the previous oppressive family form, along with any surviving economic functions it might have. There was, therefore, a convergence between what Engels saw as the precondition for women's emancipation and the development strategies and goals of socialist states. These latter priorities were pursued most energetically where the tasks of development were most challenging and were considered most urgent.

Patriarchal Socialism?

State socialism's accelerated project of development and nation building did not eventuate in the prosperous modernity that was promised. Indeed socialist modernity, like its capitalist antagonist, had both a dual character – one with some positive and many negative features – and a contradictory one with respect to modernity. Communist rule was associated, on the one hand, with revolutionary policies that sought to achieve major transformations 'at a stroke'; yet on the other hand, it revealed an inherent tendency towards bureaucracy, repression and stasis. Centralised planning came increasingly to be associated with inefficient and paralysed economies, which suppressed the longed-for economic growth while a stifling conformity prevailed in an all but stagnant cultural life.[50] The conservatism that Bauman identified as the long-run fate of utopias was strikingly evident in the communist case.

For all its initial radicalism, the revolutionary project of state socialism came to preside over cultural formations which retained many of the practices and prejudices of the 'old society' that were destined to be swept away. The ambivalent nature of communist modernity and the creeping paralysis of the state and economy had important implications for gender relations. Communist states did introduce revolutionary changes which profoundly affected women's lives – sometimes in positive ways, sometimes with disastrous results. Yet, despite the power that was concentrated in these states and the control they exercised over their populations, their effective capacity to transform social relations was more limited than was claimed to be the case by their ruling parties and by their detractors alike. What party cadres identified as 'superstition', 'old ideas' and 'feudal' authority patterns, while far from impermeable to the onslaught of the state, retained some resilience and vitality, as Soviet and Chinese ethnographers tirelessly documented.

Socialist modernity offered women a rupture with the past and a corresponding freedom from the fundamental constituents of female subordination, class exploitation and patriarchal oppression. If social inequalities had been lessened, and patriarchal authority had been weakened and challenged in law, lived gender relations within family and community were often slower to change. Numerous sources suggest that a significant proportion of women in the rural areas of China, Vietnam and Central Asia were in the 1980s still denied freedom from their father's control over marriage and were subject to violence at the hands of male kin (and mothers-in-law) for failing to comply with their wishes. This was due in part to a lack of political will within ruling parties on gender issues, following the consolidation of the revolutionary state. As long as women were mobilised and incorporated into the communist project, party elites were seldom stirred to go further than the orthodox programme on the woman question. Autonomous women's organisations were not permitted and the official women's organisations were kept firmly under state control. Even where they were active, their programmes depended on state support, which was not always forthcoming. All too often, once their top-down modernisation programmes were put into effect, 'the woman question' as an emancipatory project was considered closed, as was the possibility for debate over its impact or the reasons for its failures.[51]

Moreover, the assault on traditional, patriarchal, loci of power was sometimes an ambivalent one. It was delivered with varying degrees of conviction, depending on the priorities at the time. It produced such a range of diverse effects that it cannot be convincingly stated that state socialism dealt a decisive blow to the formations of patriarchy in the legal, economic or social realms. The societies which communist parties confronted with their modernisation programmes were infinitely varied, and patriarchal relations, where they existed, were based on a diverse range of kinship and property systems. In some cases classic patriarchy in its most absolutist forms was weakened where its material base within property and kinship relations was eradicated, in others not.[52]

Elsewhere, whether as a result of deliberate policy or as unintended consequence, party policies acted to freeze rather than transform kinship and authority relations. While official documents spoke of 'survivals' that would in time succumb to the forces of progress, more sympathetic treatments argued that 'traditional society' had escaped the regulation of the state and had thereby preserved its 'authentic' character. However, the reality was often more complex. Once these societies had been subordinated to party rule, an accommodation between society and the state was found. The formations of tribe, clan and patriarchal authority, as much as the rituals and habits associated with the pre-communist past, could be found in coexistence with, or rearticulated within, the modern system of rule. The collectivisation of agriculture in China and in parts of Central Asia, for example, destroyed the earlier property system, but continued to rely for labour upon extended kin networks under paternal authority;[53] in China, after the radicalism of the 1952–3 period of the Marriage Law reforms, the Communist Party sought to halt the pace of women's deliverance from patriarchal power, even attempting to restore these powers to the male peasantry in order to keep their political allegiance.[54] A striking indicator of the woeful limits of party policy with regard to women was that of female infanticide in China. Though discouraged, it was never eradicated, and indeed the bias against girls was aggravated by the one-child-per-family-policy, adopted after 1978 in order to reduce population growth. Here development goals had an inverse effect on the status and life chances of the female sex in a context where the state's powers to change the kinship relations that lay at the heart of son preference, were limited by the fact that the conditions of social life made it rational for parents to favour the survival of their male children. Girls were given away in marriage; it was the sons who were responsible for their parents' wellbeing in later life.

In the urban, industrialised regions of the northern communist states patriarchy resided most evidently in the nostalgic longings of conservative peasant associations and religious authorities. Yet it has been argued in relation to Russia and some of the Eastern European states that it was a broken reed among the urban populations. Sociologists spoke of a 'crisis of masculinity', a by-product of the twin castrations of an authoritarian, emasculating system, and of women's emancipation which had resulted in masculinised women. If this view expressed regret for the passing of the days when men and women conformed to their 'traditional' roles, it also pointed to a more general feature of modernity

– the detachment of male identity from patriarchal roles and authority in the absence of a more satisfying and egalitarian alternative.[55] Yet, if in domestic relations patriarchy was residual, absent or weakened, its imprint was reinscribed by the state itself in the gendered division of labour and in the concentration of political and administrative authority in male hands. Patriarchal assumptions, derived from theory and society alike, intersected with the communist development model and with the pattern of authoritarian state-building that accompanied it. This was a feature that traversed the socialist world and was constitutive of the gender order of state socialism.

The interlocking of gender inequality with the overall structure of power was starkly evident throughout the authority structure of state socialism. The important posts were occupied by senior party and state officials, civilian and military, the majority of whom were male. Even in the mid-1980s most countries' Politburos contained no women, some had a token one, others a few 'candidate' members. At the apex of power, this all-male elite wielded immense, virtually unchallenged decision-making powers combining elements of paternalism with patriarchal rhetoric and symbols of office. In some cases (Stalin, Ceauşescu, Mao), party leaders self-consciously promoted an image of fatherly power at once terrifying in its authoritarian absolutism and reassuringly familiar in its claim to take care of everything from health and education to internal and international 'enemies of the revolution'. Less ferocious, but self-consciously masculinist, models of authority were evident in the faceless bureaucrats of Eastern Europe and in the charismatic military leaders of Third World revolutions.

The gendered distribution of power in society is always more complex than a simple dichotomy between powerful men and disempowered women. Under communism, women also occupied some positions of influence and privilege; those who by their own right were senior officials, typically ministers in Health and Education, or, as in many cases from Bulgaria and Romania to China and Cuba, the most prominent women occupied their posts less by virtue of individual merit than by family ties. Such women enjoyed far greater access to material goods and other benefits administered through the party system than did those on low incomes in the rural areas, many of whom were still subject to the operations of a more directly tangible, patriarchal set of personal controls. The place of women in the social structure while one of comparative disadvantage was therefore dependent upon the way that the gender order intersected with political favouritism and family structure and upon the social relations that prevailed in different regions. The degree of male advantage and of female subordination therefore varied significantly according to locality, region, class and ethnicity. Moreover, if men remained advantaged by the system in certain ways, many were also victims of it as the rising rates of male suicide, alcoholism and morbidity testified. If the *survival* of patriarchy helped to account for the inverse sex ratio in China, some analysts suggested that in the Soviet bloc, the decline from 1970 in male life expectancy was linked to its *erosion*. Masculine anomie and feelings of worthlessness were the counterpoint to the female condition of being indispensable and overburdened, while both conditions were the product of an untransformed social division of labour.[56] Male advantage was therefore relative.

A similar ambivalence of result was evident in women's entry into employment, on which so much emphasis was placed in the emancipatory rhetoric of communist states. Policy proclamations reiterated that work was the foundation and rationale of the new society, and it was routinely claimed that through work women were achieving equality with men. The new laws would guarantee the end of discrimination against women at work and social provision would take care of child-rearing.[57] But here, too, the instrumentalist character of policies diminished the positive implications traditionally associated with female employment. Development goals depended to a crucial degree on women's contribution to the labour force, and women became equally liable to full time work and joined their national labour forces in enormous numbers. Many women already worked before the advent of communist parties to power and many chose to enter the workforce, but low wages made work universally necessary for family survival. There was no place for the dependent housewife outside some sectors of the party elite. In some cases the law penalised those who remained 'idle', with 'housewives' at times denied the albeit dubious right to vote.[58]

But the formal equality such employment bestowed was vitiated by the arduous, and sometimes squalid, conditions under which women worked, a contrast especially evident in the modern industrial heartlands of Soviet communism. Despite a commitment to various forms of protective legislation, such as the exclusion of women from many hundreds of jobs to safeguard their 'maternal function', this covert paternalism was remarkable for its inconsistency. In most of these societies women performed heavy labour in the countryside, where no laws protected them – even from the growing hazards of chemical poisoning. In the towns, women often performed such work as rubbish collection as a matter of course, and in factories frequently carried far heavier loads than permitted by law, working in unsanitary, polluted and noisy conditions. In the USSR in the 1980s, for example, the majority of janitors and street cleaners were women, as were 26 per cent of highway construction crews. Moreover, although women were formally banned from nightshifts, some 70 per cent of Soviet nightshift workers were female, a result of a loophole in the law that permitted women to be employed for short-term emergencies only. With a wage gap everywhere in the communist world of upwards of 30 per cent in the earnings of men and women, it is little wonder that few women in these circumstances could feel wholly positive about their participation in the labour force.

Women attained some measure of autonomy and social mobility under communism, but sexual divisions had been reinscribed within the radical economic model that communism pioneered. It was therefore not just a question of communist states putting in a greater effort to bring about sexual equality, as if this was amenable to quantitative measures, but of tackling inequalities within the very foundation of the system itself. In communist states a gender bias was therefore inscribed in the organisation of the economy, with features and effects that were similar to those that characterised the capitalist world.

The Alternative Gendered Economy

In its accumulated effects, this bias – most evident in the gendered division of labour with its clear distinctions between 'male' and 'female' forms of economic activity – acted against the interests of women, both as mothers and as workers. In its more stable form, one which endured in the USSR for more than half a century and in Eastern Europe, China and Cuba for some 30 years or more, the economic system reproduced certain biases against the kind of work women traditionally performed. These inhered in the economic premises built into the successive five-year plans that valued certain kinds of work over others. As workers, women were for the most part represented in agriculture, or if in industry were concentrated in the typically feminised light industries in the areas of food production and textiles. The emphasis on rapid accumulation through policies favouring heavy industry, large units of production and productive work, served to rank light industry, services and agriculture as low priority areas; thus, while some of women's traditional occupations and income-generating activities were abolished outright, others were defined as less important.

This planning bias was further reinforced by the adoption of various kinds of incentive that privileged workers in those areas of production considered priorities and which were also those in which men tended to predominate. In contrast to capitalism, where wage levels are to a large extent determined by market forces, in CPEs they were fixed through the state planning agency. Although wage differentials were more compressed in planned economies, they were nonetheless significant and based on the values placed on different economic activities. Thus, in theory, wages served as a means of regulating the flow of labour to certain sectors of the economy, according to the priorities of the plan. Wage levels for different sectors were based on the broad rule – one that Marx had formulated in his 'Critique of the Gotha Programme' – that reward was commensurate with productivity and the social value of the work performed – 'to each according to his work'. In this schema, the least prioritised areas were those in which women were concentrated, thereby ensuring that they would be the least well paid members of the workforce.[59] Wage policy, therefore, had the effect of supporting a dualistic employment structure, which at household level confirmed cultural expectations about men's relation to work being more important than that of women. Because men earned more on account of their structural advantage in employment, they were considered the household's main earners, while women performed the lower paid, less valued work along with the household tasks, in effect performing a double shift.

The regulated wage structures of CPEs, which maintained incomes at a relatively low level, together with the reliance on an extensive use of labour in the economy, meant that virtually all adults had to work to achieve a minimum standard of living. Long hours of work, a five-and-a-half-day week in many countries, travel time to work and inflexible schedules all added to the difficulties of combining wage work with family life and domestic responsibilities.

It is in this light that another dimension of the economic model, with its emphasis on accumulation at the expense of consumption, acquired a special significance on account of the difficulties it caused for the management of everyday life. The contraction of private markets and independent services, and the severe restrictions placed on the manufacture of 'non essential items', translated in the urban areas into scarcity, queues and slow progress in the provision of domestic appliances. Difficulties in obtaining even simple repairs, poor urban planning and transport all compounded the problem. Since the full-time working woman, more often than not a mother too, retained the main responsibility for domestic servicing, inadequacies of provision hit her particularly hard. Difficult enough at the best of times, combining full-time work with keeping house and raising children was made all the more so by lack of goods and services which could otherwise ease the burden.

This situation was compounded by the neglect of the non-waged reproductive work that women continued to perform. These activities were crucial to household survival in a shortage economy, but were recognised only to the extent that women were sometimes given a day off a month for household duties. In general, scant value was placed on non-productive activities and this had been the case since the time of the Bolsheviks. Lenin followed Marx and Engels in expressing a concern to liberate women from 'the drudgery of domestic work'. He anticipated a time when the Soviet state would deliver women from servitude through labour-saving devices and the socialisation of housework. The Bolshevik economist, Strumulin, calculated in the 1920s that each day some 36 million hours were expended on cooking in the Russian Republic alone. If this work were collectivised, over 4 million housewives would be released for genuinely valuable, that is, productive, labour.[60] The optimistic vision of the liberating potential of technology and the productive power of a socialised economy did not materialise, and efforts to alleviate the reproductive work in the home were half-hearted, while the value of the work itself remained unacknowledged. An ironic failure of state communism lay in this – women so long urged to think of themselves as the equals of men, were still performing on average more hours of paid work and as much as three times more housework than were their Western counterparts, while also experiencing low pay, arduous conditions and discrimination at work.

These economic policies had gendered effects and produced inequalities which received confirmation in the political and ideological domains. A tenacious disposition on the part of officialdom and public alike to rationalise and essentialise gender attributes sustained a more enduring tolerance of gender inequality than prevailed in the West, in the absence of any challenge from feminism. With women apparently emancipated from tradition and full members of the modern nation-states of the socialist world, the instrumental link between policy on women and state priorities as a whole prevailed. Defenders of the system were quick to argue that socialism's end goals, including the full emancipation of women, could not yet be attained in what was still an uncompleted, 'transitional' process. However, this was to confuse what was, in theory at least, a valid point – namely that any process of emancipation involved material preconditions and correlates – with a more questionable one, that the theoretical and political conceptions upon which policies were based were such as to lead automatically to emancipation. It was the premises which remained unchallenged and unchanged, as was to become equally evident in the context of 'reform', when, far from the transition leading to developed or advanced socialism, the system as a whole entered a serious, and terminal, crisis.

The Onset of Crisis and Dissatisfaction from Below

The centrally planned economies of both North and South were judged by many observers as capable of delivering some positive results in terms of their own development objectives, and were initially considered to have secured some of the conditions for further growth. Over time, however, the system proved unsustainable. Taken as a whole, the economic situation of CPEs was, from the late 1960s, one in which growth had slowed to a point of stagnation. Bureaucratic inefficiency, over-centralisation and the lack of competitive market pressure all took their toll. A number of countries consequently introduced market reforms designed to stimulate higher levels of growth and greater efficiency. Whereas the USSR waited until after Gorbachev's advent to power in 1985 to introduce major economic and social changes, some of the communist parties in the South had begun these well before – China after 1978, Vietnam after 1981 and Mozambique after 1983. In Eastern Europe, Poland and Hungary had begun to liberalise – and to rethink some of their other policies, including those concerning women – in the 1970s. With the launching of *perestroika* in the USSR after 1985, the great majority of the communist states became involved in one way or another in this process, and it became increasingly evident that formerly prevalent views on 'the woman question' were being revised, sometimes radically.

Ultimately, it was the failure of the ruling communist parties to deliver enough of the promised material progress that provided the decisive impetus to attempt the reforms of the 1970s and 1980s. In the sphere of social life the crisis consisted in a growing awareness on the part of both leadership and population of the failings of the system, even though compared to earlier periods the situation was easing. Yet it is useful here to distinguish between the actual development and intensification of these problems and the increasing intolerance towards them of their long-suffering peoples. This dissatisfaction from below had several causes: an extension of the real economic malaise into other areas of life; a greater impatience with the shortcomings of the system as a result of higher levels of education and the relative relaxation of political controls; a decline in the opportunities for social mobility as economic growth slowed down; and, evident in all matters to do with everyday life and social affairs, an increasing sense that the socialist countries were falling further behind the West. To this was added the widespread cynicism at the corruption and privilege among the higher reaches of party power and at their vacuous claims and empty promises. All these factors had their impact on popular attitudes toward gender issues. The slowing down of the economy and the stagnation of output and productivity levels rendered the idea of equality through employment increasingly implausible; at the same time, and as demand grew, the failures of social services, provisioning, transport, and so forth, became more evident. The sheer difficulty of making ends meet, in terms of both time and money, placed households under acute strain. These material pressures were duly reflected in the rising number of divorces and – in the countries of the North and in Cuba – in the falling or persistently low birth rates dubbed, with some accuracy, the 'Mothers' Strike'. Policies had been revised to address this problem, but without sufficient success.[61]

The scarcity and financial hardship that prevailed among much of the population deepened the division of labour and mutual dependency in the family. For many households living on the edge of economic viability, both men and women performed a 'double shift': where possible, as in Hungary, men took second jobs or worked in the informal economy, while women put their remaining energies after a day out at work into managing the household, bartering scarce goods and services and caring for children and relatives. The family, despite all its tensions, was still popularly regarded as a refuge or as a site of resistance against the authoritarian state and suffocating public life.

Thus, in the conditions of reformist policies, traditional gender divisions were reinforced through the structural and ideological biases inherent in economic policy and in the organisation of society. These factors taken together implied that reforms aimed at reinforcing women's ties to the family would find substantial resonance within the populations of these states, even if their effect was to intensify gender segregation and inequality. This, then, was the paradoxical outcome of seven decades of post-revolutionary commitment to solving the 'woman question' – the 'right' of women to employment was questioned, essentialist ideas of woman as mother and home-maker were reinforced and the societies emerging from decades of state intervention to promote gender equality were engulfed in a tide of gendered change, religious and traditionalist at one end of the spectrum, pornographic and exploitative at the other. This, arguably more than the limits of the communist project, was the 'Nowhere' to which communism had brought its subjects.

Conclusions

This chapter began by recognising a historical verdict, that from the perspective of the post-communist era the attempt to construct a revolutionary communist alternative to capitalism has been universally read as a failure. Such a verdict applies not only to the general project of creating a viable, superior socioeconomic system, but also to the specific record of these states with regard to equality between the sexes. Yet it was not so long ago that a significant portion of scholarly opinion across the political spectrum viewed the efforts of these states in a more enquiring and sympathetic light. For some, their state-centred development model was necessary for the tasks of nation building; for others these states represented a challenge to imperialist hegemony, a cultural break with Western values and a return to an authentic national culture.[62] Perhaps the most widely held of these more sympathetic views was that which saw their social achievements more positively, arguing that at a cost to individual rights that was held to be temporary and defensible, they had provided their populations with economic and social rights that comparable capitalist societies did not, and could not, deliver.[63]

The balance of judgement has shifted to a more critical consensus on these states. Their failures are more evident, and the collapse of the birthplace and heartland of communism in 1991 decisively concluded the debate over how these states might evolve. Recent decades have been characterised by the return of a self-confident liberalism, with the market enthroned as the guarantor of progress. The post-war era of statist projects, whether of the developmental state, socialist, national-reformist or welfare state variety has arguably come to an end.

Yet the clarity of this verdict may be contrasted with the imprecision and uncertainty accompanying other questions that are raised by the analysis of the communist record. Arguments have been too easily drawn, or allegedly drawn, from this history: that the state should play no role in economic development or social policy, that all attempts to bring about equality are doomed, that collective social action is self-defeating, and more broadly, that all conceptions of progress, historical advance, even development itself, are best abandoned.

There is no need to claim definitive answers to these questions to challenge the alternative dogmas that have replaced those of authoritarian Marxism-Leninism. A retrospective analysis of the communist record does not mean rejecting everything associated with this history, any more than it must defend its 'gains'. Rather, it entails drawing out, in a tentative but open-minded way, the issues which this history raises. The questions that it opens, not those it closes, are the most important intellectual legacy of the communist period.

Here it is appropriate to consider how far the problems identified, and the goals proclaimed by the communist project of women's emancipation, remain relevant. Deep inequalities between the sexes in the home and workplace, and the reproduction of those inequalities by social and international forces, were certainly as much a feature of the world at the end of the twentieth century as they were at its beginning. That communism provided a false utopia, and in its own programme reproduced gender inequality, does not detract from the continuing validity of the critique of gender inequality which both it, and feminism, shared.

Equally, it is important to reassess the history of women's responses to the communist project and its aftermath in these countries. The claims made by communism about historical advance and mass support were deceptive. Yet this does not mean either that the communist project did not receive widespread support at some points, not least from women, nor that its interventions did not, in certain respects, benefit women.[64] Emancipatory discourses and policies were contained within the socialist project, none so radical as its modern promise of an equality which opposed all forms of despotic power and privilege. State communism's authoritarian modernisation did not fulfil that promise, but as part of its mixed legacy it improved the life chances of many of those at the bottom of the social scale.

However, the argument has been made here that the significance of such achievements cannot be abstracted from the political conditions under which they were realised. If these states followed a western vision of modernity, it was one that broke radically with the political and economic order associated with the liberal Enlightenment tradition. Modernisation from above, without the market and without democracy. resulted not in strong integrated economies and societies but in syncretic and stagnant ones.

Yet some measure of development occurred, and in most cases extreme poverty and its correlates were significantly reduced where not eradicated. Anticipating the goals articulated globally during the United

Nations Decade for Women, communist states were the first to introduce structural transformations enabling the mobilisation of women and their 'integration' into development. From being regarded as marginal members of their societies, women were brought into the public realm and were made both agents and targets of social reform. Perhaps the distinctive achievement of state socialism was its accelerated inclusion of women into its modernising project, even as its greatest disservice to one of the causes which it claimed to promote – women's emancipation – was to create harsh, hypocritical and in some ways counter-productive means of achieving it.

In the end, of course, no final judgement on state socialism is possible, if only because the criteria of assessment are themselves ever open to dispute, as is the empirical evidence offered in support of them. The 'record' of communism cannot be rendered in the unqualified language of progress, 'gains' and 'advances' that marked the more self-confident developmentalism of the past. Nor have the populations who lived under its rule been able to deliver a complete or unambiguous verdict on its history. This brings us to the issue that underlies the discussion of the communist revolutionary experiment and the one that ties it most closely to contemporary analytic and policy debate: that of development. In the aftermath of communism's collapse, and in the broader questioning of rationalist and 'Enlightenment' assumptions within social theory, we are far from the confident historical vision that inspired communism itself, as it did many strands of feminism. History is *not* moving towards a single, clear, modern goal. Social practices and forms of power are *not* expressions of one historical totality. The oppression and emancipation of women are *not* conditional upon, or directly tied to, the progress of society as a whole, or a particular form of modernity. It was this vision which underlay the communist project and which inspired its greatest aspirations, as well as its most terrible crimes. Today development remains an aspiration for the poorer nations of the world, but development alone, without structural change in the global order and within society itself, has not delivered, and arguably cannot deliver, on the promise that it has held out. Contemporary debates reflect a more cautious and critical understanding of development, one that downplays any concepts of transcendent progress and unqualified technological advances, and also allows for a different modernity, one that is diverse not uniform, is subject to democratic accountability and is based on principles of justice and fairness.

Communism promoted a vision of human emancipation that, in the end, frustrated that vision and created new forms of oppression. At the same time it sought to mobilise its supporters and transform society within the framework of competition with another social system, that of capitalism. As we have seen, on both counts it failed. Yet this need not entail either that the achievements of capitalism are exempt from critical analysis, or that the aspiration to freedom and development encompassed within the concept of emancipation does not retain a certain validity. Feminism, as Sabina Lovibond has observed, has developed its goals in a critical relation to the culture from which it springs.[65] That critical relation remains as valid now as it ever was in regard to both contenders for global hegemony during the twentieth century. In such a critical assessment, the study of the record of the communist states, and the re-evaluated assertion of those aspirations, which they embodied, can – and should – retain an important place.

6

Analysing Women's Movements*

Despite the appearance of an extensive literature on women's movements and the steady growth since the mid-1970s in works which offer a critical, feminist engagement with political theory,[1] discussion of the broader implications of women's politics remains a relatively unexamined aspect of the literature on development. There have been some recent attempts to redress this absence,[2] yet it is as if the debates within feminist political theory and the field of development studies have pursued parallel paths with little real engagement with each other. This is all the more remarkable given the impact of women's movements on policy-making and politics in the developing world.

Meanwhile, the analysis of women's movements both historically and cross-culturally, has demonstrated the range and diversity of the forms of solidarity women have engaged in and has alerted us to the factors, both structural and symbolic, which are significant in particular cases.[3] Yet it could be said, without too much fear of exaggeration, that the attention devoted to women's movements has had at least two negative consequences. In the first place, it has tended to marginalise discussion and analysis of other political phenomena which are of at least as much significance, both for what they have contributed to our thinking about institutional arenas for advancing women's interests and for what they have achieved in practice.[4] Second, some of the dominant assumptions about women's movements found in the development literature remain quite problematic. In what follows I shall offer some thoughts on the ways in which contemporary debates about women's movements might be moved on to address the new context which gender politics confronts in the developing countries.

*This chapter first appeared as an article in *Development and Change*, vol. 29, no. 2 (1998).

Women's Movements and Female Collective Action

The interest in women's movements has a long history. Its more recent origins go back more than 30 years, to the work of feminist historians such as Sheila Rowbotham and Olwen Hufton,[5] whose aim was to recover a 'hidden history' of female activism. This early work was not only concerned to establish that women were participants, and not bystanders, in the events of history, but it also suggested that women's political involvement was of a distinctive character and significance. As political actors women were seen to impart to their struggles, practices, strategies and goals, certain gender-specific qualities. In subsequent and continuing debates these were variously explained as expressive of some essential feminine attribute or derivative of the specific social positioning of women as carers and as those responsible in the domestic sphere for the work of social reproduction.

This literature has been particularly concerned with three types of women's movement. In the first place, there was an interest – coincident with the appearance since the 1970s of a reinvigorated and international feminist movement – in tracing the history of feminism and the work of feminist groups and organisations in various parts of the world. Second, there was a parallel concern with the struggles of low-income women over consumption needs and their protests against social injustice. During the 1970s and 1980s these struggles gained a particular momentum in Latin America, India and some African and East Asian countries as the combined effects of political repression and economic recession took their toll.[6] In the 1980s during the period of economic recession, debt crisis and stabilisation policies, women's movements became an object of policy concern, as their potential as vehicles for the delivery of goods and services to those in need was realised. A third, more recent, cluster of studies on women's movements has focused on the mobilisations of women within 'fundamentalist' movements, beginning with the analysis of the Iranian Revolution.[7] These studies opened up a range of questions about female mobilisation, which had remained on the margin of the earlier discussions and outside the scope of most of the comparative literature on women's movements.

While much of the work on women's movements in the development literature has been largely descriptive in character, there has also emerged a current of ongoing theoretical work. This has been concerned with three types of issue: first it has begun to examine the factors – historical, social and institutional – which condition both the emergence of female activism and the specific, gendered forms of collective identity.

A second form of enquiry, found more commonly in the planning and development literature, has engaged with questions of categorisation, in order to find adequate criteria for differentiating between the various types of women's movement that have come into existence. A third and more recent theme has been that of examining the relationship between women's movements and democracy, an issue which has become pre-eminent in the developing countries in the aftermath of authoritarian rule. These three sets of issues will be reviewed in summary fashion below.

Why Women's Movements Appear When They Do

The comparative analysis of women's movements shows considerable variations between regions in their timing, character, influence and effectiveness. This suggests that the appearance of women's movements and of different forms of organisation and resistance has been contingent on five main factors: prevailing cultural configurations, family forms, political formations, the forms and degree of female solidarity, and the character of civil society in the regional and national context. One implication of this historical and comparative work is that women's movements are essentially modern phenomena. Although there have been forms of female collective action in pre-modern societies, these have tended to be either small-scale or spasmodic eruptions of social protest. The mass, relatively sustained entry of women into the field of politics, the emergence of women's movements and of particularistic conceptions of women's interests and citizenship rights are developments which were associated both with the spread of Enlightenment ideas, and with the multiple processes of socioeconomic modernisation and forms of political activity that accompanied them. Among the many effects of these processes can be instanced a redefinition both of the meaning of the public and of the private spheres and of women's lived relationship to each.

While women's movements in this sense first emerged in the political and social conditions of eighteenth-century Europe, it was in the nineteenth and early twentieth centuries that women in many other regions of the world began to organise against inequalities based on sex and to demand legal reforms aimed at removing patriarchal rights within the family and in society at large.[8] Modernising nationalisms and socialist thought played their part in these early claims on the polity, and self-proclaimed feminist movements sometimes achieved substantial legislative reforms. In other contexts, women's rights were handed down from above by liberal constitutionalists, by socialist states or by populist regimes anxious to broaden their political base. They have also sometimes resulted from the influence of colonial powers on subject states and from dominant powers over defeated states. Finally, women's rights have also been won as a result of more than half a century of United Nations influence in the international arena.

If women's movements have a historical association with the multiple processes of modernity both in its capitalist and socialist variants, they have not always expressed demands for full citizenship and equal rights. Some women's movements arose in opposition to what they saw as the corrosive trends of modernity and sought to defend women's emplacement within 'traditional society'. More recently, the emergence of militant currents of religious 'fundamentalism' has been accompanied by sizeable women's movements which seek to redefine women's rights in ways that challenge Enlightenment notions of equality and universal rights of citizenship.

Whatever form female mobilisation has taken, the twentieth century has been marked by the growing absorption of women into the public realm, not only into education and employment, but also into the particularly resilient realm of politics.[9] We see a steady progression in women's political involvement in the diverse range of political experiences from revolutionary upheavals, fascist and populist regimes, Islamist movements and in social movements more generally, while the numbers of women involved in liberal political processes as voters, candidates for election, members of parties and governments has continued to rise.[10] Yet women's entry into positions of power within formal, institutional politics has everywhere been fraught with difficulty, and this is despite women's extensive incorporation into the public sphere as the century has progressed. While there have been some notable exceptions, the upper echelons of political power have remained a remarkably resilient bastion of male exclusivity. This is true even in countries where other formal or structural constraints limiting women's access to the public realm have been considerably weakened, and where formal structures and legislation have been put in place to support women's participation.

What are Women's Movements?

These are some of the background issues of history and politics which have helped to contextualise the extent and character of female mobilisation in given countries or regions. I shall turn now to look at the second set of analytic issues identified in the literature on women's movements, that of the salient factors that differentiate between them. There have been numerous attempts at typologising women's movements and organisations (or practices within them), some of these within the development literature itself.[11] Needless to say, many of the underlying issues remain, and will remain, unresolved, given the differences in theoretical approach.

To start with, there are contrasting views as to what constitutes a women's movement. On the one hand, there are clearly identifiable women's movements which, like those which mobilised to demand female suffrage, have a leadership, a membership, a broader following and a political programme. On the other hand, there are more diffuse forms of political activity, which can also qualify as a movement and, therefore, are distinct from other forms of solidarity such as those based on networks, clubs or groups. The definitional boundaries are complicated by the fact that networks or clubs sometimes develop into, or form part of, social movements. However, it seems preferable to reserve the term 'movement' for something that involves more in size and effectivity than small-scale associations, if these are few in number and have little overall impact. But a large number of small associations, even with very diverse agendas, can in cumulative terms come to constitute a women's movement. Much of the literature on Peru during the 1980s speaks of a 'women's movement' made up of diverse currents, including grassroots mobilisations organised around basic needs. Tens of thousands of women were active in this way.[12] Oduol and Kabira (1995) describe a similar development in Kenya in recent decades, where again thousands of women were engaged in activity aimed at 'improving their situation' in a variety of ways. While this kind of activism is not a women's movement in the terms noted above, in that it has no central coordination and no agreed agenda, nonetheless, the extent of participation and its overall significance suggest that popular women's movements often take this more diffuse and decentred form.

To speak of a movement, then, implies a social or political phenomenon of some significance, that significance being given both by its numerical strength but also by its capacity to effect change in some way or another, whether this is expressed in legal, cultural, social or political terms. A women's movement does not have to have a single organisational expression, and may be characterised by a diversity of interests, forms of expression and spatial location. Logically, it comprises a substantial majority of women, where it is not exclusively made up of women. Some authors have identified women's movements with particular organisational forms and goals. Sonia Alvarez suggests that women's movements 'pursue women's gender interests ... [and] ... make claims on cultural and political systems on the basis of women's historically ascribed gender roles'.[13] Wieringa identifies women's movements with resistance to 'the dominant system', and with a commitment to 'diminishing gender subordination'.[14] Alvarez adds the rider that women's movements are also defined by their autonomy from control by other social groups. Excluded from this definition therefore are all forms of, to quote Alvarez, 'state-linked mass organisations for women, women's branches of political parties, trade unions and other organisations of civil society that are not primarily organised to advance women's gender specific concerns'.[15]

These criteria, however, denote a particular kind of women's movement, and, while such movements have been significant in the development of feminism, they have not been the only kind, or even sometimes the most important kind. As Alvarez shows in her study of Brazil, many forms of female collective action are in effect marked by the absence of one or other of these criteria.[16] Moreover, general treatments of women's movements have tended to exclude consideration of right wing mobilisations of women, even though there are by now some important studies of these.[17] Are fascist mobilisations of women, or Islamist women's movements, not women's movements *in any sense?* And what do we do with the women's organisations and their sizeable memberships in the existing and former socialist states? These are usually excluded from being considered women's movements on grounds of autonomy, if not on grounds of interests. Yet they deserve consideration in order to evaluate their significance both as political phenomena and for what they signify for their participants.

I shall return to examine these criteria in a moment, but suffice to note here that the definition of women's movements as autonomous and expressive of women's gender interests does not usually encompass what Sheila Rowbotham (1992) has called the phenomenon of 'women in movement', that is, women acting together in pursuit of common ends, be they 'feminist' or not. Yet it is important to acknowledge that these other forms of female mobilisation, excluded from consideration as 'women's movements', nonetheless constitute a large proportion, possibly the greater part, of female solidarity in much of the modern world. Women have been an active, if not always acknowledged, force in most of the political upheavals associated with modernity, as members of trade unions, political parties, reform and revolutionary organisations and nationalist movements. Such formal and informal relationships with political processes and institutions are significant for what they can tell us about the terms and character of women's incorporation into political life.

In order to recognise these diverse forms of female political action, we might rehabilitate a concept deployed in the literature on political movements, that of collective action. To paraphrase Charles Tilly (1978), this connotes solidarity in pursuit of common goals. This term can more easily encompass the variety of forms of female mobilisation that have accompanied the process of modernity. As far as women's movements are concerned, Alvarez's criteria involving the pursuit of women's interests and independent self-activity raise two issues which have tended to be conflated – that of organisational autonomy and 'women's interests'. However, it is at once evident that in analysing different forms of female collective action and interest representation, the question of how to define a women's movement is a more complex one than first appears and the boundaries are less clear cut than is often implied. This is because both core definitional criteria, not only autonomy but also women's interests, remain problematic, as is evidenced by their contested histories.

Female Collective Action and Types of Institutionalised Agency

The Autonomy Issue

From its inception as a social movement, feminism has been engaged in a long and unresolved debate over organisation. Two issues have been particularly contested; that of autonomy and that of what principles should govern internal organisation. From the earliest moments of women's political mobilisation, women activists in political parties, trade unions and social movements have argued that they needed a place within which to elaborate their own programmes of action, debate their own goals, tactics and strategy free from outside influence.[18] Flat, non-hierarchical organisational structures were also considered more appropriate ways of ensuring democratic principles and allowing greater debate and participation in the formulation of objectives. However, creditable though such principles may have been, the varied history of female activism reveals a considerable diversity of institutional arrangements, within which autonomy figures as only one of many possible forms, while genuinely non-hierarchical organisations have been the exception rather than the rule.[19] For many women's organisations the urgent problem was how to reconcile principles of democratic consultation with effective leadership, an issue that was increasingly felt to determine the success, even the survival, of the organisation concerned.

Underlying feminist concern with organisational structure, and expressed in the demand for autonomy, is the question of authority. More specifically, the question that is engaged is: from where does the authority to define women's goals, priorities and actions come? Here it may be useful to establish an initial set of distinctions between three ideal types of 'direction' in the transmission of authority:[20] these may be called *independent, associational* and *directed*, corresponding to the lines of authority that have crystallised in relation to female activism. I shall briefly consider each in turn.

Independent Movements

First are those referred to above as autonomous organisations, characterised by *independent* actions, where women organise on the basis of self-activity, set their own goals and decide their own forms of organisation and forms of struggle. Here, the women's movement is defined as a self-governing community that recognises no superior authority, nor is it subject to the governance of other political agencies. Its authority resides in the community, and that community has what Dahl (1982) calls 'final control over the agenda'. As we have seen, this is the form that is most closely identified with feminist definitions of women's movements.

It is often assumed that if collective actions by women issue from within an autonomous organisation then they must be expressive of women's real gender interests. Yet this is a problematic assumption, since autonomous organisations of women have been associated with a very diverse range of goals, demonstrating apparently conflicting definitions of interests. These have ranged from self-help activities of various kinds, to protest movements, to those associated with a self-conscious feminism, to ones entailing the abrogation of women's existing rights and envisioning the greater dependence of women on men and commitment to family life. There have also been apparently spontaneous movements of women in favour of practices such as *suttee* and female genital mutilation.

It is, moreover, important to note that there is an extensive record of female participation in independent collective actions in pursuit of universalist goals, that is, ones that are *not* related directly to women's gender interests.[21] An example is provided by some nationalist struggles, where women organise independently to help realise the broader goals of nationalist or revolutionary forces, such as the women's clubs that appeared in Cuba in the late nineteenth century supporting independence from Spain.[22] Such forms of activism may have a special meaning and clear implications for women (which accounts for why they gain their support), but the goals of such movements are typically formulated in universalist terms and are seen as indissolubly linked to national independence and development. Such movements are not, therefore, pursuing gender-specific interests, but they have involved independent collectivities of women in the field of national politics.

Independent organisational forms are therefore compatible with a variety of different political positions and goals; and even when women do organise autonomously, they do not always act collectively in pursuit of their gender interests. Women's interests cannot be 'read off' from the organisational form in which they are expressed; the mere fact of an organisation's autonomy or internal organisational structure does not indicate that it is a privileged vehicle for the expression of women's interests nor, indeed, that it is entirely free from authority, either internally with respect to the organisation concerned or with regard to external influence. The latter raises interesting questions concerning 'autonomy' in that an autonomous movement typically designates some discourses and/or principles as *authoritative*. Thus, while not recognising a 'higher authority' it might recognise an authority in the form of a privileged interpretation of reality. The question then becomes one that is less to do with authority *per se* as to do with the values and purposes with which it is associated. Autonomous organisation does not, therefore, exist in any necessary relationship with the character of the goals or the interests which are articulated – or even with the identities of the actors involved. Furthermore, autonomous organisations do not necessarily lead to the empowerment of women: first, because informal power structures can operate 'tyrannically' in the absence of formal limits or procedural rules governing the exercise of power; second, because autonomy can in some contexts mean marginalisation and a reduced political effectiveness.[23]

Associational Linkage

A second type of organisational principle and a different conception of authority is expressed in what we could call *associational* forms. Here, independent women's organisations with their particular goals and institutional autonomy choose to form alliances with other political organisations with which they are in agreement on a range of issues. These forms may be seen as *associative* in recognition of their quasi-independent status within an alliance of interests; their actions are not directed by a superior power, as women remain in control over their own organisation and set its agenda. In this situation women's associations may also choose to delegate power to outside agencies such as parties or public officials, an arrangement which, if it is to work, must be based on trust and established procedures of accountability. Power and authority in this model are negotiated, and cooperation is conditional on some or all of the women's demands being incorporated into the political organisation with which the alliance is made. Vargas (1996) notes in her reflections on women's movements in Latin America that this process of negotiation from an autonomous base is the key to democratic politics; it acknowledges that interests are diverse and sometimes conflictive, and that they cannot be defined in unitary terms and imposed from above.[24]

This kind of associative linkage escapes the polar dilemma of 'autonomy or integration' which has long divided the different currents within women's movements and it has the potential to be an effective means of securing concrete agendas for reform. It does, however, run the risk of cooptation resulting in the women's organisation losing its capacity for agenda setting. In order to minimise this danger, some autonomous women's movements have set conditions on organisations with which they are prepared to cooperate. In Brazil, in the 1980s some feminist groups made it clear that they had no interest in legitimising any agency where criteria for participation were not based on democratic parameters, where resource issues were not resolved according to principles of transparency and where the institution was 'not an ally of feminist causes'.[25] Such conditionality, a necessary feature of this kind of arrangement, clearly depends as much on a conducive political environment for its realisation as on the effective capacity of women's movements to be in a strong bargaining position.

Directed Mobilisations

A third ideal typical form is what could be called *directed* collective action. This applies to those cases where the authority and initiative clearly come from outside and stand above the collectivity itself. The women's organisation or movement is therefore subject to a higher (institutional) authority and is typically under the control of political organisations and/or governments. There is little, if any, room for genuine negotiation over goals. This means that either one or both of the following tend to occur: (i) that the goals of women's associations do not *specifically* concern women other than as instruments for the realisation of the higher authority's goals; and/or (ii) that even if they do concern women, control and direction of the agenda does not lie with them as an identifiable social force. Female mobilisation is therefore *directed*, with the proviso that the degree of direction involved can vary substantially, as can the forms taken by the directing authority. There may also be considerable fluidity in a given historical context: in one situation there may be a movement from direction to greater autonomy as the collective actors acquire more political resources and influence over the political process; in another situation the reverse could occur, with a once-independent movement coming increasingly under the control of a party or the government. A critical factor in the assessment of concrete cases of this directed form of collective action is the nature of the party or state concerned: social democratic governing parties with women's sections need only to be compared with the official women's organisations in state socialist variants to underline the point that there are major differences in the quality and type of direction involved.

While directed mobilisation of this kind represents the antithesis of independent women's organisations, it has in many parts of the world, and for a substantial period of history, constituted the principal form in which female mobilisation has taken place. It is important, however, to establish some distinctions between the main forms that have arisen, three of which can be mentioned here. In the first type, women are mobilised to help achieve a general goal, such as overthrowing a dictatorship, or bringing a particular party to power. In this case, there is no explicit commitment to enhancing women's specific interests. For a Latin American example, the Nationalist Revolutionary Movement (MNR), a left-wing guerrilla organisation in Bolivia, managed in the 1970s to mobilise many thousands of women and even had female commanders of armed militias. Yet according to one analyst, 'there [was] not one single political or ideological document belonging to the MNR that addresse[d] or propose[d] the matter of women's struggles'.[26] In effect, women were used by the party to repress popular discontent.

A second type of directed action is that which, while primarily concerned with securing broader political goals, nevertheless does express a commitment to advancing women's interests, but within the context of a general commitment to social change. This is the case of those modernising nationalisms and socialist movements which sought to advance general goals that included the emancipation of women from traditional forms of oppression and that supported some conception of women's rights. Such movements aimed to mobilise women and encouraged them to promote their own interests through official women's organisations. Yet these interests were defined in advance by the party as the overarching authority, and no alternative definition of interest or independent associations were permitted. In socialist conceptions women's interests were to be realised as a necessary part of the overall project of national development and social modernisation, formulated in opposition to 'traditional' forms of patriarchal oppression. They may indeed have had an emancipatory function in that they bestowed rights on women which were previously denied; however, the point remains that women's organisations were subordinated to the authority of the state and their actions were dictated by the party.[27]

A third form of directed collective action is where women are mobilised for causes which may abrogate rights they already have in the name of collective, national or religious interests. Examples of the latter include those religiously inspired movements where some groups of women have been mobilised by political parties in support of redefining the 'gender regime', rejecting liberal conceptions of gender equality in favour of more traditional notions of the 'patriarchal bargain'.[28] This form of female collective action has been studied in relation to authoritarian regimes of various types, such as Nazi Germany or contemporary Iran, where it has been shown that such apparently 'irrational' mobilisations of women are not usefully seen in terms of 'false consciousness'. Rather, they suggest that there are marked variations in the ways that women's interests and politics are defined. I will return to this point later.

These, then, are different ways of identifying some preliminary distinctions with regard to women's movements and collective actions. We have seen that as far as women's interests are concerned, there is no necessary relationship between forms of organisation and interest articulation. While there are good reasons for the feminist emphasis on autonomy and non-hierarchical forms of practice, such principles, even when applied, cannot be seen as guarantors of some 'pure form' of women's movement expressive of 'women's interests'. Moreover, there are cases where the agenda for women's associations is dictated from above and includes a commitment to enhancing women's interests. Finally, there are cases where the agenda set by the organisational authority has little to offer women in terms of enhanced rights or greater political representation, yet it can succeed in mobilising substantial numbers of women. In other words women's gender interests are not always transparent, or even primary for women, any more than their gender identity is their sole identity.[29]

Women's Interests

This takes us to a second area of analytic distinction employed in the discussion of women's movements, that of 'women's interests'. This issue came to occupy a place of considerable importance in the debate on gender and development, following the diffusion into planning contexts of some conceptual distinctions I elaborated in the mid-1980s.[30] The history of the 'interest paradigm' as some have termed it, is a curious one; what began as an attempt to render the discussion of interests more sensitive to the complex issues at stake[31] ended up as an oversimplified model, which was sometimes applied in such a schematic way that the usefulness of thinking about women's interests at all was, for some, put in considerable doubt.[32]

All theories and concepts run the risk of being misapplied, but this is not usually reason enough to abandon them. The notion of interests has a long history in political theory and calculation, and, as Jonasdottir (1988) concludes in her critical evaluation of the concept, it is difficult to dispense with in accounts of politics, agency and collective action, let alone of political representation. What is needed, however, is some greater refinement in its treatment and caution in its deployment. Returning for a moment to my original article (reproduced as Chapter 2), the aim here was to problematise the way in which women's interests were formulated. I argued against certain constructions of women's interests and critiqued the notion that sex was a sufficient basis for assuming common interests. Instead, women's interests were seen as historically and culturally constituted, reflecting, but not reducible to, the specific social placement and priorities of particular groups of women; they were also seen as politically and discursively constructed. This allowed for the possibility of questioning the ways in which interests are formulated and the uses to which arguments about interest are put, both by women themselves and by those seeking to mobilise them.

Two sets of heuristic distinctions were introduced: the first involved identifying a category of 'gender interests' as distinct from those generally referred to as 'women's interests'. This sought to distinguish between those general or specific interests which women's organisations may claim as their own but which are not identified with gender issues. *Gender* interests referred to those arising from the social relations and positioning of the sexes and therefore pertained, but in specific ways, to both men and women.[33]

A second, more contentious distinction identified two ways in which women's gender interests could be derived: these were termed respectively 'practical' interests, those based on the satisfaction of needs arising from women's placement within the sexual division of labour; and 'strategic' interests, those involving claims to transform social relations in order to enhance women's position and to secure a more lasting repositioning of women within the gender order and within society at large. The intrinsically political, potentially transformative nature of strategic interests needs re-emphasising. Kate Young suggests the notion of *transformatory potential* to indicate the 'capacity ... for questioning, undermining or transforming gender relations and the structures of subordination'.[34]

Before proceeding further it may be helpful to recall that my original discussion of women's interests was within a work of political sociology, in this case an analysis of the Nicaraguan Revolution and its policies concerning women. Some later usages of these distinctions detached the categories from their explanatory context and adapted them in an effort to develop guidelines for the purpose of policy and planning.[35] These guidelines in turn were sometimes banalised by applications 'in the field', where they were treated, in the words of one practitioner, as a 'magic key', or deployed as a mechanical prescription for women's organisations to follow.[36] This is not to say that questions of interest have no pertinence for gender and development policy. The issue is one of the role they are designated in the planning process and by whom, and what relationship is established between the planning agency and the population with which it aims to work. This is as much an issue of good practice as of good theory.

If, in the evolution of the 'interest paradigm', some elements of the original analysis as well as the theoretical intent were misunderstood or lost in translation, two issues in particular could usefully be clarified: that of the way interests are conceptualised and that of the relationship between interests and needs. In the first place some authors assume a conception of interest which is at variance with that proposed in my original article. My article began by acknowledging the impossibility of deriving women's interests from a generalised account of women's subordination, akin to Marx's theory of proletarian exploitation. Yet Kabeer and Wieringa in their critical discussions automatically assume a Marxist derivation, while Wieringa believes that interests are necessarily equivalent to 'objective interests' and are thus given *a priori*.[37] The 1985 formulation, however, explicitly rejects this conception because it rests on essentialist assumptions and 'explains collective action in terms of some intrinsic property of the actors and/or the relations within which they are inscribed ...';[38] this conception implies that women's interests are given in their structural positioning and simply need to be read as an effect of the division of labour, reproductive capacities or, more generally, from women's social/structural location.

This theory of 'objective' interests has been criticised on a variety of other grounds both political and epistemological.[39] It presumes that interests can be identified irrespective of the subjective inclinations of agents and thus opens up the possibility of outside agencies imposing their version of objective interests on subject peoples. Such conceptions presume that interests can be identified as in some way 'true', as in correspondence theories which posit a direct relationship between the agent's interests and reality. Such truth claims can be contested from a variety of positions and there is consequently little support for such absolutist notions of truth in contemporary political debate. Interests and the struggles that arise in pursuing them are not usefully seen as an effect of some structural (or indeed biological) determination. While material needs or social positioning are important in explaining certain forms of mobilisation and resistance, their reductive deployment in terms of a 'structural effect' neglects the processes involved in the construction of meaning and hence of subjectivity itself. The formulation of interests, whether strategic or practical, is to some degree reliant on discursive elements and is always linked to identity formation. This is especially pertinent in the case of women whose interests are often closely bound to those of the family or household. This suggests that claims about women's objective interests need to be framed within specific historical contexts, since processes of interest formation and articulation are clearly subject to cultural, historical and political variation and cannot be known in advance.[40]

If reductive accounts of objective interests have their limitations, the solution is not to substitute a purely contingent and subjective construction of interests as this has little explanatory power or political pertinence.[41] Fierlbeck expresses the dilemma: '[To] say that women ... do have "objective" interests which must be addressed despite individual preferences devalues their own subjective articulation of what is important to them; while to admit only that women have "subjective" interests makes it all but impossible to address the disparities and attitudes that disadvantage women *qua* women.'[42] Jonasdottir (1988) suggests a compromise, arguing that any definition of interests must recognise agency and subjectivity, but they must also be understood to be formulated within determinate contexts which affect the way agency and choice are exercised. In this sense, only subjective interests can be said to exist, but since these are formulated within specific, bounded, historical contexts and constraints, it is possible to see interests as socially defined in ways that allow the calculation, with due reflection on the particular context, of something like objective interests. Objective interests could be said to correspond to the outcome which is of the most benefit to the agent concerned and should be pursued with the most appropriate strategies to realise them.

These issues are pertinent to the distinction between strategic and practical interests, one which has been objected to on several grounds. Wieringa opposes the distinction because it privileges one form of demand-making over others as an appropriate basis for feminist strategy. She argues against distinctions of any kind as they contain 'hierarchical overtones', and she is against these in particular because she sees them as unhelpful 'binaries', which are an attempt to 'control and normalise reality'.[43] Yet we surely need distinctions as heuristic devices if only in order to reveal how much more complex reality is.[44] This does not imply that they should be turned into dichotomous essences. Moreover, in policy contexts such distinctions can have a dynamic role, if they are introduced as a way of stimulating debate and discussion. To argue against distinctions is surely to argue against theory itself, rather than to debate the uses to which theory can be put. Wieringa's position seems inconsistent; distinctions are hierarchical, yet practitioners are urged to carry out 'feminist activity' with 'feminist-informed analysis'. What is this other than a privileged theory and discourse? Wieringa at times seems to conflate the role of theory with that of practice. We can all agree that it would be bad practice in moral and instrumental terms to impose change on an unwilling collectivity. But as Wierenga herself says, it would also be bad practice to avoid confronting difficult questions of politics and strategy on the grounds that what exists must be right.

With regard to the uses made of the strategic/practical distinction in planning contexts, the problem is that it has apparently been deployed in the form of a too rigid binary, with practical interests set against strategic in a static, hierarchised opposition. If this has occurred, it is far from what was intended and misrepresents the original theory. Clearly, practical interests can, at times should, be the basis for a political transformation. Indeed, the evidence shows that this evolution has sometimes occurred in the process of struggles around practical interests, as in the case of 'popular feminism' in Latin America.[45] Here, poor women mobilising around practical gender interests have sometimes engaged in strategic struggles which simultaneously enhance their ability to satisfy their practical needs and their strategic interests. However, it is equally important to stress that this transformation may not occur and that it is not simply given in the nature of struggles around practical interests. As many commentators have shown, such struggles more often than not do not proceed to demands which would challenge the structures of gender inequality, or enhance women's rights. Whether they do or do not is to a large degree contingent on political and discursive interventions which help to bring about the transformation of these struggles.

What purpose then is served by the distinction between practical and strategic? The distinction does differentiate between ways of reasoning about gender relations; in the formulation of practical interests there is the assumption that there is compliance with the existing gender order, while in the case of strategic interests there is an explicit questioning of that order and of the compliance of some women with it. Such a distinction between what Gramsci called a 'practical consciousness' and what we could term a 'strategic vision', has always been important to politics, especially to emancipatory politics. How else, other than through what Foucault calls 'the critical labour of thought upon itself', could claims to think differently, and to see the world in different terms to that which is presented in conventional stories about social relations, occur? If, in the formulation of practical interests, women take inequality or male authority over them for granted, then this is a different way of seeing the world to that which evolves in the course of political discussion premised on alternative, egalitarian visions.[46] If feminism, like other forms of critical theory, insists on seeing this reality as containing oppressive relations and social injustices, and if its practice is concerned with challenging it and changing it, then it depends on some measure of critical, alternative thought and hence on some means of making value judgements about the social order.[47] Needless to say, if such political and analytic distinctions are inevitable, they do not sanction practices which display arrogance or lack of respect for alternative views and ways of living. That is not only poor practice but self-defeating politics. The political *links* between practical and strategic interests are ones which can only emerge through dialogue, praxis and discussion.

Finally, in other usages of 'the paradigm', some, following Moser (1989), have preferred to interpret 'interests' as 'needs' because the latter does have a more direct applicability to planning and policy. The idea of need is a more categorical, less political and less fluid construct, even in the hands of those, like Fraser (1989), who give it a more political meaning by emphasising how needs are discursively constructed. Interests are conceptually different from needs, in that the former are more clearly intentional, belong within a political vocabulary and are the product of a process of reasoning which assumes instrumental agency. In simple terms, needs are usually deemed to exist, while interests are willed. Jonasdottir (1988) has suggested that in some needs discourses the question of authority acquires a particular salience: needs tend to be defined by and acted upon by expert others – planners, the political elite – while interests imply some greater degree of agency. While I can agree that there is a difference in the application of the needs/interests discourses, the latter, too, can involve questions of external definition and authority. In any event, Jonasdottir (1988) is surely right to suggest that what is required for the purposes of political calculation is some way of combining a discourse of needs with that of interests. This is essential in the planning field. Moser (1989), in fact, suggests that the planning process requires the identification of women's interests by women themselves, so that they can be translated into planning needs. Needs and interests should therefore be closely related in the planning process, with the proviso that the caution that should be deployed in relation to interests is equally necessary in relation to needs. Fraser (1989) uses the term 'the politics of needs interpretation' to emphasise the contested, contextual and discursive character of needs, resulting from a political process of interpretation, much as has been said in relation to interests.

Democracy and Interests

The identification of different kinds of interests raises other issues that are rarely considered in the development literature, namely, what are the *politics* (not just the power relations) involved in the articulation of women's diverse interests? It is evident that women's gender interests can be instrumentalised by political forces which claim to be promoting women's interests in general – as if they were self-evident, unproblematic and uncontested. In recent times, governments and development agencies have mobilised women into voluntary welfare work on the basis of their practical interests; such appeals have also been deployed to solicit women's support for neo-conservative campaigns around 'responsibilising the family'. The point is not to deny that women might identify with these definitions of their interests, but rather to ask questions about their broader political pertinence and their longer-term policy implications within specific contexts.

The question of broader political objectives is especially pertinent in the formulation of strategic interests, because the latter imply a process of politicisation in which particular transformative visions and strategies are elaborated with the aim of enhancing women's position overall. Feminism has itself provided several kinds of strategic vision, each articulated within different political discourses – these include socialist, liberal, nationalist, radical, anarchist, communitarian and maternalist versions, to name but some. The context of my original discussion of interests was a socialist revolution, that of Nicaragua. It was concerned with the emancipatory politics of feminism and socialism and of their shared and conflicting theoretical universes. Within the Latin American context of the time, feminism was associated with general principles of equality and with the classic feminist programme, which aimed to minimise the social differences between the sexes.[48] However, it is clear that other forms of strategic vision have been elaborated within women's movements, ones which are premised on different assumptions to 'equality feminism' and which sometimes depend upon radically opposed conceptions of gender relations. A critical distinction which can be made is between women's movements that premise their strategic visions on principles of equality and on the reducing of differences between the sexes, and those which argue for the enhancement of women's place in society through an appreciation of the differences between the sexes.

The latter view finds expression in a variety of political strategies, some of which are quite opposed to classical feminist conceptions of autonomy and equality. Women's movements based on this kind of difference politics have included certain kinds of motherist movements, housewives unions and some strands of religious fundamentalism, which attempt to retrieve a special place for women in the private sphere. Here a distinctive conception of women's interests is at play: it sees protection by men (or the state) and economic dependency on one or other, or both, as the necessary correlate of women's withdrawal or conditional presence within the public realm. A 'separation of the spheres' argument, supported by essentialist views of sex difference, is often an explicit component of women's interests conceived in this way.

Such conceptions of women's interests can be argued against on the grounds that they do not, nor can they, enhance women's socio-economic and political status in the context of major, gendered social inequalities. This would be the 'equality' feminist view.[49] Yet, these movements may share some long-standing feminist preoccupations – a belief in women's informal power in the home and the need to valorise women's work in the domestic sphere and in those areas supposedly most suited to women's 'special attributes'. In the case of some recent appropriations of this discourse, there is an attempt to politicise these interests, to extend the realm of women's juridical rights in the home and to empower women within this context.[50] When women's interests are formulated in this way as a vision of how to transform and enhance women's place in society, within terms of debate premised upon 'difference', then there may be grounds for speaking of them as being 'strategic' in character. However this question is resolved, it reveals that what is at stake is not only the difference between strategic and practical interests but that between different conceptualisations of women's interests and the politics consequent upon them. In other words, the kind of strategic vision which animates women's politics crucially denotes the terrain of debate and intervention for feminism.

Do we need a theory of interests for women's politics? It has been objected by some analysts that the notion of interests derives from a masculine model, connoting male values of rational goal-oriented behaviour premised on utilitarian political assumptions. Women, it is argued, are animated by emotion, by values which are altruistic: women's love and care for others is not based on rational self-interest but on other, moral, imperatives.[51] It is true that theories which conceive of interest in narrow utilitarian terms do not help in understanding such phenomena as 'maternal altruism' and care work, but this is chiefly because such theories are premised on ideas of the individual as abstracted from social relations. If individuals are seen as *social* beings, it becomes easier to explain why women might identify their interests more closely with the family and neighbourhood ties. Yet while the embedded character of women's social positioning might make it more difficult to separate affect from interest, it does not mean that women's commitment to family and kin is purely moral and entirely without self interest. The recognition of women's 'embeddedness' in the social realm, as well as an analysis of the social relations of carework, are perhaps more useful starting points than essentialist notions of 'woman the carer'.[52] Indeed, for many women the issue is not one of selfless altruism, of giving up their interests, but rather that of how to reconcile the conflicting desires stimulated by affect and caring on the one hand and by self-fulfilment outside the home on the other.

So if interests can be adequately and acceptably defined within discussions of policy and politics, what is their broader significance for women's political practice? Can women's interests be a sufficient basis for politics? Or should we consider how, and indeed if, women's *gender* interests can be defined in relation to broader goals and political processes? We have already considered how women's movements have developed diverse forms of association with other political agencies; sometimes women's gender interests have been defined and fought for by themselves, sometimes they have been defined, authorised and supported from above. In the same way, gender interests can be struggled for within a variety of different strategies. Two of these are particularly salient here: the first is the pursuit of women's interests within the framework of particularistic demands; the second is the reframing of women's gender interests as part of a redefined general interest.

Feminism is often cited as an example of identity politics charac-terised by single issue and particularistic demands.[53] Yet this does not accurately describe the trajectory of modern feminism, which has seen much overlapping of strategies and diversity of goals, many of them directed at achieving greater social equality and public provision. Within this diversity, particularistic demands have played an important part in the struggle for women's rights, most evidently in relation to such issues as reproductive choice and domestic violence. The pursuit of particular-istic interests (the right to protection from marital abuse, the right to reproductive choice) is of course not necessarily at variance with strategies that pursue broader goals and interests and may be framed in terms of general principles (the right to protection from violence, the right to one's bodily integrity). Indeed, this framing of women's gender interests within a broader set of political and ethical principles has been an important component of women's struggles within liberal, socialist and nationalist states. Yet, as a tactic it is perhaps double-edged; it runs the risk that the specificity of women's situation and demands are crowded out by other claims and that principles of autonomy are threatened or sacrificed to the expediency of alliance building. But the process of taking women's interests out of the personal, private and non-political sphere into the public terrain of political demand-making and then of framing those demands in terms of a redefined general interest can be an effective way of giving feminist demands a more general salience. It may also give them a central place in discussions of how to incorporate women's interests into visions of a reordered, more just society. In this way interest-based politics do not have to be renounced altogether, as some have argued.[54]

Conclusions: Women's Interests and Strategic Visions

The possibility of achieving an appropriate balance between particularist and univeralist demands, autonomy and association, is greatly enhanced by favourable political circumstances. In many developing countries women's movements have been working with the consequences of a double transition to economic and political liberalism, one which has brought a measure of democratisation but has been slow to deliver on its promise of greater prosperity for all. Deepening social inequalities and persistent poverty levels have challenged women's movements to contribute to the elaboration of a workable formula for the delivery of social justice within which women's interests, diverse though they be, are given recognition. Meanwhile, the female sex, over-represented among the least privileged groups, remains under-represented within policy-making arenas while continuing in the main to lack effective representative organisations.

The issue of women's strategic interests is necessarily bound up with what broader political project women's organisations or movements are engaged in or are associated with. As will be seen in the case of Latin America, examined in Chapter 7, many women's movements have framed their demands within an overall project of democratisation. Operational definitions of women's interests have come to include demands for women to be acknowledged as full citizens – a vision which depends for its realisation on the attainment of social, as well as civil and political rights and upon gaining institutional power. In the conditions presented by the return to democracy, women's movements have been able to contemplate forms of association and alliance with other political forces and organisations with which they sympathise. This entails a shared commitment to an agenda which transcends while it still encompasses particularistic interests, by reframing these where possible as part of a redefined social project. The critical issue for those women involved in these efforts is to ensure that the radical insights and transformatory vision of gender analysis, feminist theory and demands, has some purchase in the policy domain. Among the most significant contributions of feminism has been the development of a new perspective on social and political life, one which not only reveals its profoundly unequal and gendered character, but which requires a reassessment both of the priorities of states and of the normative social order. Gendered analyses of policies, and of their social consequences, have transformed the debate over poverty and over the impact of macro-economic policies on developing countries. Feminist theory has shown why the sphere of reproduction needs to be placed firmly within the planning process, not just to acknowledge women's invisible labours but to identify social needs more generally within conditions of racialised and gendered social inequalities. As was evident from the resolutions of the Beijing Conference, for many feminists in the developing countries, the important issue is how to develop a feminist politics which can also promote a general project of democracy and social justice. This may be one of the ways in which women's movements will define strategic interests in the decades ahead.

7

Gender and Citizenship in Latin America: Historical and Contemporary Issues*

Citizenship has, since the 1980s, become the currency of much political and historical analysis, with work from within this perspective appearing in virtually all regions of the world.[1] It is however not surprising that this concept has come to occupy such a special place within contemporary political and theoretical debates, or that its appeal has spread so steadily across the world. It not only signifies a way of problematising the politics and policies of liberal democracy, the dominant political form in the modern world, but it can encompass a wide range of social and political issues raised by the new post-Cold War international and national context. Citizenship provides a political language for thinking about broader questions of social membership which have been sharply re-posed by global trends such as migration, nationalism, indigenous claims and social marginalisation.

The concern with citizenship and democracy is one to which feminism has made a significant contribution. The work of Elshtain, Pateman and others sparked a renewed interest and engagement with political theory, through interrogating the premises of liberalism and democracy, and revealing the workings of political exclusion and inequality within the heart of its universal principles of equality, universalism and impartiality. This feminist critique has inspired a wide range of historical and contemporary scholarly work on citizenship, while it has entered and given direction to political and policy debates

*This discussion is informed by interviews and conversations with women's movement activists in Latin America over many years. I am grateful to all of them for their time and hope that my interpretation does not do violence to their views. A version of this chapter was first presented as a paper at a conference on Women and Citizenship held at the Autonomous University of Mexico in 1996, organised by the Centre for Gender Studies (PUEG).

on the processes of gender and ethnic exclusion. At the same time, the irruption of women's movements of various kinds into the political arena has provided a challenge of a different kind to normative definitions of political practice and of the meanings of citizenship itself.[2]

Yet citizenship is a concept with a considerable anterior history; it has been, and remains, a contested and constantly evolving concept. Differing notions of what is implied by struggles around the issues it raises often prescribe contrasting political priorities and strategies, ones that change with time. The classical Graeco-Roman ideal contained three central elements: equality, the rule of law, and participation in political, including military, life. With the birth of political liberalism there developed new arguments over the proper balance between civic responsibilities and individual freedoms, while in the twentieth century liberal conceptions of citizenship themselves came under attack from, on the left, Marxism and other theories of collective identity; and, on the right, from nationalism. The founding of the welfare state also signalled a new conception of citizenship rights, which stressed social membership and social rights as a necessary complement to political rights.

In more recent decades, citizenship has regained ground as an authoritative political concept. This advance has reflected the collapse of other forms of political community, most evident in the transitions from authoritarian rule, both capitalist and communist. Debates over citizenship have been rekindled and further extended by radical and social liberalism and by the engagement of a post-Marxist left with democratic theory. Liberal individualist conceptions of citizenship have been challenged by republican conceptions of active citizenship and by communitarianism, while Marshallian concepts of social rights have been defended against libertarian critiques of welfare within the policy arena. Thus, in the absence of a socialist alternative to liberal capitalism, the field of engagement indicated by 'citizenship', like liberalism itself, has broadened; left and right alike appropriate its language to discuss a range of apparently similar concerns.

Yet if the politics of citizenship are a matter of dispute, so too are its founding assumptions. Post-modern critics have attacked its rationalism and universalising premises while denying the validity and usefulness of the concept altogether in a world characterised by fragmentation and globalisation, and where the citizen, it is claimed, has been replaced by the consumer. Within citizenship studies itself, there is a sceptical re-evaluation of the Enlightenment legacy and a critique of the classical conception of citizenship. This has been shown to operate with an implicit language of privilege played out in relation to class, 'race' and gender. Yet, sound though this critique may be, it has itself posed further questions on which no consensus exists. For some, it requires that citizenship be stripped of its universalist pretensions and reformulated instead as a means to promote other principles, those of localism, pluralism and difference. For others, however, this universalism is seen as a necessary and essential defence against the growing threat to women's and minority rights posed by right-wing nationalism, fundamentalism, communalism and theocratic despotism. Here, regional and cultural specificities necessarily pose different questions and elicit different political responses so that the *meaning* given to citizenship struggles is, to a significant extent, context-dependent. In sum, it would be fair to say that the field of engagement indicated by citizenship has become thoroughly pluralised and its meaning highly varied.

The Variability of Citizenship[3]

There has, therefore, been a growing recognition of the significant variations in what citizenship entails both in terms of the rights it confers and in terms of the meaning it has for those inscribed within it. Less well-understood or analysed are the ways in which these understandings are themselves deeply gendered, as are the specific obstacles which women have faced in claiming full citizenship.[4] Citizenship, understood as the legal foundation of social membership, is context-dependent in three main ways: as a system of rights it defines a citizen's entitlements and responsibilities within a particular legal tradition and social context; in signifying the social and political membership of a nation-state it makes claims on loyalty and identity within the framework of a specific set of cultural understandings; and, as noted above, within political struggle, citizenship claims may assume a variety of different means and ends depending on particular political discourses, priorities and opportunity contexts.[5] To complicate matters further, the considerable diversity that exists *between* regions of the world in matters of law, nationhood and politics, may be replicated *within* these regions and even within countries themselves. In these various respects, Latin America is illustrative: Peru differs from Argentina, but Ayacucho also differs from Lima.[6]

Such spatial-cultural variability in matters of citizenship is also found with regard to gender formations. Culturally specific representations of gender difference and identity have become encoded in political discourses concerning citizenship and social membership. They have implications for the way in which women's interests and obligations are formulated in citizenship discourses. The character of gender formations also influences the entitlements which women have demanded and the kind of political presence they have sought and achieved. Gendered accounts of citizenship therefore presuppose an understanding of the gender regime that prevails in given societies.[7] This provides an insight into the mechanisms by which women have been marginalised, excluded and subordinated within particular states and forms of civil society.

A gendered account of citizenship also requires us to distinguish between the formal rights it confers and what we might term 'really existing citizenship', that is, between the legal-political and the social aspects of citizenship. Implicit in the latter is the recognition that, for one reason or another, many formal rights are not realised. This gap between formal and substantive rights invites analysis of how citizenship is lived in practice – in the courts, in the polity, in the household, as well as in the understandings different sectors of the population have of their rights and of the terms of their social participation or exclusion. Such an analysis benefits from the techniques of thick description. In providing an understanding of the social context and meaning of citizenship it can cast light on the different factors – some gender-specific, some not – which have served to define what citizenship means for women, as well as to reveal how this varies according to social position and according to other factors such as age and ethnic identity. Crucial here, too, is the identification of the historical and political forces and rhetorics that have come to influence such definitions. As with other political constructs, for example national identity, the definitions that prevail are both contested and change over time. While citizenship has been a goal of feminist political struggle for over a century, it has been an ever-changing one. Gendering citizenship requires us to see both how women's agency has been involved in defining that goal, and also how, over time, its meaning, as well as that of the rights with which it is associated, have changed.

Within the growing body of literature on gender and citizenship, changing legal discourses about rights and entitlements have generally been analysed in relation to feminist movements on the one hand, and state interests on the other. Where these three elements – law, female activism, and the state – have been found to intersect most tellingly for a gender analysis is in the interface between the public and private spheres. The meanings given to the public and the private and the boundaries between them, whether constituted in discourse or in practice, have been (and continue to be) a site of struggle for and within feminism. At the same time what is designated spatially as 'the public' and 'the private' has changed, as a result, *inter alia*, of the broader processes of social and economic development associated with modernity. Women's mass, visible entry into the public sphere and into modern forms of employment has destabilised the classical opposition between women's and men's social placement. But it did not dissolve gender differences, for as women entered public space the latter was recoded into masculine and feminine territory. Even as women breached the ultimate bastion of male exclusivity, that of institutional politics, they entered it on different terms to men and occupied positions in accordance with what were seen as their 'special feminine attributes'.

This moving frontier, both real and symbolic, between the public and private is nowhere more clearly evident than in the rights and laws pertaining to women, which in various ways have inscribed the female body in legislation. This, and indeed the concept of 'femininity' itself, has given meaning to how the 'private' was defined – whether with regard to motherhood, sexual rights in marriage or reproductive rights – thus forming the bedrock of the case for differential rights of citizenship. Yet in the early struggles for citizenship, the idea that women had 'special attributes' was deployed both for and against their admission into public and political life, and was both opposed and supported by feminists. Indeed from the nineteenth century onwards, women's struggles for citizenship – whether in Latin America, Europe or Asia – have expressed an unresolved tension between the principles of equality and difference, evident in contrasting assumptions about femininity and biology. With these general points in mind, we will turn now to consider some of the gendered meanings of citizenship in Latin America.

Gender and Citizenship in Latin America

Latin America had a significant feminist movement from the late nineteenth century to the early decades of the twentieth century.[8] However, the struggle for citizenship was shaped to a considerable degree by the colonial experience on the one hand and a political history of unstable democracy and military dictatorship on the other. Spanish rule left its imprint in its legal codes and in a cultural configuration which gave Catholicism a particular influence over women's lives. Colonialism also bequeathed a legacy of ethnic division and racialised inequality, which delayed the inclusion of black and indigenous people within the political calculus of citizenship.[9]

The Wars of Independence from Spain allocated women a place in the pantheon of republican virtue as mothers and guardians of the hearth, despite a more complex reality which gave many women firsthand experience of war, as nurses, troop followers, even soldiers. The leaders of the Independence movements were liberals but not democrats, and envisioned only a limited, male enfranchisement. Women were to remain 'outside citizenship' until well into the twentieth century on the grounds that their domestic virtues and 'special attributes' did not equip them for it. Yet women learnt to deploy this language of difference in ways that challenged the public–private schism that was used to disqualify them from political citizenship and legal equality. They took their feminine virtues out of the home and into the public space and demanded that they be recognised as a service to the nation.[10] This was a theme which animated Latin American women's movements and gave them an enduringly distinctive cast. [11]

Women's movements of various kinds emerged across the sub-continent in the nineteenth century as radical ideas borne by immigrants from Europe began to exert an influence. Women of different classes and shades of opinion began to challenge their treatment in the law and to contest the terms of their social and political exclusion.[12] They did this in ways that gave special significance to their role in the family, in a discourse which drew in direct and indirect ways on referents derived from Catholicism.[13] This gave meaning to constructions of femininity that bore on the way in which the issue of difference was played out with respect to women's rights, social policy and political participation.

As in Europe, female suffrage was an early demand of feminism, appearing in the Latin American movements in the late nineteenth century.[14] Here the two-sided potential of difference became clear. While opponents of female enfranchisement argued that women were variously too passionate, ignorant or domestic to exercise political judgement, its supporters also deployed this language of difference, inverting its terms to argue that women's innate qualities of altruism and morality would serve to improve political life. Thus, female biology and psychology were pressed into service in the pursuit of equality. When the Argentine suffrage law of 1912 denied women the vote on the grounds that they could not bear arms, the most ancient test of citizenship, feminist campaigners replied, as their revolutionary sisters in France had done a century before,[15] that they bore children, and sacrificed their sons to the nation in war. Motherhood was thus claimed as an equally valid test of their loyalty to the nation-state.[16]

Latin American feminists and their male supporters therefore high-lighted the issue of difference, and demands for citizenship were often played out through idealised representations of motherhood and wifely duty. While in parts of Europe women strove to individuate themselves from the family in matters of identity and rights, this strand of feminist thought was less evident in Latin America.[17] The politicisation of motherhood, often linked to ideas of the nation and nationalism, were recurrent themes in Latin American twentieth-century history. However, feminists extended the meaning of these terms: the home as women's sphere of interest and competence was resignified to embrace neighbour-hood and municipal issues and the protection of child and female labour. By extension, philanthropic activities became an acceptable mediation of the public and private for women. The 'sacred qualities' of motherhood could be deployed in the service of society, and with women claimed as 'genuinely altruistic' in opposition to a masculine self-serving individualism, their efforts were seen as assisting in the reform of public life. While these arguments were also made in other parts of the world, in Latin America motherhood and domesticity were endowed with an enduring moral and political significance, even as what they signified varied over time.

As in the USA, feminism allied itself with civic maternalism in the pursuit of social reform and protection for women.[18] Many Latin American feminists were active in the eugenicist social hygiene move-ment,[19] supporting the introduction of public and child healthcare and becoming the first social workers in the late 1920s. This affinity between difference and public service lay behind the granting to women of the vote in municipal elections (often denied at national level), on the grounds that they would be working close to their homes and on issues close to their domestic interests.[20] Even the most sympathetic reformers and champions of female equality did not aim to de-couple women from the family; the development of 'compensatory feminism' in Uruguay, which in the 1940s became popular in the Southern Cone (Argentina, Uruguay and Chile), represented a step forward for women in many ways.[21] It sought to have motherhood recognised and protected in the law by making welfare provision for mothers and children, while the government would remove obstacles to equality in education and employment. Yet as some feminists argued at the time, it was not compensation they sought, but equality.[22]

For contemporary feminists versed in the arguments over difference this history raises some intriguing questions. Were the claims of difference and motherhood the most effective strategic discourses available to women at the time? Did they indeed achieve greater equality and dignity for women, or did the attempts by Latin American feminists to address social and political issues through 'a different voice' in an effort to reconcile rights, social justice and motherhood cede too much ground to difference at the expense of equality? It is worth noting that the reform of the civil codes in the Southern Cone countries, which, by the late 1920s, finally gave women control over their own property and earnings, was justified as giving mothers the rights they needed to better perform their role in the family. Decades before that, women workers had defended and gained their right to work in precisely the same terms.[23] In effect these were concessions granted to women primarily for the sake of their children.

Some of this ambivalence over women's individual rights was also evident in the issue of female enfranchisement. In many cases female suffrage was granted by states, from above, and often for reasons more to do with state interests than the pursuit of social equality or the strength of feminist movements.[24] Significantly, the first Latin American government to enfranchise women was a conservative administration in Ecuador, which, fearing a challenge from more radical elements, felt it could rely on the 'natural conservatism of women' to deliver its votes safely. As a result women received the franchise in 1929, almost a quarter of century before revolutionary Mexico which had denied women the vote for fear of the self-same quality, their 'conservatism'. In Argentina, with the support of Eva Perón, women were enfranchised in 1947 principally as a means of enlarging the Peronist vote. Eva Perón mobilised thousands of working-class women who were addressed as the 'wives of the soldiers of Perón'. Her emotive discourses were a notable example of the public exaltation of difference, one which drew on familial symbolism: she identified herself as the loyal wife of the great leader and mother of the 'great Peronist nation', and called on women to support their men (who were supporting Perón), by minding the hearth and home.[25] Argentine populism may have been a step in the direction of greater mass participation but its message was resolutely patriarchal. Even as it sought to bring women into national political life, it did so in terms that dignified and politicised traditional gender identities. In this spirit Eva Perón anticipated the wages for housework campaigns of the 1970s, when she called for women to receive some financial reward for the work they performed in the home. That women from the working classes were themselves stirred by these appeals is evident from the enduring loyalty 'Evita' commanded after her lifetime,[26] as well as being reflected in the size of the membership of the Peronist Women's Party which she headed; this reached half a million in 1951, the year before she died.

There was, therefore, a clear continuum in Latin America between women's roles in the family and in struggles for citizenship rights. This identification of women with the family led to Latin American women acquiring an array of social rights and entitlements designed to protect the family and the 'race'. Women were treated in law as in need of protection rather than equality. This approach was only challenged by some socialist feminists in the first wave of the early twentieth century, and later, from the mid-1970s onwards when equality feminism acquired a following within second wave feminism and analyses of patriarchy gained ground.[27] In the 1980s and 1990s, when many Latin American countries embarked on a process of reforming women's legal rights, equality *and* protection were combined in the new codes. Women were seen as requiring equality as a consequence of their responsibilities within the family. The individuation of women's rights *from* the family remained a contentious issue, associated with extreme equality feminism and as a political goal, liable to fail. Feminist campaigners themselves therefore continued to deploy familist arguments to secure women's rights, as the only means by which a consensus over reform could be achieved.[28]

Women's social roles of wife and mother were woven through the history of women's citizenship in Latin America. The theme of motherhood was present most evidently in feminism itself, but it also appeared within populism, and in the socialist iconography of revolutionary states such as Nicaragua. The idealised *guerrillera*, emblem of the Sandinista women's organisation, the Luisa Amanda Espinosa Association of Nicaraguan Women (AMNLAE), was portrayed bearing both gun and infant in a combative refiguring of women's earlier claims on citizenship as mothers. These maternal identifications also animated the grassroots mobilisations of women that are such a characteristic feature of Latin American civil society. No necessary politics followed from an identification with motherhood: these motherist movements were associated with politics that ranged across the spectrum, from the human rights movements of the Mothers of the Disappeared to those which supported General Pinochet in the shanty towns of Chile. Moreover, for all its pervasiveness as a symbol of femininity and as a constitutive element of female identity, both the meaning of motherhood and the investment of women in its idealisations varied considerably according to social class, age and ethnicity. Nonetheless, despite these caveats, motherhood was a pervasive and enduring 'referent of female mobilisation' in Latin America,[29] as well as a significant factor in helping to account for the distinctive evolution of the region's women's movements.[30]

If a strategic mobilisation of difference arguments and an identification with motherhood within political life were features of Latin American women's movements, there were two further characteristics which can be noted for their salience in respect to contemporary citizenship debates: the *social* character of feminism in the region and the emphasis placed on participatory politics. With regard to the first, there were always significant currents within Latin American feminism which, at various points in its long history, sought a distance from the kind of approach commonly identified with North American feminism, one in which a rights-based individualism has driven much movement activism. Latin American feminist movements laid considerable stress on individual rights and more on social rights, partly as a consequence of the cultural significance of difference noted above, partly because of the role played by vibrant currents of social feminism, ones which were nourished from the different sources of socialism, populism and social Catholicism.

Latin American women's movements contained a range of distinct tributary streams or currents – autonomous popular movements, activists in political parties and trade unions and feminist organisations – each representing different social strata with a distinct political evolution. Popular grassroots activism evolved largely through mobilisation around, and politicisation of, women's role-based needs and identities. Those active in political organisations comprised both working-class and middle-class women, while the core of the feminist movement was composed of university-educated women whose political origins lay within the student movements of the later 1970s and in the organisations of the left.[31] Despite this diversity Latin American feminism exhibited two common features: a concern to advance a broader project of social reform and to realise women's rights within it, and forms of activism which involved the popular sectors – both as objects of mobilisation strategies and as subjects of their own activism. Overall, the feminist movement in Latin America stands in contrast to that which emerged in parts of Europe and in North America, in that it did not on the whole engage in the kind of identity politics which made the pursuit of single issue, particularistic interests its primary goal. The greater stress that was placed on issues of collective and social responsibility make the Latin American movement one that might best be described as a kind of 'social feminism'.

Related to the above, and a particular feature of its second wave, was Latin American feminism's engagement in participatory activism. As will be discussed in more detail later, ideas of community activism, empowerment and participation originating within social Catholicism and the left animated women's and feminist movements in Latin America from the 1950s onwards. Although tensions existed between popular women's movements, (comprised of those on low incomes) and the largely middle-class feminist activists, there can be little doubting the degree of interaction between the two that occurred. A notable development from the 1980s was the growth in popular feminism among female activists from low-income settlements and within the organised working class who either openly identified with feminist aspirations or, if not, had nevertheless absorbed feminist discourses into their rhetoric and strategising.[32]

In sum, the Latin American women's movement in its heterogeneous and distinctive forms has been a more diverse and vital force than has often been recognised. As Jaquette has noted, its contemporary political contours were shaped by three sociohistorical components: a feminist movement with demands broadly similar to those of European, Canadian and US women; a women's movement which mobilised against dictatorship and authoritarianism and against the violation of human rights; and a popular movement which turned survival strategies into sociopolitical demands.[33] To these can be added the significant mobilisations of women by political parties, some of which, as in Peronism, absorbed elements of feminist discourse (and some of its demands), but reworked these within a politics which explicitly identified itself as anti-feminist.

Redemocratisation, Social Movements and Citizenship: *Desde la Protesta hasta la Propuesta*[34]

These constitutive elements of Latin American feminism were present but reconfigured in the changed circumstances and political discourses of the 1980s and 1990s. Second-wave feminism matured in Latin America in a period of political crisis and dictatorship. Unused at first to the machinery of democracy, those active in the women's movement followed a course which some participants have described as a shift, albeit hesitant and conditional, 'from the margins to the centre'. In the 1970s, women activists – disillusioned with the exclusionary, authoritarian and masculinist organisations they were involved in, including those of the left – sought to create autonomous spaces within which to develop an alternative politics. Autonomy became a principle of political organisation, and with the 'end of politics' imposed by the authoritarian regimes, feminist and many other women's movements went underground and identified themselves as oppositional and anti-state.[35] As we shall see, autonomy was to remain a central issue and an increasingly conflictive one within the movement throughout the transition period and afterwards.

During the 1980s, while feminists in the Western liberal democracies were able to turn their attention to the state both as an arena of struggle over policy and as an object of feminist theorising, in Latin America the political and theoretical space was occupied by social movements. With the ending of authoritarianism and the revitalisation of democratic politics, ideas of citizenship gradually gained a hold in Latin America, but within a context in which social movements remained important both as political phenomena and as signifiers of what politics meant to many activists in the region. Thus, while the Western feminist engagement with citizenship theory was coincident with the gradual return to democracy, in Latin America it grew out of a different political context. As we shall see, citizenship activism went through several shifts of emphasis corresponding to the evolution of priorities within the movement more broadly. In this process an initial emphasis on social movements and *active* citizenship was followed by an increasing engagement with rights and with the state as an arena of struggle over policy.

A predominant concern of the early work on citizenship within feminism was to provide a gender analysis of the grassroots movements concerned with basic needs and human rights that were active both under the authoritarian regimes and during the transitions to democracy. One of the first and most widely diffused texts was Elizabeth Jelin's edited collection *Women and Social Change in Latin America*, published in 1990. A product of a comparative project funded by the United Nations Research Institute for Social Development (UNRISD) on popular participation, this volume examined the organised efforts made by an 'excluded social group (i.e. women) ... to increase their control over the regulative institutions of society'. Jelin defined the project as forming part of a 'search for identity and citizenship'.[36] This work represented a timely intervention in a debate on social movements. Until that moment the debate had been conducted as if women were not participants in these movements and in the absence of any recognition of the gendered character of such activism.[37] In the forward to the volume, Lourdes Arizpe located the work as motivated by a 'current worldwide eagerness for democracy', but made it clear that she meant a particular kind of democracy, one 'which goes beyond traditional political structures and institutions'. This caveat signalled what was arguably a distinguishing feature of Latin American feminist politics and writing in the 1980s, namely the endorsement of active, that is, participatory, citizenship.[38]

Latin American feminist theorists and activists joined critical theorists of the left such as O'Donnell, Lechner and others in criticising the liberal utilitarian conception of citizenship. They questioned the principle of privileging individual rights over questions of social responsibility, rejecting the version of citizenship that defended a narrow interpretation of rights and the 'thin' versions of social and political membership that such definitions of citizenship entailed. Instead they argued for a more substantive version of citizenship which was both more participatory and more socially responsible. There was therefore, agreement between feminists and those social movement and civil society theorists who stressed the virtues of 'active citizenship' or 'participation'. These latter forms of activity were seen as a counter to the corrupt and alienated politics of the state and as a virtuous activity in their own right, contributing to the building of civil society and hence of firmer foundations for democracy.

In this period, calls to develop a strong civil society through encouraging social and active citizenship appeared across the political spectrum in Latin America. The left saw it largely in terms of leading to greater public participation and capacity for advancing a project of social and political reform; proponents of social Catholicism saw in it a means of reconfiguring and revitalising the communitarian ethos which characterised the Christian base communities in their heyday. For their part, women's movement activists saw it as a way of furthering women's interests and empowerment, by allowing work in neighbourhood associations to be given appropriate recognition and support.

Feminist analysts focused their attention on making women's participation both visible and valued, while they debated the gendered character of the forms of mobilisation and demand-making that accompanied it. They insisted that citizenship had to take account of what Latin American theorists called *el cotidiano* – the quotidian – or everyday life, because it was only in that way that women's worth could be identified and valued and that their distinctive political subjectivity could find expression.[39] Democracy was understood not only as a practice of institutional formal politics, but one which concerned everyday life and which permeated the family and the wider society. This implied redefining the meaning of democracy itself. Thus the gendered dimension of active citizenship was discussed in terms of five principal and evolving concerns: its potential for enhancing women's capacity for self-determination and achieving equality, the question of whether 'women's politics' differed in any meaningful way from 'men's politics', the significance of communitarian versions of active citizenship, the dilemmas posed by difference in the 'new' democracies, and the relationship between active citizenship and state institutions. These five issues will be addressed in turn below.

Engendering Active Citizenship

If active citizenship was viewed positively in Latin American women's movements, there was extensive discussion of the meaning of women's participation in activities like the *comedores populares*, the *ollas comunes* and the *vaso de leche* schemes,[40] which in Peru and Chile during the 1980s and early 1990s achieved high rates of participation, with tens of thousands of women involved. While few doubted the social significance of women's entry in such substantial numbers into these activities, or the experiential value of the kind of activism and female solidarity and cooperation that could result from it, some questioned whether it constituted an important part of women's struggle for their collective interests *as women*.

Here analysts were divided between optimists and pessimists. For the former such activism had three positive effects. In the first place these schemes served as 'apprenticeships' for women whose experience of solidarity and leadership 'empowered' them in a way that enabled at least some of them to take up a role in the formal political arena.[41] Second, they led to the creation of 'new spaces' which women could occupy in the public sphere, effectively reconfiguring the boundaries between, and meanings of, the public/private spheres. Third, the confident occupation by women of these new spaces allowed them to challenge their subordination in the home. Caldeira saw the significance of this development in terms of a cultural transformation, a new way of experiencing womanhood, one which contributed to a process in which relations between the sexes and female identities were redefined.[42]

This positive view of participation as leading inevitably to desirable change was shared by the early social movements literature, but both failed to engage in any systematic way with questions of politics and to analyse the consequences, individual or social, of the activities concerned.[43] As social movement activism declined, or at least changed, with a move towards greater institutionalisation in the late 1980s, more sceptical views about the claims made for such activism were voiced. Again, while few doubted that female participation in the world outside the home broadened women's experience, it was more difficult to demonstrate that it made a tangible or lasting impact on the majority of women's lives with regard to the division of labour and power relations in the home. Such evidence as existed on this issue was inconsistent; it showed that activism or participation could make a difference, as the testimonials of many key activists verified. But outside this group, often it did not, or did so for only a short time, with participants returning to the familiar oppressive patterns of before. One conclusion that could be drawn was that activism alone, in the absence of a transformative politics and supportive material circumstances, did not lead to 'empowerment'. This issue therefore revealed to women activists both the potentiality and the limits of active citizenship, indicating that its significance and outcome were more contingent processes than had been assumed.[44]

If the effects of activism on gender relations were variable, so too were its political effects. As contributors to this debate stressed, an active civil society was an integral component of democratic life, indispensable for a healthy society. In Latin America women often took a prominent role in efforts to create active forms of citizenship and civic responsibility. They were frequently identified as a principal force in the reconstitution of civil society in both the authoritarian and post-authoritarian periods.[45] Women's activism sometimes came to be seen as the *equivalent* of a democratic politics, one which was by definition all the more radical because it was not political in the conventional, institutional sense. Yet, whatever validity such an analysis was seen to have when applied to the period of transition from authoritarianism (when such activism was located within an oppositional and a democratic politics), could this experience be generalised to include *all* such activity irrespective of context? Questions were therefore raised as to whether this model of active citizenship was adequate to the task of building a democratic society, and whether it should be treated as a substitute for such a project.

Moreover, although active citizenship was often associated with radical politics in Latin America, and could constitute an essential element of such a politics, ideas of active citizenship could be annexed to a range of sharply differing political interventions and objectives. Social citizenship, understood as community activism, participation or moral regeneration was not always, or indeed necessarily, linked to projects for democratic reform or greater social cohesion. It could also serve the purposes of more conservative forces, as was evident in contexts where nationalist and religious fundamentalists of various kinds had sought to create a political community, in the furtherance of objectives which would lead to authoritarian, patriarchal, racist and chauvinist policies. Right-wing parties in Latin America had themselves been quick to jump on the active citizenship bandwagon; the Partido Acción Nacional (PAN) in Mexico made explicit use of this language in efforts to mobilise support for conservative family policies. In the literature on these issues, the boundary between active citizenship, social movements and top-down mobilisation was rarely clearly drawn.

Thus, while active citizenship continued to be upheld as a principal element of the work of women's movements, it was increasingly recognised that its politics, practices and outcomes were contingent on the broader social context and political meaning that was given to it. A general endorsement of active citizenship, in the absence of a political strategy, or without attention to the politics and policies with which it was associated, ran the risk of generating false expectations of what active citizenship could deliver. As Arizpe had warned: 'The demands made by the women's movement are not as yet far reaching. We should remember that "participation" is the weakest of the links in the chain of equality in contrast with the "taking of decisions". To demand participation and not decision-making powers is ... a rather modest way of engaging in politics.'[46] Moreover, if active citizenship was a necessary condition, it was not a sufficient condition for any meaningful democracy. For it to serve as a crucial element of a democratic politics it needed to be distinguished from political currents and policy initiatives which had different objectives and priorities. Therefore, some tough questions began to be posed about the broader significance of the concerted calls for active citizenship in the climate of neo-liberal policies and, as we shall see later, such calls existed in considerable tension with feminism. With these general issues in mind, I turn now to look at the way in which citizenship discourses were deployed in the debate over the gendering of activism.

The Gendering of Activism: Mothers and/or Citizens?

As noted earlier, Latin American feminism evolved in a cultural context in which female political activism was often explicitly role-based. In the 1970s and 1980s, with the appearance of grassroots mobilisations of women around basic needs provision, and of the 'motherist' human rights movements such as the Madres de la Plaza de Mayo, the gendered meaning of such activism became a subject of debate within Latin American women's movements.[47] Such mobilisations by women were seen by many analysts as illustrative of the quintessential women's movement and of the essence of feminine politics. They arose on the basis of specifically feminine moral values, ones which were variously attributed to women's social positioning within the division of labour, or the primordial experience of mothering, or were simply seen as an outgrowth of female biology.

For some analysts these situational and/or natural attributes of femininity produced a politics that was more democratic, more altruistic and less hierarchically disposed as far as organisational forms were concerned. As Jelin expressed it, women 'did' politics differently to men. While 'men's politics' was defined by self-interest, hierarchical power relations and competitiveness, women's were oriented towards family or community, and were based on democratic and cooperative values. Femininity was therefore offered both as the basis for a new way of doing politics and as representing the values of a good society overall. Latin American treatments of citizenship from within this perspective drew on the work of Italian feminist Rossana Rossanda, French theorists of *la différence* such as Hélène Cixous and others such as Carol Gilligan and Sara Ruddick. As the theoretical debate within feminism over citizenship evolved, a feminised version of citizenship was postulated which was committed to a conception of a different female political consciousness or 'voice', one grounded in virtues that were unacknowledged in normative understandings of politics.[48] Thus, in stressing the 'female' value of caring and belonging within the community, women's politics were placed in opposition to 'male' values of autonomy expressed in rights-based contractarian liberalism.[49]

The feminist advocacy of female virtue found its counterpart in some religious quarters in Latin America. Leonardo Boff, an influential theorist of the theology of liberation, helped to disseminate a critique of liberal capitalism as based on a masculinist rationale to which he counterposed female virtue and the world of affect rather than profit as the basis of public morality.[50] In some versions of ecofeminism similar assumptions prevailed, with creative woman-nature counterposed to destructive man-culture epitomised by capitalism.[51] Some Latin American feminist analysts of social movements came to see the issues of daily life and struggle for basic needs, and the commitment to democratic forms of organisation, as illustrative of the virtues of (feminine) social movements over conventional (masculine) forms of organisation, in an evocation of

Habermas' advocacy of 'lifeworld' against the functional reason of state and bureaucracy.

The terms of these arguments can be seen as a development of the earlier Latin American debate over women's accession to citizenship rights, in which as we have seen, feminine virtues were at its centre. First-wave Latin American feminists had argued that such virtues needed to be carried over into the public sphere,[52] where they would re-moralise and transform an over-rationalised or corrupt social and political life. Juan Perón placed this discourse at the service of the state when he designated Evita's place in politics as the 'heart' of Peronism with himself, in a predictable binary, as the 'head'. More than 20 years later, Salvador Allende, from the left, also appealed to the female voter by praising the superior feminine morality which would cleanse the public sphere.

While such invocations of superior feminine values may be experienced by those so addressed as 'empowering', may deliver political dividends and may at times be strategically deployed within feminist campaigns, there were dangers in an uncritical acceptance of the gender ideology on which such views rested. In the first place calls to re-moralise society always found strong support within the right and through the Catholic Church, where the appeal to feminine virtue was cast in terms which invoked traditional family values based on conventional roles and authority patterns between the sexes. It is a short step towards making women responsible for the moral values of society, with the attendant castigation of those found deficient by these standards, whether these are women who work outside the home, single mothers or others judged deviant by such standards.

Critics of difference feminism have argued that a feminist politics necessarily problematises the relationship between gender, politics and morality rather than assuming that it is ontologically given. This allows for the recognition that women's politics are not only, or necessarily, 'maternal politics', democratic or caring.[53] These values, often associated with 'women's morality', are positive ones, but they may best be treated as ones that cross the gender divide, even if they are not equally distributed. Moreover, if women are treated as the sole bearers of moral virtue and made responsible for the public good, masculinity remains unexamined, its negative identifications unchallenged and men absolved from responsibility in this domain. In this way the sexual division of morality, like those of labour and politics, persists as an intrinsic feature of wider social inequalities.[54]

A different approach has been signalled by shifting the terms of debate from 'women's values' to a broader consideration of what women typically *do* and what their responsibilities in this regard are. Whether conceptualised as reproductive work or as care, it has been a matter of feminist concern to render it visible and in so doing to locate it within the structures of power and privilege which define its gendered modalities.[55] A gender analysis of this issue has become central to feminist theorising about citizenship and has relevance as a social policy concern.[56] By thinking about these responsibilities, the feminist debates about morality can be shifted from the terrain of essentialism to that of politics and policy, and issues of care can be combined with issues of rights, *both* of which are necessary to any project of social justice.[57]

This is not to say that questions of morality have no place in contemporary political debate, but they may be better reframed within the context of criticisms of modern state policies and practices and of the deepening divide between rich and poor. If the debate about morality is moved from the private to the public sphere, it could find a place in the struggle against corruption, and bureaucratic and political self-interest.[58] Such struggles do not depend on ideas of 'female values'. While there are reasons to be sceptical regarding government-led efforts to moralise public policy, bringing ethics into the state could mean reordering its priorities in a more humane, egalitarian and democratic manner, something which political theorists in Latin America have seen as a priority if disillusioned electorates are to overcome their distrust of the political system.[59] However, this is not something that merely increasing the numbers of women deputies in parliament would resolve on its own, or at all.

Morality, Communitarianism and Citizenship

Questions of morality re-entered debates over public policy in the late 1980s and 1990s through the revitalisation of another tradition of political thought, that of communitarianism, a politics associated with the values and forms of cooperation identified with 'community'. In the changed circumstances of the 1990s, this refocused debate on the uses to which female activism was being put. If the debates within Latin American feminism over citizenship and participation arose in the climate of social movements and redemocratisation of the 1980s, in the decade that followed they acquired a new significance with the decline of social movements and the rapid extension of NGO activity. These two processes were themselves linked, as many social movement activists began to work in NGOs, in a process which Alvarez has described as the 'NGOisation' of the Latin American women's movement.[60]

In the conditions of structural reform that accompanied the region's redemocratisation process, ideas of active citizenship and participation from below were appropriated by international agencies and governments and refashioned as policy tools. Invoked as much by politicians as by the World Bank and NGOs, they were now seen as a way of tackling a range of social and political problems by establishing a more widely shared sense of social responsibility and a firmer basis for political legitimacy. Regional UN agencies such as the Economic Commission for Latin America and the Caribbean (ECLAC) called for the development of more 'community level' networks and ties of social solidarity. These were to serve as a counterweight to the anomie caused by poverty, informalisation and persistent levels of unemployment. Meanwhile, the World Bank advocated 'greater efforts to take the burden off the state by involving citizens and communities in the delivery of core collective goods'.[61] Some of the new agencies of welfare delivery which emerged in the conditions of crisis of the 1980s, such as Social Investment Funds, were designed to function not as mere dispensers of social assistance but as a means to strengthen civil society: the beneficiaries of such welfare schemes were not seen as the passive recipients of 'assistentialist' programmes as in the past, but were now to be active participants in the policy process, formulating their own needs and engaging in the design and implementation of projects – hence active citizens. An increased concern over the rise of crime and related social problems spurred politicians and policy-makers alike to promote greater social participation in community projects as a means to promote greater social cohesion and public responsibility.

This support for citizen participation in community work coincided with an increased interest in international political and policy debates in the ideas of what in North American political theory came to be called 'the new communitarianism'. The reference to 'new' indicated a recognition of the historical antecedents of these ideas, ones that could be found in a diverse array of critiques of liberalism within nineteenth-century political and social theory.[62] The growth of interest in these ideas reflected developments in political philosophy and social, especially urban, policy during the 1970s and 1980s. Indeed some of the core ideas of the 'new' communitarianism provided a supportive rationale for active citizenship within the Latin American debates, so that ideas that were distinct in origin converged in practice. This convergence was evident in a shared critique of liberal individualism and of its corrosive social effects and the shift of emphasis away from the state towards the creation of local initiatives, community values, social integration and solidarity.

In Latin America such ideas were far from new. They had long been present in the continent's political and social life and formed an integral part of its historical evolution. From the late nineteenth century, French positivism, together with Catholic corporatist ideas and Social Catholicism, stood in critical opposition to utilitarian liberalism, while it helped to give direction to Latin American social policy and political practice. The corporatist regimes of the inter-war and post-war period drew on communitarian ideas to promote organicist conceptions of state–society relations.[63] Later, communitarian ideas achieved a secure implantation in the left by virtue of the role of the Catholic Church after the Medellín Conference of 1968. They inspired the Christian base communities and helped to animate local development agency practices of community participation. From the 1980s, concern over the social costs of the adjustment policies was accompanied by a growing interest in ideas of social cohesion and social capital as indispensable elements of social life.[64] In the Latin American context many felt that social movements and community activism, rather than institutional politics and corrupt parties, had potential for creating new forms of sociability and generating trust. The Papal visit to Castro's Cuba in January 1998, incomprehensible to many outside observers, was in part a confirmation of a common stance that conservatives and socialists alike could adopt in a rejection of liberal individualism in its neo-liberal form, through an affirmation of collectivist moral values.

In Latin America community activism could, and did, result in tangible benefits. For the poor, in the absence of adequate social provision, it was perhaps the only way to secure food, health and improved housing and services. Movements which promoted active participation could also result in cleaner and safer neighbourhoods, greater respect for public utilities, greater civility in social interaction, improvements in the fabric of social life as well as a measure of self-administration or 'empowerment'.[65] The expansion of NGO activity in particular provided an important site for the channelling of such activism, outside the realm of political parties and state. These various elements converged in the practice of women's movements, many of which were directly involved at the interface of active citizenship and communitarianism.

Within feminist political theory there were positions which shared elements of the communitarian critique of utilitarian liberalism. Liberal individualism was argued to be premised on a masculine ideal of freedom, one to which women, bound by the ties of family, could not, or did not, aspire.[66] Indeed, it was sometimes claimed that women were the natural communitarians, either because they were less motivated by a self serving individualism, or – because of their social 'embeddedness' in family and neighbourhood together with their responsibility for provisioning – more materially predisposed to grassroots activism and community work. The latter view carried some force in the Latin American context, where a resilient tradition of community mobilisation around basic needs provision involved a substantial proportion, where not a majority, of women. One study showed, for example, that in Bolivia in 1987 there were 3844 grassroots women's organisations; in Chile in 1991, 10 496; and in Peru in the same year, 14 851.[67] Moreover, it was arguably women who were especially vulnerable to poverty, the deterioration of civility and spread of crime that occurred during the period of debt and adjustment. As such they had a special disposition to become involved in community activism. It was hardly surprising, therefore, that women came to be so central to the success of post-adjustment poverty alleviation strategies[68] in a curious alliance between communitarianism and neo-liberalism.

If there was a convergence between these otherwise opposed traditions it arose through a common distrust of the state, one which was both justified and fairly widespread in Latin America in the 1990s. Communitarians and neo-liberals supported policies that stressed the virtues of self-help and voluntary work as a way to develop greater self-reliance and autonomy from the state. However, such strategies were freighted with gendered assumptions. As 'natural communitarians' women were relied upon for voluntary work. They were more often than not good networkers, they joined associations, cleaned up neighbourhoods, supported churches and school activities, managed and staffed poverty schemes and played an active part in grassroots politics.

Self-help projects and voluntary sector work implied a considerable, often unacknowledged, dependency upon women's unpaid labour, all too often seen as a natural extension of their responsibilities in the family. Women's work was consequently taken for granted rather than being examined as an effect of unequal social relations. In essentialising sex attributes, social responsibility also came to be seen as the preserve of women. These assumptions had been widely criticised in the development literature. Projects which assumed that women were free and available for such unpaid work, and were designed to increase women's labour productivity or intensify their caring responsibilities, frequently failed because they overloaded exhausted women without offering them any support in the form of childcare or any training in skills that many needed to obtain a paid job.[69] Such assumptions, however, persisted unchallenged in communitarian theories and their kindred development approaches. Moreover, the latent (sometimes overt) anti-statism of these visions, inherent in the advocacy of the 'virtues' of self-help, carried other risks. Necessary and laudable though self-help was when complemented by other forms of provision, if it was to serve as a substitute for them it was a different matter.

A further critique came from Foucauldian analyses of neo-liberal governmentality. In this vein some Latin American writers and activists saw a troubling convergence between the efforts of women's movements to 'incorporate women into citizenship' and the new technologies of governance associated with the 'neo-liberal state'. The discourses of citizenship and empowerment were as integral a part of neo-liberalism's market driven formula of rule, as was the devolution of state power to other agencies including professionals, the family and NGOs. Veronica Schild, referring to Chile, argued that these elements coalesced in the new approaches to poverty alleviation. An essential part of the cultural project of neo-liberal governance was the creation of a new economic and social subjectivity in which the language of citizenship, individual rights and responsibilities was deployed to secure greater self-reliance, thereby taking some of the fiscal pressure off the state and diminishing its responsibilities. Individuals were thus free to become 'masters of their own destiny', but were subject to the regulatory discipline of the market.[70]

Participation, active citizenship and female activism around basic needs were therefore seen as taking place under the terms of a new social contract, one posited on the political technologies of market governance. Such analyses of neo-liberalism cast valuable light on some of its cultural modalities and reinforced the need to set the activities of social movements within the broader context of policy shifts that were taking place and the power relations in which they were imbricated.[71] Yet the political economy of neo-liberalism in Latin America has been a site of conflict and contestation with varying, not necessary, political and social effects. In assuming the coherence and effectiveness of 'neo-liberalism' and in reducing the policies adopted to their political functionality, such approaches sometimes downplay the politics involved, especially in regard to demands from below for citizenship and poverty alleviation. In this perspective, social movements seem positioned as the complicit allies or 'cultural dupes' of neo-liberal hegemony, a view that had the potential to disarm and demobilise political initiatives.

If, in Foucauldian approaches, power is everywhere, it is scarcely addressed by communitarians, new or old. The community (or civil society) is more often than not envisaged as a space without structured power relations and conflict. Yet, for those at the sharp end of power relations, if working 'selflessly' within communities implies an uncritical acceptance of their inequalities and prejudices it may be necessary to question the premises on which such communal solidarity is built. Communitarians argue that individual rights should be subordinated to social responsibility and hence enter into conflict with feminists on social policy issues and rights advocacy work. Communitarian theorists such as Etzioni express similar views to sections of the Catholic Church in Latin America when they lament the socially corrosive effects of women's mass entry into paid work.[72] Feminism is routinely blamed for fostering a 'selfish individualism' among women who 'only care about their rights not their responsibilities'. These views reflect a broader anxiety about the changes in relations between the sexes and generations and are associated with calls for a 'retraditionalising' of the domestic sphere and a revitalising of moral life.

But within Latin American feminism there is some scepticism, as there is elsewhere, over calls to moralise or to 're-norm' society. For in such a process the issue is what values are to be imparted in the construction of the good citizen? Communitarianism, whether expressed through the Catholic Church, as in Latin America, or in the theoretical work of the new communitarians, is associated with a conservative morality.[73] Moller Okin (1991) has argued that if morality is to be taken seriously, it must be founded on principles of justice and equality within the family itself. *Par contra*, in communitarian visions 'family values' are advocated in a way which prescribes 'traditional' roles and authority patterns between the sexes.

These ideas have been challenged not just by feminism but also by social trends whose structural causes are unlikely to be offset by returning women to the home or by attempts to moralise society. Such views simplify the causes and underestimate the depth of the social changes that contemporary societies both in the advanced and less developed worlds have undergone. The 'detraditionalising' of the family,[74] and the reconfiguring of a new sexual contract premised on female autonomy, requires more creative responses from policy-makers than a call to return to the 'traditional' family, one premised on the subjection of women to patriarchal authority and to the requirements of the domestic sphere. With growing numbers of female-headed and extended households, and up to 40 per cent of married women (or more) in work in most countries – more often than not in poorly rewarded and insecure jobs – the idea that women are 'dependants' or available to engage in unpaid community labour, daytime childcare, full-time care of the elderly or, indeed, permanent 'participation', are as mistaken as those that imagine that men are the main breadwinners, involved in full-time stable employment. More broadly, it is doubtful whether modern civil society, with its deeply structured social inequalities, can become the moral community imagined by communitarians. Gellner (1994) among others sees as futile attempts to 'moralise' a mass society that by its very nature cannot serve collective moral ends.

Communitarian versions of active citizenship, therefore, for all that they can have a popular appeal, rest on assumptions that from a variety of perspectives are questionable. In Latin America feminist theory and practice has often conflicted with, but at times converged with, communitarianism. The domain of social action which both have occupied – the neighbourhood, district and municipality – has helped to create and sustain vigorous forms of social cooperation. Such associational activity is a vital force in any society, but its potential is enhanced through linkage with departments of the state, with democratic politics and organisations and by being part of a broader project of socioeconomic reform. In such contexts equality issues and struggles for rights need not be in contradiction with broader societal goals, or signal rampant individualism, but form part of the fabric of a democratic culture.

Difference and Pluralism

In the 1980s the internal politics of Latin American feminism entered a new phase. An apparently consensual movement was increasingly fractured by differences of class, ethnicity and generation, as prevailing feminist strategies were critiqued for failing adequately to take account of that diversity. The continent's movement emerged from the period of authoritarianism, as difference or otherness (*otredad*) came to be recognised as a basis for a more pluralised movement. This was a product both of the spread of feminist ideas and aspirations to wider sections of the female population in Latin America and of new debates taking place within the international arenas of the women's movement. [75]

With the consolidation of civilian rule in Latin America the focus on identity shifted to embrace issues of citizenship. The central question which feminism from its inception had posed of citizenship was that of whether, and if so how, its universal principles could accommodate difference, but without sacrificing equality. [76] Feminist theorists debated whether women's movements should strive for equality within a universalist framework or work for a change in the rules in order that difference be recognised and accommodated within a more pluralised legal and political system. Such debates over the political implications of difference occurred mostly in Europe and the USA and had a muted impact within Latin American feminism until the 1990s. This may have been due to the fact that neither a radical separatist feminism nor a black/ethnic politics, both driving forces in difference debates, had developed a strong presence in Latin America at the time. Yet as indigenous organisations gained strength and voice, an increasing acknowledgement of diversity and plurality marked feminist writing and activism from the mid-1980s onwards. Conceptions of citizenship began to be recast both as a means to deal with some of the dilemmas posed by the return to democracy and to redress its more exclusionary mechanisms. Within the women's movement itself, a greater sensitivity to issues of difference began to be worked into its internal practice and its political strategising.

Not surprisingly, the degree to which difference should be a principle of demand-making was contentious, and many practical as well as political issues remained unresolved. There were those who argued that sex difference and the female body should be the basis for completely revolutionising the way that law, rights and politics were conceived,[77] but these were minority views. In most cases a pragmatic approach evolved, allowing a degree of consensus on a range of issues. One such issue was the campaign to secure group rights, in this case with regard to quotas to increase female representation in the legislature. In the 1980s, women made up an average of only 6 per cent of the lower house in Latin America, a figure bolstered by the high rates of female representation in socialist Cuba and Nicaragua. The campaign to improve on this achieved some support from parties and governments, and legislation in regard to quota systems for national elections was, by the late 1990s, drafted or passed in more than a dozen Latin American countries with a corresponding rise in female representation.[78] This was a measure which opponents saw as inconsistent with fundamental principles of equality and impartiality and as a threat to the universalist premises of citizenship. However, the granting of rights of representation to groups historically marginalised from political power was justified by its supporters as an expedient designed to secure, if belatedly, something of citizenship's egalitarian promise. This endorsement of the principle of affirmative action was applied equally to the group rights of black and indigenous people, who also saw some improvement in their political representation as a result of constitutional changes and through quota laws in parts of Latin America at this time.

There were, however, difficulties with the assumptions underlying group representation, ones that arose from the experience of the women's movement itself – that of how to secure the representativity that the quota system presumed. How was an 'interest group' such as women, with a diversity of needs and preferences, to find a political voice in the absence of agreement over underlying issues of principle? Moreover, how was it possible to ensure that the representatives themselves did not simply act as a particularistic or party elite imposing policy on its constituency? The issue of representativity had always troubled Latin American women's movements as evidenced by the disputes in regional *Encuentros* (approximately four-yearly regional meetings), where charges were sometimes made that some groups were attempting to establish the primacy of one version of 'the woman's voice' over another.[79] More fundamental challenges were posed by the recognition that the idea of representational quotas rested on reductive and essentialist assumptions, ones that underlay most versions of identity politics. The justification for block representation was seen as resting on the fragile foundations of the irreducible, 'unfixed' character of identity itself.[80] Yet, as several studies attested, such diversity did not prevent women legislators from being those who were more likely than their male counterparts to support legislation dealing with family issues and women's rights.[81]

While none of these questions could find any resolution, in the 1980s and 1990s issues of sex difference were contested daily in the arenas of social policy and juridical reform. While there was strong support within feminism for difference to be recognised in the formulation of social policy and law, there were equally strong arguments against the legal codification of such essentialist assumptions. An opposition to essentialism within much feminist theory suggested that the logical goal of feminist legislation was to favour equality over difference as the guiding principle of reform.[82] Yet in their practice Latin American women's movements refuted the conventional framing of the question in terms of an alternative, of equality *or* difference.[83] Many campaigners felt that both principles – equality and difference – were important to retain, but also to prioritise. A commitment to the general principle of universality often went along with a recognition that social inequality required measures that assumed differential capacities and entitlements. This was evident in the practice and interpretation of those laws which recognised difference in matters of divorce, domestic violence, provisions on childcare and the rights of working mothers. In Latin America, the passing of laws which discriminated in *favour* of disadvantaged groups was long considered necessary to address social injustice.[84] It found expression in the compensatory feminism of the 1940s, and had served as the principle underlying other measures of social reform. Here the principle of equality was combined with issues of protection, which at times resonated with an uncomfortable paternalism. Yet campaigners for women's rights and entitlements, faced with the realities of building alliances to gain support for reform, often found themselves adapting their discursive strategy to accommodate the circumstances. In some cases a strategic essentialism was successfully deployed, as in the earlier first-wave movements, to secure greater equality of outcome. In Venezuela, for example, where claims for women's individual rights were regarded as 'unacceptably feminist' by opponents, reformers mobilised a familial discourse to argue that to support democracy in this important institution (the family) was to affirm a societal value. Venezuela's 1990 Labour Law thus enshrined the 'social function of maternity' as the 'underlying justification for gender-sensitive workplace legislation'.[85] It made clear that no differences were permitted that denied women's equal rights to men in the workplace, only those that allowed them to combine work and motherhood. Citizenship could thus allow for principles of equality *and* difference to be respected even as it retained a broader commitment to universality of principle. Thus, in the 1990s, feminism, both in Latin America and elsewhere, moved beyond the framing of women's demands in terms of simple oppositions between equality or difference[86] to exploring how they might be reconciled within a broader commitment to equality.[87]

Difference issues also arose, and with less resolution, in relation to the claims of indigenous and black women for recognition within the broader women's movement. The 1982 *Encuentro* in Lima attempted to face up to racism and to the racialised patterns of exclusion which characterised not only the broader society but, in certain measure, the region's women's movement itself. Representation from these groups and communities was woefully small at first and in the main, feminism made little initial impression on them. As many long-active members of the women's movement acknowledged, the claims of racialised minorities on the discourses of citizenship represented one of the most significant developments of the 1990s, but one that the Latin American women's movement as a whole was slow to respond to.

It would, however, be misleading to characterise the Latin American women's movement as made up exclusively of white, middle-class and highly educated women. From the late 1970s and throughout the 1980s, women from the popular classes including mestizo, indigenous and black women were increasingly active in campaigns on women's issues. But the idiom in which politics and identity were expressed in the earlier period was that of class, and hence 'race' and colour were neglected. This changed with the decline of class politics and as issues of culture and identity came to the fore, especially among Amerindian populations where a refigured notion of what was meant by 'indigenous' emerged.

That political identifications among racialised minorities underwent significant changes during these decades is most strikingly illustrated by the autobiographical *testimonios* of the two most celebrated female figures from within ethnic communities, published in 1978 and 1983 respectively, the Bolivian miner's wife and activist Domitila Chungara, and the indigenous rights campaigner Rigoberta Menchú.[88] The first showed a clear identification with a class politics and subjectivity, while in the second, published five years later, ethnicity and identity politics were the principal authorial referents.[89] This mirrors the trajectory of Latin American radical politics, one which was accelerated by the contentious marking of the quincentenary of Columbus' 'discovery' of the 'Indies' in 1992, and by the policies of international aid organisations which encouraged the revitalisation of indigenous culture. Whether ethnic identity politics would prove effective in giving indigenous women greater political voice to formulate their own demands remains to be seen. Such politics in Latin America has been very diverse and has spanned the political spectrum, with corresponding gains and losses for indigenous women. The dangers of women's interests being subordinated to communitarian goals, which stressed social harmony and downplayed internal inequalities, were familiar enough concerns, and as black and indigenous women themselves acknowledged, assertions of collective identity could pose problems for women's rights within such collectivities. Citizenship discourses were deployed by black and indigenous feminists to assert both their right to *be* different and their right to equal treatment in law and society. By the time of the Beijing Conference, these questions not only came to occupy a major place in discussions of the women's movement but had led to the redefinition of the movement itself as multicultural and multiethnic.[90]

Underlying these multiple struggles for citizenship, the issue for many Latin American feminists at the close of the millennium was not only how to reconcile these tensions over difference, and create a multi-layered movement but also how to develop a politics which could promote a general project of social justice. Such a project depended upon a radical reworking of the state, making it at once more socially

responsible and democratically accountable by ensuring that organisations which voiced demands for social justice and equality were guaran-
teed institutionalised channels for influencing law and public policy.
Here, Latin American feminism faced the limits, challenges and opportunities offered by liberal democracy in its attempt to reformulate the
politics of participation and of citizenship itself. This, then, returns us to
the question of feminist practice and its relationship to the body politic
and its representative agencies – the issue which came to dominate
feminist debates in the 1990s.

From the Margins to the Centre – via the International

The return to civilian rule in Latin America presented women's movements with a favourable opportunity context to press for political and
legal reform, especially as it occurred at a time when issues of democracy
and good governance formed part of the repertoire of international
policy instruments. The 1980s and 1990s saw Latin American governments repeatedly affirming their commitment to democracy in international and regional meetings of such bodies as the Organisation of
American States (OAS), where they signed agreements pledging to
strengthen democratic representation and institutions. This allowed
questions of female representation to be placed on the agenda of reform
– as occurred within the OAS itself when its Women's Commission
sought (and gained) approval for a broad range of recommendations to
improve policy sensitivity to gender inequality. Effective advocacy on
gender issues was to a considerable extent also impelled by the presence
of the growing women's movement within the region. The events and
preparatory meetings occasioned by both the UN Decade for Women
(1976–85) and the regional *Encuentros* of the women's movement
(beginning in Colombia in 1981), provided gender issues with a public
profile and stimulated continental debate over policy.

Thus, partly under the influence of a growing international women's
movement,[91] partly due to the greater self-confidence and concerted
efforts of some national women's movements and partly the result of an
effort to comply with international pressure and present a modern face
to the world, post-authoritarian administrations recognised women as a
constituency which required greater representation within the government and policy process. Latin American governments en bloc accepted
the proposals for promoting gender equity which resulted from the UN
Decade for Women, contained in the *Forward Looking Strategies*
document. Gender issues were increasingly absorbed into the discourses

of politicians, who promised reforms in their electoral campaigns and if elected were pressed to deliver them. In Argentina for example, Raúl Alfonsín supported the liberalisation of divorce and the reform of *patria potestad* in his electoral campaign of 1983; Alan García's government in Peru explicitly referred to the promotion of women's interests in his National Development Plan of 1986–90; all the contenders in Chile's and Uruguay's first post-dictatorship elections in 1989 included in their campaigns specific reference to gender issues and endorsed the need for a female presence in the country's political institutions. If for most of the century women had been excluded from power, now it seemed that power was interested in women.

However, as noted earlier, the issue of whether and how to deal with the state had a special resonance in Latin America. The return of democratic governments and reactivation of political parties required feminist movements to reassess how they positioned themselves, not only in relation to political institutions but also to NGOs and international development agencies. With regard to working in or against the state, this issue was one which Julieta Kirkwood had identified a decade before as one of the key knots (*nudos*) of feminism. It remained contentious throughout the 1990s, as was evident in the debates that divided both the national movements and the regional *Encuentros*,[92] none so bitterly as in Chile in 1996 where movement representatives split three ways on how to deal with the state – for integration through political party activism, complete autonomy and conditional collaboration from an independent base.

Latin American feminists tended to be sceptical about the capacity of states to alter their procedures, cultures and masculinist conception of the polity in such a way that women's concerns could be accommodated within its framework. The evidence showed that the rules of the political game were weighted against women's influence over policy and participation in government.[93] Growing concentrations of institutional power and the resistance of many governments to implementing genuine democratic reform were themselves formidable obstacles to cooperation, lending support to a view of the state as impermeable and its concerns remote from those of the citizenry. Moreover, within the left of the women's movement theoretical approaches to the state combined elements of Marxism with feminist analyses that viewed the state as an irredeemable site of patriarchal power.

Such negative views of working within state structures had led many women's organisations to welcome the role increasingly played by NGOs in the areas of welfare, development and women's rights. Some indeed argued that the proper space for the revitalisation of politics was within civil society rather than within the conventional institutional arenas of states and parties. They saw the support for projects designed to 'empower' women through consciousness-raising, education and training as delivering direct and immediate benefits in contrast to the more remote, sometimes merely formal, gains associated with conventional politics.[94]

This approach converged with other positions within the movement. An enthusiasm for working in small projects or within social movements justified the development of a separate sphere of feminine politics, which would correspond with, as well as give expression to, 'women's politics'. This argument, discussed earlier, was, however, based on suppositions that had often worked to keep women out of politics altogether. It assumed that since women's virtues, and hence politics, were different to men's, women's work in politics should be within a 'women's space', that is, within a female community, one that was preferably not subject to 'masculine' forms of authority – meaning separate from formal institutional arenas. This vision of a female politics implied that women should be active in the affective world of grassroots activism which eschewed the cold rational masculine world of politics, law and institutions. Yet, apart from the essentialism of such views, the dangers of abstention from that masculine world were ones that women had long experienced in what amounted to a political division of labour where men controlled real power; to argue in favour of its perpetuation and legitimation was somewhat self-defeating.

The proliferation of NGO activity from the 1980s and the resulting concentration on small projects and local communities reflected, and in some cases deepened, the pluralisation and fragmentation of the women's movement. While this was welcomed by some as a sign of a healthy diversity, for others it highlighted a general failure to make any kind of coordinated response to policy.[95] At a more general level, the mapping of the public–private binary on to male–female spheres of politics (neighbourhood/state) continued a sterile separation of the two spheres, preventing necessary forms of dialogue and strategic linkage between the two.

By the end of the 1980s, however, many feminist activists across Latin America saw themselves as having been able to transcend some of the false polarities that had hitherto informed thinking about politics. Crucial here had been the experience of Brazil where the women's movement had achieved a productive synergy with state agencies, by working in collaboration and creative tension with these and with new or revitalised political parties. From 1983 an energetic State Council on the Status of Women (Conselho Estadual da Condição Feminina) was active in São Paulo promoting debate and policy on women nationwide, and two years later a National Council on Women's Rights was created, which combined presidential support with an autonomous remit. This body pushed for a broad range of reforming strategies encompassing health, education and women's rights.[96]

Partly as a consequence of this positive experience and others elsewhere, the 1990s saw a shift in the direction of taking the state more seriously as a site of feminist intervention, and this in turn led to a strengthening of three linked developments in the strategy of Latin American women's movements. First, there was an effort to increase female representation in the various institutions of the state through such measures as quota laws and women's policy units. Second, there were efforts to build broad coalitions (*bancadas femininas*) and networks (*redes*) across different sectors including movement activists, NGO workers, state functionaries, legal and educational professionals and women in political parties.[97] Such coalitions could be effective in securing political reforms. The congressional approval of domestic violence and quota laws in Argentina, Chile, the Dominican Republic, Mexico and Peru was a result of such cross-party, cross-sectoral co-operation. Third, practical efforts were made by feminist NGOs to combine the principle of organisational autonomy with a greater degree of collaboration with the state and its agencies to secure reform on certain issues. Associations which pressed for legal reform, for example, not only worked for change at the grassroots, but lobbied for legal change and even helped in the drafting and popularising of new laws.[98] Such developments were novel in the context of the Latin American women's movement and signified two conceptual shifts: the abandonment of a monolithic conception of the state for a pragmatic approach which saw it as more permeable; and a relinquishing of a negative and unitary view of democratic liberalism, in recognition of its potential for reform and its different political modalities.[99]

The process of greater female representation in state agencies gathered momentum in the course of the 1990s, again propelled to some degree by broader international and interregional developments. The cluster of UN conferences which took place during the decade galvanised both women's movements and governments and provided a context within which discussion and regional networking took place: the United Nations Conference on Environment and Development (UNCED) in Rio de Janeiro in 1992, the World Conference on Human Rights in Vienna in

1993, the Population and Development Conference in Cairo in 1994, the World Summit for Social Development in Copenhagen in 1995 and the Fourth World Conference on Women in Beijing in 1995, all contributed to this process.[100] Intergovernmental regional meetings such as those of the Summit of the Americas and ECLAC were also key moments in the lobbying process, providing women's movements with an opportunity to gain governmental recognition and support for their activities and agenda, as well as to confront the attempts of hostile forces to seize control of the policy agenda.[101] Thus, the international context helped to sustain and give direction to the new opportunity context for the region's women's movements, stimulating public interest and contributing to changing public attitudes.

Latin American feminists were far from sharing the experience of those working within Scandinavian social democracy or in the European Union, who were able to speak of 'feminising the state' through the establishment of women within positions of influence and through party support for women-friendly policies. But there was in the 1990s, in a number of countries, some increased scope for efforts to extend the agenda of 'good governance' to include feminist concerns.[102] One index of this increased commitment was the strengthening of women's commissions, some of which acquired presidential support.[103] By the end of the 1990s no Latin American country was without a women's policy unit, many staffed by former women's movement activists. At the same time, redemocratisation was accompanied by demands for a revitalisation of institutional politics while the exhaustion of the neoliberal extremism of the 'lost decade' led to a rethinking the relationship between state and economy, with a corresponding stress on greater devolution of powers to local and regional government agencies and civil society. This resulted in a considerable female presence in some countries' local level institutions. Public attitudes towards feminist demands had also undergone something of a sea change in this period. Surveys conducted in a number of countries showed that the majority of those interviewed viewed women's entry into government favourably, and a sizeable minority even thought that women were preferable to men as politicians as they were more honest and worked hard.[104]

Another aspect of the reform process to which women's movements were able to contribute was that of the law and the legal system. This, too, received support from international activity on human rights, which helped to stimulate action for the reform of the law and judicial system in some states. In the period leading up to and following the 1993

Vienna Conference, the women's movement itself intensified its engagement with issues of rights and citizenship. The Vienna Declaration recognised women's rights as inalienably, integrally and indissolubly part of universal human rights and called on governments to ensure sex equality before the law. Within Latin America, human rights issues had been an integral part of the struggle against the state terrorism of military regimes, especially in the Southern Cone and in Central America. In the latter, issues of citizenship were tied directly to human rights discourses.[105] Women had been centrally involved in the campaigns for peace and for an end to civil violence, and sometimes gained considerable international attention, as occurred with the Mothers of the Disappeared in Argentina and the Widows in Guatemala represented in CONAVIGUA.[106]

From the mid-1980s, women's groups were increasingly utilising the language of human rights and citizenship to demand legal reform and state action on pressing issues such as the high indices in the region of violence against women.[107] This indeed was the issue that inspired what was perhaps one of the most popular and effective campaigns ever to have been promoted by Latin American women's movements. In terms of citizenship theory it confronted the public-private separation central to classical liberalism and insisted that the family did not remain outside the sphere of justice. Feminists in NGOs working within the popular sectors joined with organisations lobbying the state for legal reform and were able to collaborate productively on these issues, securing support for women's refuges and police stations as well as changes in the law. In the 1980s Brazilian women had led the process by organising state and national level councils of women to advise on legislation for women and pioneered the development of police precincts to deal specifically with violence against women. As a result of these campaigns, the new Brazilian Constitution of 1988 declared a state interest in the curtailing of domestic violence. Six years later, in 1994, the Organisation of American States approved the UN Convention for preventing, sanctioning and eradicating violence against women (CEDAW) and, as a result of the work of local and transregional networks (*Redes contra la Violencia*), by the end of the decade ten Latin American countries had adopted new legislation on domestic violence.[108]

Meanwhile, other issues previously regarded as too sensitive by many women's movements began to appear or reappear within feminist demands such as abortion, the lack of effective contraception and the issue of forced sterilisation – these latter, again, were given some impulsion from the international arena, this time by the 1994 Conference on

Population, as well as active support from health networks (*Redes de Salud*). More broadly, women's movements in the region were also arguing for human rights to include social rights, and were successful in some countries in securing changes in labour and agrarian laws which promoted greater sex equality in their provisions. Meanwhile, a parallel shift occurred in the development field, where the idiom of needs-satisfaction gave way to a greater emphasis on rights, citizenship and empowerment.[109]

In short, from the mid-1980s onwards women's interests acquired greater representation within the region's states at both local and national level, as well as within supranational bodies on grounds of both equity and social justice. Women made gains in representation,[110] in rights and in policy terms. These gains were secured by means of effective argument, advocacy and active regional and international strategising They were made possible through the opportunities for lobbying and bargaining afforded by democratic processes, especially elections which were important moments for demand-making and alliance-building. The effectiveness of such interventions was, however, contingent on more than the securing of 'women's spaces' within the political arena. It depended to a large degree upon a favourable political climate and on the nature of the state and government – contingencies which remained critically important in determining the continued success of women's movement's claims on the state for resources and policy changes.

The gains made in this process, for all that they were impressive, were neither secure nor would they necessarily prove incremental. They had more often than not resulted from tireless lobbying and organising, sometimes by small numbers of dedicated activists. While gender issues had become part of the 'common sense' of the age, and while governments may have been happy to concede to some formal changes in women's juridico-political status, women's representation in the state was still characterised by an inadequate institutionalisation. Moreover, the sympathy which governments expressed towards women's issues and the direction of policy depended crucially on the party in power, on its own political ideology and hence openness to gender equity issues. Gains achieved under one administration could all too easily be set back by a change in government or president. Finally, as the Brazilian case demonstrated, the allocation of institutional space alone was not a sufficient condition for meaningful change; women's representatives were most effective when their capacity to push actively to keep their demands on the political agenda was organically linked to the pluralised forces within civil society.

In reflecting on the obstacles that stood in the way of women – along with other marginalised sectors – being able to realise citizenship's inclusionary promise, analysts returned to six persistent problems: the lack of a political culture and sustained programme which could nourish and promote the democratic and egalitarian spirit of feminist demands, inform citizens of their rights and encourage them to pursue them; the corresponding lack of attention to the need to democratise the institutions of state and party, rendering them more internally democratic, 'woman-friendly', transparent and accountable to their constituencies; the lack of a critical mass of women in positions of authority who could give support to bringing about these changes; a pervasive resistance, both bureaucratic and personal, to fully integrating women into the arenas of public power as 'subjects of public policy';[111] the tendency of some governments to impose their own agenda on women's policy units; and the risk of such units losing touch with the movement as a whole. In other words, without a broader consolidation of meaningful democracy, campaigns for women's rights were in danger of losing force and direction.

Conclusions

This chapter began by discussing the regional and political variability in the meanings given to citizenship and in women's claims for inclusion within it. In Latin America, as in Europe and North America, first-wave feminism challenged the double standard of early liberalism, which promised equality while preserving masculine prerogatives. Women were kept out of political power for much of the century, but they could not forever be denied the formal rights of citizenship, even if they acquired them slowly and on terms that differed from men's. While they contested the assumptions on which their exclusion rested, they also claimed their rights in terms which respected difference, arguing for the recognition of the value of women's work for society, in both the private and public realms. The challenge to prevailing notions of citizenship from the earliest movements was to have difference valued rather than ignored or denigrated, and to have the work in, and responsibility for, the domestic sphere recognised. This demand was partially realised over the course of the century as women gained social rights and some political representation, but its radical and egalitarian potential was rarely realised, or when it was, it was all too often subverted in practice.

The interventions that Latin American women's movements were able to make and the strategic resources, both symbolic and political, that were available to them at any one time were governed by the vicissitudes of the continent's political history. The consequent reframing of the terms and language of citizenship claims across a century of different state forms not only illustrates a certain instability in some of citizenship's referents but also how destabilising the assimilation of women's demands has been for some of the abstract principles that it embodies. Most evidently, the critical engagement with citizenship from the standpoint of those excluded from it forced difference on to the political and policy agenda, but in ways which never fully resolved the tension between abstract and embodied conceptions. This remains the case despite the fact that feminist campaigns for justice and rights have shown a notable creativity in reconciling equality principles with traditional role-based conceptions of difference.[112]

As discussed in the second part of this chapter, difference defined the very meaning of 'women's politics' for many Latin American activists. Assumptions about women's special attributes grounded the strategies and priorities of an identity politics that provided the impulsion for vibrant and novel forms of women's participation in the public sphere. However, there were risks inherent in such primordial assumptions. In accepting gendered divisions in social and political practices as natural, there could be no effective challenge to the inequalities on which they rested. What needed addressing was how to achieve a proper and equitable balance between the spheres of 'feminine' and 'masculine' endeavour, between care and work and between local and national politics. Such a balance entails the dismantling of the structures of inequality; it does not entail the end of differences between men and women, but rather the end of the unequal social effects that are legitimated in terms of that difference.

In the conditions of liberal democracy that prevail in Latin America, programmes for equitable social change depend upon a politics of engagement with public policy. This was impossible or unthinkable under military regimes, where women's movements directed their energies instead to civil society. However, as political conditions changed, remaining outside the state entailed certain costs and carried certain risks. Women's movements increasingly worried about being instrumentalised through the forces of neo-liberalism; communitarianism, sometimes seen as a bulwark against its corrosive effects, relied on an acceptance and reinforcement of an inegalitarian normative gender. While such risks could be offset by a commitment to a transformatory gender politics within local projects, for a feminist voice to be heard in the arenas of public policy, an engagement with the state was required.

This came increasingly to be the focus of a part of the women's movement's energies in the period of redemocratisation and resulted, as we have seen, in some important changes in law, policy and representation.

The Latin American case demonstrates that the vitality and success of the women's movement in the post-authoritarian period has depended upon a creative interaction between civil society and the state, a move not only *from* the margins to the centre of politics but *between* the margins and the centre. But there had also occurred a growing engagement with institutions in the international and pan-Latin American arenas over this period. The former, in the shape of humanitarian development agencies, proved a particularly vital resource for women's movements and provided many of the legal instruments and much of the funding which fortified their varied claims. The degree to which this implies, as some analysts have argued, that citizenship cannot be thought of only in relation to the nation-state, is a matter which requires consideration in the light of the Latin American experience.[113] However, even if such globalised arenas have acquired an important role in politics and policy, it is the nation-state that governs, legislates and implements policy. In matters of politics, legality and social justice it remains a critical site of intervention.

Latin American citizens, in having a state of law restored to them, have once again acquired 'the right to have rights', itself the precondition for the attainment of other citizenship rights. The efforts made over recent decades to contest the terms of women's citizenship rights have so far succeeded in bringing significant changes in the legal and political domains. Yet while these have had to be fought for, and may remain insecure, liberal democracy has often been more willing to concede equality in law and political rights than economic and social rights. The perplexing reality of the post-authoritarian transitions which women's movements confronted at the end of the millennium was one of increased opportunities for participation in the formal political arena, but in a context of deepening structural reform and social inequality. The international shift from the social state to the contract state of neo-liberalism produced a context in which there occurred a significant diminution of social rights, the condition for the full realisation of political equality. Citizenship enshrines ideas of political freedom, impartiality and equality before the law, but as many liberal theorists have themselves acknowledged, these ideals were threatened in a system founded on great inequalities in wealth and income. The tension between market principles and the claims of citizenship could only be reduced by deliberate policy interventions to secure social equality, what T.H. Marshall (1950) referred to as the subordination of market price to social justice. If Latin American women's movements are to realise the full potential of the rights conferred by citizenship, a useful starting point might be a gendered reading of this fundamental insight.

Notes

Introduction

1. The results were published in Young (et al.) (1984).
2. Research for these various projects was undertaken in South Yemen, Ethiopia, Afghanistan, Nicaragua, Cuba, Russia, Azerbaijan, Hungary and Iraq. The resulting publications include: *The Ethiopian Revolution* (Halliday and Molyneux, 1982); *State Policies and the Position of Women in the PDRY* (Molyneux, 1982); 'Women's Emancipation under Socialism: A Model for the Third World?', *World Development* (Molyneux, 1980); 'Legal Reform and Socialist Revolution in Democratic Yemen', *International Journal of the Sociology of Law* (Molyneux, 1986a); ' "The Woman Question" in the Age of Perestroika', *New Left Review*, no 183 (Molyneux, 1990); 'The Woman Question in the Age of Communism's Collapse', in Mary Evans (1994); and 'Women's Rights and Political Contingency' (1995).
3. *La Voz de la Mujer* (1997).
4. These include De Beauvoir (1953), Mitchell (1965), Rowbotham (1972).

Chapter 1. Anarchist Feminism in Nineteenth-Century Argentina

1. The research on *La Voz* was carried out in the archives of the Institute of Social History, Amsterdam.
2. See Abad de Santillán (1930), Nettlau (1971) and Oved (1978).
3. *O Jornal das Senhoras*, for example, appeared in Brazil in 1852 and was dedicated to the 'social betterment and the moral emancipation of women' (Hahner, 1978).
4. Ferns (1960).
5. Bourdé (1974).
6. On the eve of World War I, 30 per cent of the Argentine population were immigrants in contrast to 14 per cent of the US population in 1910 (Solberg, 1970).
7. *Ibid.*
8. Anarchist ideas were not all imported. There were indigenous anarchist currents in Argentina and forms of spontaneous popular resistance – but these were unable to achieve a stable organisational expression. Gauchesque culture became a central theme for anarchist playwrights and poets from the 1890s onwards (see Franco, 1973 and Yunque, 1941).
9. Rock (1975).
10. Solberg (1970).
11. Marotta (1960).
12. Bourdé (1974).
13. Teresa Mañe, the Spanish teacher and activist, often wrote under the name of Soledad Gustavo. She was born in 1866 and was married to another anarchist, Juan Montseny.
14. Solberg (1970).

15. Unfortunately, there are too few listings to form an accurate picture. Oved (1978) argues that in Argentina, as elsewhere, anarchist support was primarily from unskilled and semi-skilled workers.
16. *Segundo censo* (1898).
17. Marotta (1960).
18. *Segundo censo* (1898).
19. All translations by author.
20. Mentioned in the literary journal *Caras y Caretas*, 1901. According to Abad de Santillán (1930), Creaghe was 'much loved' by the Argentine anarchist movement. Before leaving Britain, it seems, he had been active in the workers' movement in Sheffield and had brought out a newspaper called the *Sheffield Anarchist*.
21. This ambivalence in the movement's attitude toward feminism and women anarchists' successes and failures is discussed in the context of Spain up until the Civil War by Kaplan (1971) and Alvarez Junco (1976).
22. Rowbotham (1972).
23. From the 1900s onwards, the statutes of some of the workers' groups in which anarchism was strong contained demands for equal pay for women and for the abolition of marriage. The latter demand appeared in the anarchists' proposals for the statutes of the Federación Obrera Argentina, Argentina's first workers' federation, but was dropped from the final list of demands, probably on account of socialist opposition (Marotta, 1960).
24. Marotta (1960).
25. According to *Cavas y Caretas*, María Calvía also founded a group called 'Los proletarios'.
26. Quesada (1979) reports that one of the editors turned up in Rosario between 1900 and 1903. He writes that the visitors to the newly built Casa del Pueblo included Pietro Gori, and many others used to gather there: 'the Marchisio woman, who together with Virginia Bolten founded "La Voz de la Mujer", the latter publication called the Rosarian (Louise) Michel due to the ardour of its oratory'. (From other sources it would appear more likely that it was Bolten, not *La Voz*, who was dubbed 'the Rosarian Michel'.)
27. No. 6 is unavailable. The first four issues measured 26 cm by 36 cm, whereas the remaining ones were slightly larger and varied in size, suggesting the use of different presses.
28. Some of these poems were written to be read at meetings. No. 8 of *La Voz* carried a 207-line poem by 'Pepita Gherra' that was, according to the editors, to be read at the Spanish Workers' Union meeting.
29. See Alvarez Junco (1976) for a discussion of the family, free love and feminism in Spanish anarchism.
30. The Santa Cecilia Colony in Brazil is the best known of these. *El Oprimido* was at the centre of a debate on this question, having apparently sponsored the publication of the pamphlet *An Episode of Love in the Socialist Colony 'Cecilia'*, which advocated multiple relationships, abolition of the family and communal care of children. Ruvira (1971) says that these Argentine anarchists did have their free unions and that their children appear in the civil register with names such as 'Anarquía' (Anarchy), 'Acracia' (Free spirit (fig.)) and even 'Libre Productor' (Free Producer).

31. Rock (1975).
32. In 1900 Cecilia Grierson founded the National Women's Council and five years later a feminist centre was set up in which the core members of the Argentine suffragist groups came together.
33. Little (1978).
34. Two English writers of the period, of Church of England persuasion, lamented that by 1891, 37 per cent of all marriages in Buenos Aires were civil ceremonies, following the legalisation of secular marriage in 1887 (Mulhall and Mulhall, 1892).

Chapter 2. Women's Interests, the State and Revolution in Nicaragua

1. Author's interview (1982). Nora Astorga was Deputy Foreign Minister at the time.
2. The Association of Women Confronting the National Problem was founded in 1977 to counter Somoza's excesses and promote gender equality. Its general secretary was Lea Guido, who later became Minister of Health. See AMNLAE (1981) for an account of AMPRONAC's history and its list of aims; and Randall (1982).
3. For firsthand accounts of these activities see Randall (1982), Deighton et al. (1983), and Ramírez-Horton (1982).
4. The women writers have been more interested in this question. See especially Maier (1980).
5. Corraggio, (1983). Corragio's paper was also published in Slater, (1985).
6. Randall (1978, 1982).
7. This is usually translated as 'poor neighbourhoods'.
8. This organisation is involved in various anti-imperialist and pro-peace campaigns and gives support to the bereaved.
9. For examples of women's attitudes. See Hansson and Liden (1983).
10. Quoted in MacKinnon (1982). For critical discussions, from differing perspectives, of the record of socialist states, see Markus (1976) and Stacey (1983).
11. This discussion necessarily leaves out the specific situation of women in Nicaragua's ethnic minorities. The Miskito Indian communities in particular require separate consideration because they have, and have had historically, a very different relationship to central government than that which is described here.
12. There are differing definitions of patriarchy, but most of them agree that patriarchy describes a power relation existing between the sexes, exercised by men over women and institutionalised within various social relations and practices, including law, family and education. I return to the issue of patriarchy in Chapter 5.
13. There is a third usage of the term 'interest', found in Marxism, which explains collective action in terms of some intrinsic property of the actors and/or the relations within which they are inscribed. Thus, class struggle is ultimately explained as an effect of the relations of production. This conception has been shown to rest on essentialist assumptions and provides an inadequate

account of social action. For a critique of this notion, see Benton (1982) and Hindess (1982).

14. Zillah Eisenstein, editor of *Capitalist Patriarchy and the Case for Socialist Feminism* (1978), developed a sophisticated version of the argument that women constitute a 'sexual class' and that for women, gender issues are primary. See Eisenstein (1983).

15. It is precisely around these issues, which also have an ethical significance, that the theoretical and political debate must focus. The list of strategic gender interests noted here is not exhaustive or definitive, but is merely exemplary.

16. See, for example, Kaplan (1982) and Hufton (1971).

17. Borge's speech was delivered on the occasion of the fifth anniversary of AMNLAE. It was published in *Barricada* on 4 October 1982 and is available in translation from Pathfinder Press (1982).

18. *Ibid.*

19. Approximately 20 per cent of economically active women were in agriculture, with similar percentages for personal services and marketing activities. Women accounted for only 15.25 per cent of the formal sector urban workforce. See Deighton et al. (1983).

20. Data are from the Oficina de Mujer, the office which coordinated the activities of AMNLAE with the FSLN.

21. Substantial numbers of women were in favour of conscription and bitterly resented the Council of State's decision in 1983 to exempt women. AMNLAE fought a popular campaign to revoke the decision, which resulted in women having the right to volunteer. I discuss this in Molyneux (1985b).

22. This viewpoint has to be compared and contrasted with many nationalist movements that call for the sacrifice of women's interests (and those of other oppressed groups) in the interests of the nation.

23. In some of the regions affected by the war (Matagalpa, Jinotega), where conscription was high, women had come to represent as much as 40 per cent of the workforce by February 1984 (interview with Magda Enríquez, a member of AMNLAE's national directorate, March 1984).

24. Data are from figures supplied by the Oficina de la Mujer and the Central Planning Agency (MIPLAN).

25. These provisions were contained in Decrees 573 and 538.

26. Data are from Oficina de la Mujer (1986).

27. For a fuller account of Sandinista social policies see Walker (1985).

28. For a discussion of the agrarian reform and its effects on women, see Deere (1983).

29. Data are from the Instituto Nacional de Estadísticas y Censos (December 1981).

30. Basic provisions were rationed and heavily subsidised until 1983, when it became increasingly difficult to peg prices due to mounting economic pressures.

31. AMNLAE argued that the implications of women conserving resources under a socialist government were radically different from those under capitalism, because in the first case the beneficiaries were the people, and in the second, private interests.

32. Although there were no women in the nine-member Junta that constituted the FSLN leadership, the vice-president of the Council of State (until the

elections of November 1984) was a woman, and women assumed many key positions in the party at the regional level. On three occasions between 1979 and 1990, women filled ministerial posts.

33. This argument was put forward to quash the new Family Law in the Council of State. See reports in the national press during November 1982.

Chapter 3. The Politics of Abortion in Nicaragua

1. Author's interview with representative of the Nicaragua Health Fund, Spring 1987.
2. Speech reported in the *Militant*, 19 November 1987.
3. Abortion was legal in most of the self-proclaimed socialist states, and in a substantial number was available on demand for social as well as medical reasons. However, it was made illegal by Stalin in the USSR in 1937 and was only re-legalised in 1955. It was severely restricted in Romania and Albania and absolutely illegal in the first 'Third World' socialist republic, Mongolia, where it was officially outlawed on the grounds that the population was too small at 1.5 million.
4. By 'reproductive rights' is meant women's legal capacity to exercise choice over conception and childbearing. This includes the right to use and obtain contraceptives, abortions and sterilisations or other safe methods of fertility control; it necessarily entails the loss of rights others might exercise over a woman's person.
5. Angel and Macintosh (1987).
6. This followed regional trends. Catholic Latin American countries have seen a rise in abortion rates. In the mid-1970s it was estimated that there were 65 abortions per 1000 women of reproductive age, or almost 30 per cent of known pregnancies.
7. Accounts of Sandinista policies on women and their results can be found in the following: Harris (1987), Molyneux (1985), and in *Nicaragua Today*, the periodical of the Nicaragua Solidarity Campaign. For good qualitative material see Angel and Macintosh (1987) and Rooper (1987).
8. This acronym stands for the Luisa Amanda Espinosa Association of Nicaraguan Women, bearing the name of the first woman Sandinista to fall in the fighting against Somoza.
9. Molyneux (1985b).
10. *Barricada* (15 November 1985).
11. Oficina de la Mujer (1986).
12. Author's interviews in Nicaragua. The 'theology of liberation' had been silent on these questions.
13. World Bank (1985).
14. The term 'feminist' is used in Nicaragua, both as a pejorative by those who are against its demands, but also by Nicaraguan women's rights activists. Officials, too, may use the term approvingly as in the following remarks by Lea Guido when head of AMNLAE. 'Through its participation in a popular revolution, the Nicaraguan women's movement has evolved from a patriotic, anti-imperialist and anti-dictatorship orientation to a strong feminist position' (*Women in Central America*, no. 2, 1987). As in Western feminism,

there are different conceptions of what constitutes a feminist position or practice.
15. Vilas (1986).
16. Angel and Macintosh (1987).
17. See the South Yorkshire supporters of Socialist Action dossier of Nicaraguan press articles on abortion in Nicaragua. The translations first appeared in issues 1 and 3 of *Intercontinental Press* in 1986.
18. FSLN (1987).
19. These were Tomás Borge, Luis Carrión, Bayardo Arce and Carlos Núñez.
20. This simply confirmed what had already been agreed in principle at earlier congresses. There was, however, some opposition to what was seen as the weakening of the institutionalised capacity of the movement.
21. FSLN (1987).
22. Quoted in *Perspectiva Mundial* (1987), p. 18.
23. *Militant* (19 November 1987).
24. *Barricada International* (1987).
25. Mass (1975).
26. World Bank (1985).
27. Mahon (1987).
28. Yet the degree of acceptance of Catholic teaching on this issue varied enormously between countries. The majority of women opposed abortion in Ireland, for example (Mahon, 1987), but in Poland political support for the Church was contrasted to widespread disregard for orthodox teachings on the family. Nicaragua would appear to have been somewhere between the Polish and Irish cases.
29. Author's interview with Amalia Chamorro.

Chapter 4. The Federación de Mujeres Cubanas

1. Author's interview, Havana, January 1996.
2. The policies of the 'special period', inaugurated in 1990, were a response to the foreign exchange and fiscal deficits caused by the cessation of economic support from the Soviet bloc. They stressed self-reliance, rationing, across-the-board cuts and moral incentives. (Pastor and Zimbalist, 1995).
3. On the campaign for the 'rectification of errors' see Pastor and Zimbalist (1995) and Eckstein (1991).
4. Cuban economists estimate that the aggregate fall in the GSP between 1989 and 1993 was around 45 per cent (Carranza, Valdés et al., 1995, p. 17). The global social product (GSP) differs from gross domestic product (GDP) as a measure of economic growth. Among other things, it excludes non-productive sectors such as health and education.
5. In the second half of the 1980s the Cuban economy stagnated with an average growth rate of less than 0.2 per cent. Pastor and Zimbalist (1995) calculate that the real GDP growth rate in 1990 was –3.1 per cent, in 1991 –14.0 per cent and in 1993 it was –20.0 per cent. However, by 1994 there were signs of recovery, with GDP rising by 0.7 per cent, then by 2.5 per cent in 1995.

6. *Paladar*, literally 'palate' or 'taste'; *jinetera*, literally 'jockey', denoting a form of casual prostitution engaged in by men and women.
7. The legislation of the Torricelli Bill and the Helms-Burton Act have arguably set back the prospects for Cuban democracy in several respects: economically it has retarded Cuba's recovery process; politically, it has enabled the Cuban leadership to entrench more repressive policies with respect to civil society.
8. For a discussion of this reform current and of exile politics see Molyneux (1999).
9. Thinking along these lines, from within Cuban research institutes, can be found in a volume of papers presented at an international workshop on democracy held in Havana in 1994 (Dilla, 1995, 1996).
10. '¿Cuba: Cuál es la democracia deseable?', in Dilla (1996), pp. 117–29.
11. *Ibid.*, p. 180.
12. This study draws on two research visits to Cuba – one in 1981, the other in January 1996 – as well as on other comparative work, referenced below, on social policy and regime transition in socialist states.
13. Other than the FMC, the most important interest groups represented in mass organisations are La Asociación Nacional de Agricultores Pequeños (ANAP), the Comités de Defensa de la Revolución (CDRs), the Central de Trabajadores de Cuba (CTC) and the Unión de Juventud Comunista (UJC).
14. Eva Perón's Peronist Women's Party, founded in order to mobilise support for the Argentine regime in 1949, had, at the time of the 1951 elections, 500 000 members, with 3600 branches in the country as a whole, when Argentina's total population was substantially larger than that of Cuba in the 1980s, the latter being under 11 million.
15. The unexpectedly rapid collapse of the former Soviet bloc has shown how difficult it is to make assumptions about the way that the effects of state policies are experienced by their populations. Claims regarding the legitimacy of communist parties cannot be tested and are therefore based on speculation rather than on hard evidence. Although it is probable that, despite the denial of political freedoms, such regimes can, for social and patriotic reasons, enjoy legitimacy, it is also evident from the Eastern European experiences that over time stagnation in the political field can undermine this legitimacy and that much of the regime's support can disappear, once possibilities for social advance other than through the party become available, and in a very short period of time.
16. The Sandinistas gained 41 per cent of the vote in the 1990 elections, a drop of 22 per cent on their 1984 results. For the reasons why many women defected to the opposition, see Lancaster (1992), p. 291.
17. Espín had been active in the revolutionary movement, but she was at first unconvinced about the need for such an organisation and later recalled wondering: 'Why do we have to have a women's organisation? I had never been discriminated against. I had my career as a chemical engineer. I never suffered.' Quinn (1977).
18. FMC, (1975).
19. For comparative perspectives on women and socialism see Jancar (1978) and Molyneux (1981). The strategy of 'emancipating' women by drawing them into the labour force was justified by reference to the theories of Engels on

capitalism and the division of labour, wherein women's oppression derived from their exclusion from the labour market.

20. The literacy campaign of 1961 involved thousands of FMC members who acted as 'loving mothers' to 70 000 literacy workers, performing such tasks as delivering their mail, making their beds and cooking, as well as replacing schoolteachers who were involved in the campaign.

21. The Cuban record on repression is not, however, without its gendered elements; the persecution of homosexuals, many of whom were sent to the Unidades Militares para el Aumento de la Producción (UMAP) labour camps, is among the most reprehensible instances.

22. The system known as 'people's power' was established in the 1970s and comprised local assemblies with elected bodies, first at the provincial and then at the national level. It achieved a degree of local involvement in decision-making, but fell far short of democratic change. The upper echelons of the system, at both provincial and national level, were under CCP control. The significance of the National Assembly can be gauged from the fact that it met for only a short period every year. It was noticeable that the phrase repeatedly used to identify the function of this system was *'canalizar las inquietudes de las masas'* (channel the concerns of the masses). Interview with Jorge Hart Davalos, member of the Asamblea Provincial, Havana, March 1981.

23. Hitherto, much of the FMC's international activity was developed within the context of two concerns. One arose from its membership of the Soviet bloc and involved exchange visits by delegations from 'fraternal' states and membership of international communist organisations. Vilma Espín had been active in the Soviet-controlled International Federation of Democratic Women established in 1960, and acted as vice-president for a time. The other 'regional' concern was Latin America, where efforts were directed at developing solidarity for revolutionary currents approved by the Castro leadership. See Miller (1991), one of the few analysts who has examined the importance of international links in the Latin American women's movement.

24. The FMC at first had remained aloof from the regional feminist *Encuentros*, but their members began to attend from 1988 when four delegates went to the meeting in Taxco, Mexico. There they were exposed to a variety of different feminisms (including that of the Sandinista delegates from Nicaragua), at a time when a less orthodox left was also emerging, one more sympathetic than its predecessors to feminist ideas.

25. I have argued this at greater length in 'The Woman Question in the Age of Perestroika' (Molyneux, 1990). Other developments of the time – noticeably the increased concern of states with human rights, something to which the USSR and its European allies also had to pay lip service – played a parallel role.

26. See Saporta Sternbach et al. (1992), for a discussion of Latin American feminisms and for details of the *Encuentros*.

27. That there are different feminisms as well as different women's movements alerts us to the heterogeneity of women's interests and to the varying ways in which they are socially constructed. But what most definitions of feminism agree upon is that as a social movement and body of ideas, it challenges the structures and power relations that produce female subordination.

28. Espín (1991).

29. Quinn (1977).
30. Women constituted 23.91 per cent of party members in 1988 and 18.21 per cent of the Central Committee. Until 1985 there were no women in the Politburo (Lutyens, 1995).
31. Stubbs (1994). See also Lutyens (1994).
32. Interview with author, London, 1996.
33. Smith and Padula (1996).
34. This was one of the most dramatic moments in the internal history of the Cuban Revolution. The truth of what occurred in the Ochoa trial is not yet known: that something serious was wrong and that Ochoa was shot in order to emphasise the need for unquestioning obedience of the regime were not in doubt.
35. As part of this effort, the FMC established a homeworkers' programme, that in 1989 involved some 62 000 women, many of whom were seamstresses and none of whom enjoyed the social protection enjoyed by employees. The FMC did seek redress on this issue, but without success (Smith and Padula, 1996, p. 138).
36. See Lutyens (1995) for a positive assessment of this period. Lutyens also claims that the situation of Cuban women in the rectification period contrasts with the deteriorating conditions of other post-socialist women. The point, however, is that Cuba and Eastern Europe cannot be compared because they were not at comparable stages of the adjustment process; indeed, Cuba's had not yet begun.
37. It cannot be excluded that at least part of the shift in Cuban policy was influenced by the growing discussion within the Soviet Union of how neglect of women's concerns was linked to rising social problems – marital instability, delinquency, absenteeism and crime.
38. Bengelsdorf (1994).
39. *Ibid.*
40. Smith and Padula (1996) note how those who dissented from this paternalism could be treated: 'In 1991, María Elena Cruz Varela, a 37 year old award winning poet, socialist and mother of two, publicly renounced Castro as "not my father" and protested in an open letter to the commander in chief the lack of democracy and respect for human rights in Cuba. In response, a "Rapid Action Brigade" dragged her from her Havana apartment, beat her and made her physically swallow some of her own writings' (p. 543). She was imprisoned for 18 months.
41. Interview with author, Havana, January 1996.
42. FMC official, interview with author, Havana, January 1996.
43. The report on Cuba in Valdés and Gomariz (1992) contains an insert from the FMC leadership criticising the authors for what it sees as errors and bias in the interpretation. Among the points made is the following: 'We wish to point out that it is incorrect to list the FMC under "state actor", when it is an NGO.' It is worth noting that at the Fourth United Nations Conference on Women (Beijing, 1995), the FMC was represented at both the NGO forum (the *only* Cuban women's NGO) *and* at the governmental meeting.
44. *Federadas* is the Cuban term used to denote FMC membership.
45. The percentage of adult women nominally affiliated to the FMC rose from 74.0 per cent in 1974 to 82.3 per cent in 1994. In 1994, the total number of

212 Women's Movements in International Perspective

federadas was 3 657 220 – the largest percentages made up of housewives at 42.5 per cent and workers at 38.9 per cent. Students (10.5 per cent), pensioners and others accounted for the rest (FMC, 1995).

46. Former FMC member, interview with author, Havana, January 1996.

47. This information is based on a meeting with the director, a member of the FMC for 25 years, and several staff at this Casa, Havana, January 1996.

48. When I asked the director of the Casa de la Mujer in Havana what advice a woman would be offered in the case of drug abuse or domestic violence, she replied, 'It's simple, it is a legal offence' (January 1996). This approach does not encourage use of such services, let alone enhance the capacity of individuals to deal with their problems. One official's response to my enquiry about violence against women was that 'the greatest violence is that of the blockade'.

49. Interview with author, Havana, 1996. As one critic explained, 'The FMC not only lacks analysis, it also lacks a sense of its own purpose: this is why it is perceived as irrelevant by the mass of Cuban women whose lives have changed so dramatically.'

50. Anonymous Cuban economists, interviews with author, Havana, 1996.

51. Aguilar et al. (1994), p. 4.

52. By January 1996, more than 160 000 people were registered as self-employed, and markets of various kinds were doing a brisk trade in agricultural produce, meat and crafts. Small shops selling snacks and drinks had also appeared outside people's houses, mostly run by women, as had the ubiquitous *paladares*, officially permitted so long as they did not exceed twelve dining places. Attempts were subsequently made by the authorities to regulate and restrict these activities, resulting in a sharp decline in numbers.

53. Carlos Lage, in 1993, quoted in Bengelsdorf (1995), p. 24. Castro too is reported to have said that women who prostitute themselves 'do so on their own, voluntarily and without any need for it' (*ibid.*, p. 25).

54. Senior members of the FMC, interview with author, Havana, January 1996.

55. See Pearson (1997), pp. 671–706, for an analysis of Cuba's 'crisis in reproduction'.

56. This had, in effect, occurred in the household where I was staying in Vedado, Havana. The wife had given up her job because it was too far away and underpaid and because she was looking after a sick relative. She still had a cleaner who came every day (informal domestic service is widespread in Cuba), but now did the gardening herself and spent a considerable amount of her time in doing household activities, shopping and negotiating for scarce resources and services.

57. Valdés and Gomariz (1992), p. 50. There are considerable disparities in the available data on social indicators of all kinds. Data for this section have been taken where possible from sources originating from the Centro de Estudios Demográficos at the Universidad de La Habana, and from the Instituto Nacional de Investigaciones Económicas (1995).

58. This was still the case in early 1999.

59. MAGÍN, an association of women in communications, described itself in its founding document in the following terms: 'MAGÍN es una simbiosis de los conceptos de *imagen e imaginación*, vinculados estrechamente con el quehacer de sus integrantes como creadoras y difusoras de mensajes y con la reconocida

capacidad de las mujeres para sentir que "hay un cielo sobre nuestras cabezas" ' (The word MAGIN is a synthesis of the ideas of image and imagination. [It is] closely linked both to the work of its members who create and diffuse messages, and to the well-known capacity of women to feel that 'there is a sky over our heads'.) (MAGÍN, 1994).

60. Interview with author, Havana, January 1996.
61. This is suggested by the experience of the former Soviet bloc in relation to 'the woman question', and may bear upon considerations of the prospects of the Cuban regime's institutions and its own survival into the next period. For a discussion of the 'backlash' effect in the former Soviet bloc, see Funk and Mueller (1993) and my 'Women's Rights and the International Context in the Post-Communist States' (Molyneux, 1996).
62. See Stoner (1991), for a history of women's rights activism in Cuba.
63. After the general crackdown that occurred in 1996, the emerging debate over democracy in which Dilla and others had played such a central role was silenced and the scope of NGO activity on the island was increasingly curtailed. Dilla's institute, the Centro de Estudios de Europa, was temporarily closed and some of its leading members (including the director) were moved elsewhere. Following Raúl Castro's speech to the National Assembly in March 1996 after the downing of the planes piloted by exiles and passage of the Helms-Burton Act, NGOs were seen as a fifth column working to undermine Cuban society from within.

Chapter 5. State Socialism and Women's Emancipation

1. Thesis on the Full Exercise of Women's Equality (Stone, 1981, p. 77).
2. The terms 'communist state', 'state socialist', 'Soviet system' and 'centrally planned economies' (CPEs) are used interchangeably to describe these societies in preference to the broader descriptor 'socialist', a term reserved for the movements and the parties which existed within capitalist formations. The CPEs were neither socialist (lacking democracy) nor capitalist (lacking a market), but a *sui generis* formation.
3. For discussions of this issue see Funk and Mueller (1993) and Einhorn (1993).
4. For a critical discussion of this issue see Moghissi (1994).
5. Mill (1861), Chapter 2.
6. Marx and Engels (1970).
7. Mill (1861), p. 22.
8. For a discussion of these early movements, see Jayawardena (1986).
9. Footbinding was opposed on the grounds that it brought ridicule in the eyes of the civilised world, incapacitated women for motherhood and resulted in weak children (Jayawardena, 1986, p. 178). Mustapha Kemal (Ataturk): 'I see women covering their faces with their headscarves or turning their backs when a man approaches. Do you really think that the (women) of a civilised nation would behave so oddly or be so backward?' (quoted in *ibid*, p. 25).
10. Jancar (1978), pp. 126–7, 184–5.
11. Buckley (1989), pp. 44–57.
12. Armand, in Buckley (1989), p. 57.
13. By 'monism', de Beauvoir meant the reduction of social life to economic processes.

14. Ting (1975).
15. See Randall (1994).
16. The analysis of state socialism from a gendered perspective has attracted scholars from a variety of disciplines (see, for example, Lapidus, 1978; Buckley, 1989; and Wolchik, 1979, 1994). However, it is striking how little attention was paid to this scholarship by feminist theorists and activists. Momentary engagements and glancing comments entered into broader reflections on patriarchy, the sexual division of labour, or economic processes, but the focus of attention has largely lain elsewhere, in the capitalist world, both developing and industrialised. Even socialist feminists have tended to refrain from the analysis of communist regimes, following de Beauvoir's lead in combining a general endorsement of socialism with a reluctance to analyse these formations in their specificity. Work within feminist theory on socialist states has consequently been fragmented. Socialist states have been criticised for failing to achieve the equality they promised, but the reasons given for the failures were often similar to those advanced for capitalism.
17. Jancar (1978).
18. Bukharin and Preobrazhensky (1969), p. 226.
19. *Ibid.*
20. For a discussion of this issue, see Turgeon (1989).
21. Kollontai (1972), p. 3.
22. Szporluk (1988), p.7, argues that: 'The fusion of philosophy with politics and economics helps explain Marxism's spectacular historical failure as a practical programme – but also its lasting intellectual vitality.'
23. Charles Fourier (1841), quoted in Marx (1956), p. 259.
24. Of central importance in the formulation of this later policy was the work of Friedrich Engels, *The Origins of the Family, Private Property and the State*. This historical and evolutionary account of the oppression of women posited an ideal past state of natural equality, which over time, and with the emergence of private property, gave way to deepening gender divisions, male advantage and female marginalisation and subordination, culminating in the 'world historical defeat of the female sex' (Marx and Engels, 1970, p. 488). In order to achieve their emancipation, women should join the struggle of the proletariat against private property and enter the productive labour force on equal terms to men. Capitalism was seen here as the source of female exploitation, but also as a force which undermined women's subjugation in the family by drawing them into work. Among the working class, marriage became an egalitarian partnership, but one founded on the exploitation and misery of capitalism.
25. Berman (1985), *passim.*
26. Modernity had, of course, two sides; emancipation and determination: for socialism, particularly in its Marxist form, it was the former which predominated. Socialism shared the optimism of the Enlightenment with its belief in rational material progress towards a modern secular society. Modern society, with science to guide it, tended more and more towards the freedom of social groups and individuals, a freedom from tyranny and necessity. For others, it was the authoritarian, determinist, entrapping dimensions of modernity that predominated, expressed in Max Weber's metaphor of the

'Iron Cage'. In both views, the positive and the negative, the main instrument chosen for the realistion of modernity was to a considerable degree the same, the state, but its potential was disputed. It was not only Weber who saw modernity ushering in a new form of bureaucratic (rational legal) authority. Twentieth-century critics, notably Adorno and Horkheimer in the 1940s and Zygmunt Bauman in the 1970s, were to go further and identify modernity not with emancipation at all, but with another twentieth-century political form, totalitarianism.

27. Marx (1973), p. 86.
28. *Ibid.*
29. Harding (1984).
30. These ideas are to be found in the 'Critique of the Gotha Programme', (Marx, 1974), pp. 339–59.
31. Harding (1984).
32. Lenin is seen as having introduced the element of competitive nationalist development most clearly into Communist Party thinking. See Szporluk (1988) for elaboration of this view.
33. Harding argues that this turn to a centralised authoritarian state was influenced by Bukharin's theorisation of imperialism and of monopoly capitalism, seen as an effective means of directing development in adverse circumstances (Harding, 1984), pp. 16–18.
34. This was to be complemented by the establishment of a system of reward based on Marx's principles of transitional society (outlined in the 'Critique of the Gotha Programme' (Marx, 1974)) – to each according to his work, with the privileged category of work being that which yielded the greatest surplus.
35. A legacy of the French Revolution in its moment of Jacobin extremism and modernism was its formative impact on Marxists.
36. Massel (1974), p. 41.
37. Trotsky (1967), vol. III, pp. 48–9
38. Massel (1974), p. xxii.
39. Massel (1974), pp. 86–7.
40. Massel (1974).
41. Vaughan (2000).
42. The association of reformist programmes of this kind with unpopular states – colonial- or Western-identified – led to the rejection by many of those who came afterwards of all such efforts to modernise women's situation. The identification of women with all that was backward was to result in a critique of women's emancipation as a tool for the subjugation of nations. Women's aspirations for a modern equality were all too readily seen as the 'accomplices of the destruction of indigenous culture to the benefit of imperialism' as Najmabadi (1999, p. 60) explains in relation to Iran.
43. If this was a Western vision of modernity, it was one that broke radically with the political order associated with liberalism. Indeed rulers of state socialism fashioned their governing institutions in opposition to 'bourgeois law' and its civil rights and political guarantees.
44. Democratic Republic of Afghanistan (1979), p. 19. English translation as original.
45. Even those that chose to retain some element of a mixed economy, what Soviet theorists called the states of socialist orientation (Ethiopia under the

Derg, Iraq under the Ba'th, Angola under the MPLA), followed the example of the Soviet Union in attempting to impose a state-led development model under party control. I discuss this concept in Halliday and Molyneux 1981.
46. Marx (1975), pp. 345–8.
47. The argument developed here draws on Molyneux (1981).
48. Baker (1979), p. 184.
49. The centralised collectivisation of agriculture, such a disaster in much of the Soviet Union, was never attempted in the same way in the successor socialist states. Instead, land reform strategies focused on capturing agrarian surpluses through local, rather than national, state control and through a variety of different forms of socialised labour systems. Various policies were tried in pursuit of this end: *ujamaa*, or villagisation, in Tanzania, state farms, peasant cooperatives and associations in Ethiopia, Cuba and Mozambique, family plots in China, but all were aimed at the rapid modernisation of the agricultural sector.
50. As Brus (1972, p. 32) expressed it, 'conservative modernisation was an outcome of a Soviet type development strategy ... undeniable progress in overcoming backwardness on the one hand and the lack of a continuous propensity for change on the other'.
51. This could vary, however. Croll (1995) suggests that the Chinese Women's Federation in the 1980s was given new vitality and support by party concern over the scale of female infanticide.
52. Kandiyoti (1988a) discusses the different variants of patriarchal social relations. 'Classic' patriarchy was a feature of many European formations in the eighteenth century and in Russia in the nineteenth century. In the second half of the twentieth century it could be found in a belt which spans North Africa through the Muslim Middle East, through to South and East Asia.
53. Johnson (1983), Kandiyoti (1996).
54. Stacey (1983), Johnson (1983). According to Johnson, the politicisation of gender relations occasioned by the reform period was abandoned, while conservative peasant leaders' hold of institutional powers was reinforced.
55. See Watson (1993) on masculine anomie in Poland.
56. Watson (1993).
57. The low capital base and extensive reliance on labour typical of many of these societies was an important spur behind the policies which sought women's entry into education and eventually into occupations previously closed to them. The growing dependency on women's labour gave some urgency to the provision of childcare facilities and as a result of growing state concern about population levels, women benefited from specific policies directed at ensuring higher rates of maternal and child health.
58. As in Yugoslavia under Tito.
59. McCauley (1981).
60. See Heitlinger (1979) on Soviet attitudes towards domestic work.
61. From the 1970s onwards, for reasons unconnected to the emancipation of women as such, policy relating to women was seen, throughout the Soviet bloc, to require reassessment. The most pressing issues were demographic and centred on the birth rate: many states became alarmed at its decline and took measures to make it easier for women to have more children. This was

particularly so in the more urbanised regions of the USSR, in Hungary and the GDR, but it was in Romania that the harshest measures were adopted in the furtherance of population policy objectives. Ceauşescu outlawed abortion, and pressures of various sorts were placed on women to have a minimum of three children. In a few cases – notably China and Vietnam – the opposite consideration prevailed, and coercion and incentives were used to bring down the high birth rate. These demographic considerations were directly linked to the growing preoccupation with an economic performance that was sluggish in comparison with the capitalist states. In the Soviet Union this anxiety was both external and internal, spurred not only by competition with the West but also by disparities between the low birth rates in the Russian Federation and the much higher rates of Central Asia. In Yugoslavia, a similar internal anxiety prevailed: here ethnic Albanians were seen to present a threat to the Serbian authorities and repressive measures were taken to reduce the birth rate in Kosovo.

62. See Guo (1999) for a critical discussion of the enthusiasm with which some Western theorists of the left – Foucault, Barthes, Jameson, Sartre and Althusser – greeted the Chinese Cultural Revolution.

63. This view saw the state-centred system as making an important contribution during the initial post-revolution phase towards eliminating the worst features of underdevelopment and poverty.

64. We can judge this from the oral histories and ethnographies that emerged from post-communist states, as we may infer it from the fact that, despite much invocation of tradition and a return to 'authentic' values, there has been no autonomous mass movement of women that has sought to restore patriarchal subjection or remove women's autonomy, let alone re-establish those practices of pre-modern times which caused so much harm.

65. Lovibond (1989).

Chapter 6. Analysing Women's Movements

1. See, for example, Pateman (1988), Coole (1993), and Phillips (1991, 1993).

2. For some recent contributions, see Jaquette (1994), Jelin (1990), Waylen (1996), Wieringa (1995), Radcliffe and Westwood (1993), and Safa (1990). Initiatives taken to address this absence within the development debate include the 1995 IDS conference entitled 'Getting Institutions Right for Women in Development' (Sussex University), which focused on the ways that gender issues were reflected in institutional structures, including the much neglected issue of the state and public policy. (Papers published in the *IDS Bulletin*, vol. 26, no. 3, entitled *Getting Institutions Right for Women in Development*, edited by Ann Marie Goetz, and in a book of the same name (Goetz, 1997).

3. See Rowbotham (1992) for a comparative account of women's movements and Threlfall (1996) for women's movements in the Northern Hemisphere. For recent literature on women's movements in developing countries see note 2; also Alvarez (1990), Kandiyoti (1991), Tétrault (1994), Kumar (1992), and Basu (1992, 1995).

4. Tarrés (1992) notes in relation to the Latin American literature a virtual absence in recent years of work on other forms of collective action and little

recognition in contemporary work on social movements of earlier contributions.

5. For early influential treatments see Hufton (1971), Rowbotham (1973), Croll (1978), Kaplan (1977), and Bridenthal and Koonz (1977).

6. See Omvedt (1986), Jaquette (1994), and Jelin (1990) for comparative overviews and discussion.

7. Paidar (1995) is a comprehensive analysis of the role of women in the Iranian political process.

8. Jayawardena (1986).

9. It is worth noting that the quantitative increase in women's participation has also been accompanied by the absorption of women into formerly male preserves, none more so than the army. This, however, has not implied an erosion of gender roles as such; rather it required a redefinition of women's place within society as a whole, one which added to rather than eliminated their traditional gender responsibilities, while leaving men's largely untransformed.

10. 'Other' includes state socialist attempts at legitimation through limited electoral processes.

11. Sen and Grown (1987) provide a useful typology for practitioners.

12. See Vargas (1991) and Blondet (1995).

13. See Alvarez (1990), p. 23.

14. Wieringa (1995), p. 7.

15. Alvarez (1990), p. 23.

16. Alvarez (1990).

17. An important study of female support for Nazism is Koonz (1988).

18. For a classic record of the tensions between feminist demands for autonomous spaces and political parties see the exchange between Clara Zektin and Lenin, in Zetkin (1934).

19. The participatory, non-hierarchical model of doing politics has been criticised for allowing a 'tyranny of powerlessness', that is, for failing to take account of forms of power which were exercised informally and not, therefore, subject to any regulation or control.

20. These are merely heuristic distinctions – 'idealisations', which means that they do not have to correspond to reality; a great diversity of forms of female collective action has emerged over time, and there have been changes within given movements with overlapping forms as between these three categories in given historical contexts.

21. Jean Franco has written: 'It is precisely Third World women who have insisted not only that there are differences *between* women but also that there are circumstances in which women's emancipation is bound up with the fate of the larger community' (Franco, 1989, p. xi).

22. Stoner (1991).

23. This point is made in the Latin American context by several authors. See, for example, Vargas (1996).

24. Here Vargas acknowledges Lechner's (1990) formulation.

25. Schumaher and Vargas (1993), p. 459.

26. Salinas (1986), p. 143. See also Domitila's account, in Barrios de Chungara (1978).

27. This case is explored in Chapter 4.

28. This is Kandiyoti's term (1988a).
29. See Guzman et al. (1992) on this. Also Mouffe (1988) is relevant in relation to the point that individuals generally occupy 'different subject positions' as a result of the complex process of identity formation.
30. Molyneux (1985a). (Chapter 2 this volume).
31. For discussions and applications of the concepts, see, *inter alia*, Moser (1989), Alvarez (1990), Young (1993), Kabeer (1992), Guzman et al. (1992), Safa (1990), García-Guadilla (1995), Vargas (1993), Anderson (1992), Nelson and Chowdhury (1994), and Wieringa (1994).
32. See Anderson (1992) for a considered discussion of this trajectory.
33. The issue of men's interests is considered by New (1996), who suggests that many men have an interest in maintaining the oppressive gender order which works to their advantage; however, they also have an 'emancipatory interest' in equality and in ending the oppression of women. One could add that men's interest groups have formed in opposition to what are seen as women's unfair advantages in the sphere of positive discrimination and child custody. Sarah White (n.d.) has also written interestingly on men's gender interests in the development context.
34. Young (1993), p. 156.
35. The most thoroughgoing attempt at integrating the concepts within a framework for 'gender-aware planning' was that of Moser (1989).
36. Anderson (1992).
37. Kabeer (1992) and Wieringa (1994).
38. Chapter 2, p. xx.
39. Hindess (1982), Callinicos (1987), Benton (1982), and Scott (1988).
40. Gina Vargas stresses the complex field of determination within which women's movements operate 'with regard to their own contexts, subjectivities and concerns; in relation to different realities, experiences and influences, which reveal the complexity of the relationship between contradictions, contexts and subjectivities of women. The relationship between them is complex and tense, differences of class, race, ethnicity and religion are always present' (Vargas, 1993, p. 5).
41. Scott, like Callinicos, favours a view of interests as 'discursively produced', but abdicates an entirely relativist position in favour of politics and ethical positions which 'confront and change existing distributions of power' (Scott, 1988, p. 6).
42. Fierlbeck (1995), p. 8.
43. For a spirited critique of post-modernism's influence in development debates, see Martha Nussbaum's essays in Nussbaum and Glover (1995).
44. Lynn Stephen (1998) also regards women's movements as being outside the realm of theoretical analysis on the grounds that their reality is too complex and shifting. However, this is surely always the problem with any knowledge.
45. Blondet (1995).
46. Fierlbeck (1995) makes the important point that women's adaptation to subordination is too simply read as 'consent', when the latter implies there was a real choice. In reality women's choices are often severely circumscribed placing both consent and choice in doubt.
47. A measured defence of reason would, if space allowed, be proposed here. As Gillian Rose reminds us, there is no rationality without uncertain grounds,

rationality relativises authority, 'yet this does not establish the authority of relativism, it opens reason to new claimants' (Rose, 1995, p.9.). See also Lovibond's (1989) defence of rationality .

48. Difference feminism does, however, have a long history in Latin America too, as well as an active presence within contemporary feminism (see Chapter 5).

49. As Scott (1988) and others have argued, the equality/difference distinction is unhelpful (another binary) when applied to politics and policy. Equality feminists recognise the importance of acknowledging difference for reasons of social justice in the legislative sphere (pensions, divorce settlements), as a way of redressing social injustice and hence furthering the aim of equality.

50. The German Mothers' Party, active in the 1980s, is a case in point: it called for, *inter alia*, wages for housework and increased rights to child custody.

51. Elshtain (1981).

52. Tronto (1993) and Lister (1997).

53. Jonasdottir (1988) is surely right to say that women are not just another 'interest group', because they exist in a historically determined, antagonistic and subordinate relationship to men. This has implications for issues of political representation.

54. See Mouffe (1992) and Dietz (1985) on why women's narrow self-interests should be transcended in the embrace of more general interests.

Chapter 7. Gender and Citizenship in Latin America

1. See Kymlicka and Norman (1994) for a useful overview and discussion of the citizenship debate and López (1997) for a Latin American application.

2. For theoretical treatments of citizenship from a gender perspective see, among others, Elshtain (1983), Pateman (1989), Phillips (1991, 1993), Dietz, (1985, 1987), Lister (1997), Mouffe (1992), Yuval Davis and Werbner (1999), and Young (1990).

3. This theoretical discussion is drawn from Molyneux (2000b), where Latin America is compared with the former communist states and Western Europe.

4. The scope of international law has widened in recent decades, and has extended issues of rights beyond the nation-state, thereby complicating the meaning of citizenship, and rendering it 'multi-layered' (Held et al., 1999). However, it is still understood principally in relation to the nation-state, which establishes the legal foundation of social membership.

5. This view of citizenship as an object of political struggle, which results in changes in its meaning and practices, is usually associated with Hannah Arendt's reconceptualisation of politics. See, for example, Arendt (1977).

6. Here, as in the Andean region more generally and in Central America, some indigenous communities have been argued to lie outside 'the post-Kantian canon of personhood as constituted around a hard core of universalistic rights and duties' (Menéndez-Carrión and Bustamente, 1995). If rights of membership are held by the community rather than, or as well as, by the nation, the issue of citizenship's plural character is problematised. Customary law cannot be treated here but underlines the point about the variability of the meanings of citizenship and of the social relations through which it is mediated.

7. 'Gender regime' is a term developed by Connell (1987) which refers to the ways in which gender power is mediated through specific laws, state forms, social relations and civil institutions.

8. There is a growing scholarly literature on Latin American feminism. See, *inter alia*, Lavrin (1996), Rodríguez (1997), Villavicencio (1992), Hahner (1990), Stoner (1991), Miller (1991), Alvarez (1990), Bareiro and Soto (1997), Besse (1996), Feijoó (1982), and Ramos et al. (1987). For applications of a citizenship perspective see, *inter alia*, Jelin (1987), Jelin and Hershberg (1996), Hola and Portugal (1997), Bareiro and Soto (1997) and Marques-Pereira and Carrier (1996).

9. In Peru, for example, illiterates (the majority of whom were indigenous female Amerindians) were not enfranchised until the 1980s.

10. Lavrin (1996), Stoner (1991), and Miller (1991).

11. In this chapter I use 'women's movement' to refer to the collectivity of different movements in which women are active, including feminism. The latter may however be distinguished as a specific form of women's movement. For further definitional discussion, see Chapter 6.

12. Women's legal status was virtually unchanged by Independence. They had few rights in the family, and if married had no automatic right to marital property or to child custody.

13. Franco (1989).

14. These struggles for political rights, as strenuously fought for as they were opposed, constituted only one facet of a far broader feminist challenge. From the late nineteenth and through the early decades of the twentieth centuries, feminists were also demanding social rights, education and work.

15. Female suffrage was not granted in France until 1948.

16. Lavrin (1996).

17. Sally Alexander (1995), in discussing Britain, argues that while motherhood was the grounds for women's political aspirations in the nineteenth century, 'the emphasis on motherhood, in the absence of an independent feminist voice, risked confirming women's status as one in need of protection, the association of their person with "sexual slavery" or vice. *Before 1918 ... feminists united women through the demand for the suffrage, not motherhood*' (p. xvi) (authors italics).

18. Theda Skocpol's account of the role of female agency and of civic maternalism in the formulation of social policy in the USA has been important in shifting the interpretative balance from a 'patriarchy' analysis to one which stresses politics and agency (Skocpol, 1992).

19. See Nancy Stepan (1991) on the Latin American eugenics movement and on the role of 'feminist eugenics' in the reform process.

20. As the then president of Mexico, Miguel Alemán, said of the need to grant women the right to vote and to stand in municipal elections in the 1940s: 'the municipal organisation is the one that cares most about the interests of the family and must pay most attention to the needs of the family and of children' (Ramos Escandón, 1998, p. 100).

21. The Urugayan senator, Vaz Ferreira, was a champion of feminism in the early decades of the century and developed the idea of compensatory feminism in his lectures and writings, published in Vaz Ferreira (1945).

22. Lavrin (1996).

23. See Lobato (1997).
24. For a fuller discussion of gender–state relations in twentieth-century Latin America, see Molyneux (2000a).
25. Fraser and Navarro (1980).
26. On the Housewives Union inspired by Eva Perón, see Fisher (2000).
27. This is not to say that difference feminism had no adherents, or no adherents among socialists. Mexican feminists in the 1970s were more taken with the arguments concerning difference than in other parts of Latin America where strong feminist movements emerged.
28. The reform of the Labour Code of Venezuela in 1990 achieved recognition of women's rights to protection from dismissal for pregnancy, workplace crèches and days off to care for sick family members. Campaigners used equality arguments to promote these changes. See Friedman (forthcoming, 2001).
29. The phrase is Sonia Alvarez's (1990).
30. Some Latin American feminists have spoken of the existence of a kind of 'female chauvinism' or proprietorship in relation to the home and family, which has made claims with regard to gender equality and the symbolic value of motherhood difficult issues to breach.
31. Villavicencio (1992), Vargas (1998).
32. Stephen (1998). One example among many of the latter is the avowedly anti-feminist working-class organisation the Housewives Union (SACRA), which fought for the recognition of the work women did in the home and for women's right to have this work remunerated through state transfers (Fisher, 2000).
33. Jaquette (1994).
34. A popular phrase meaning 'from protest to proposals'.
35. This view was shared by much of the left, which during the 1960s and 1970s was not only 'broadly anti-statist' (Lechner, 1990) but sceptical about liberal democracy.
36. Jelin (1990), p. xi.
37. This critique of the gender-blind character of the social movement literature can be found in Molyneux (1986b), Jaquette (1994), and Waylen (1996).
38. Turner (1986) distinguishes between active and passive forms of citizenship, that is, whether developed via the state or from below through local or workplace struggles. He also distinguishes between public and private traditions of citizenship, in which American liberalism is an example of the latter.
39. This was part of the effort to theorise domestic or reproductive labour. See Marques-Pereira and Carrier (1996) for a discussion of the debate, and Lora (1996) on the *quotidien*.
40. The *comedores* (literally 'dining rooms') operated on the basis of household membership (20–40 families being usual) and the preparation of food was done collectively, with families taking their food home to eat. They were financed by membership quotas and from the sale of food to non-members. The *ollas* (literarally 'pots and pans') involved communal cooking; the *vaso de leche* programme involved the distribution of free milk to children and sometimes to others in need.
41. Barrig (1998); and Luna 'Feminismo: Encuentro y diversidad en organiza-

ciones de mujeres latinoamericanas, 1985–1990', *Homines*, vol. 1, no. 11, cited in Marques-Pereira and Carrier (1996), p 16.

42. Caldeira (1990), Stephen (1998).
43. See Foweraker (1997) for such an analysis.
44. See Blondet (1995), and Anderson's discussion of the various phases of the *vaso de leche* campaign in Nijeholt et al. (1998).
45. Jelin (1990), Jaquette (1994), Waylen (1996).
46. In Jelin (1990).
47. There is a large literature on the motherist movements. See, *inter alia*, Feijoó (1998), Schirmer (1989), and Fisher (1993).
48. Gilligan (1982); see also Ruddick (1980).
49. Diamond and Hartsock (1981).
50. The Pope's encyclical letter, *Mulieris Dignitatem*, continues this tradition, seeking to dignify women's 'feminine genius'. Boff writes: 'We support the argument that the Virgin Mary, mother of God ... represents the feminine in perfect and eschatological form ... modernity has defined itself as logocentric, giving primacy to rationality and to the power of abstraction, [and has consequently] marginalised the feminine and with it the dimensions of human reality linked to tenderness, the symbolic and pathos' (Boff 1984, p. 187).
51. These positions were expressed at the United Nations Conference on Environment and Development (UNCED). They are critiqued in Molyneux and Steinberg (1995).
52. Tronto defines women's morality as referring 'loosely to a collection of ideas: values placed on caring and nurturance and the importance of mother's love, a stress on the value of sustaining human relationships, the over-riding value of peace' (Tronto, 1993, p. 1).
53. One example will suffice to make the point, that of those Serbian nationalist women who blocked food supplies to starving Muslims in the Bosnian and Kosovan wars.
54. Tronto (1993).
55. As expressed by Tronto: 'care as a relational activity rather than just as labour, as well as the balancing of needs of carer and care recipient, often in situations of dependence and inequalities of power and resources' (Tronto, 1993, p. 61).
56. Lister (1997), Showstack Sassoon (1987).
57. Tronto (1993).
58. Alex Wilde has referred to the efforts made by the Aylwin government to introduce an 'ethics of responsibility' into Chilean political life (Wilde, 1999). This is also suggested by O'Donnell's (1993) call for a second transition from democratic government to a democratic regime.
59. O'Donnell (1993), Jelin (1997).
60. Alvarez (1998).
61. World Bank Report (1997).
62. There are significant areas of overlap but also of difference between the North American/British and South American forms of communitarianism. They share a critique of individualism and liberalism and stress the importance both of shared social values and of active cooperation below the state level, in particular in urban neighbourhoods. They both respect the idea of a moral

community often derived from religious belief. The writings of sociologist Amitai Etzioni have, for instance, been taken up in the USA and Britain to think about ways of reversing alarming trends of social decomposition in the inner cities.

63. Stepan (1978).

64. Putnam's work (1992) was influential here. For an application to Latin America and other developing countries see Evans (1997).

65. Ideas of community interest helped to animate social movements for civil peace and social renewal such as the multiclass alliance supporting the Viva Rio movement in Brazil in the 1990s. This brought tens of thousands on to the streets demanding community policing and police reform, public safety, and improved housing for the poor (Gaspar Pereira, 1996).

66. For a discussion and review of feminist engagements with communitarian ideas see Frazer and Lacey (1993).

67. FLACSO (1995).

68. Micro-credit was a favoured anti-poverty strategy of the 1990s following the success of the Gramene bank and the move of its founder to the World Bank.

69. Kandiyoti (1988b) draws attention to the reliance of participatory strategies for health delivery on mothers to administer and even finance initiatives that are directed at improving child health – oral rehydration and immunisation, among them. The onus is on women to extend their traditional responsibilities in the family to include provision of basic healthcare.

70. Schild (1998).

71. For a discussion of this issue see Alvarez et al. (1998).

72. See Etzioni (1993). The British feminist Bea Campbell sees this as 'speak[ing] to an anxiety about the seismic shifts in relations between the genders and generations ...The call for a return to "basics" permits white men to exempt themselves from the critique of the masculinities that make life a misery' (Campbell, 1995).

73. McIntyre indeed insists that 'tradition' is a necessary part of the good society (McIntyre, 1981, 1988).

74. Giddens (1990).

75. See, for example, the Mexican journal *Debate Feminista*'s special issue on *Otredad*, year 7, vol. 13, April 1996. Stephen's (1998) interviews with low-income activists show how feminist ideas had been taken up, even by those who described themselves as non- or anti-feminist.

76. Phillips (1991), Lister (1997).

77. Carole Pateman's (1988) work was influential here. A parallel application of difference arguments can be found in the rise of ethnocultural movements in this period.

78. 1998 data from the Inter-Parliamentary Union shows that only 11 per cent of cabinet-level posts and seats in the national legislature of Latin American states were held by women. However, quotas did push up women's representation in Congress in Argentina from 5 per cent before the laws to 28 per cent by 1998. Parties with women's quotas include: Mexico's PRD (30 per cent) and PRI (30 per cent); Chile's Partido Socialista (40 per cent), Partido por la Democracia (20 per cent) and Democracia Cristiana (20 per cent); Costa Rica's PUSC (40 per cent); Brazil's PT (30 per cent); Venezuela's Acción Democratica (20 per cent); El Salvador's FMLN (35 per cent) Nicaragua's FSLN (30 per cent); and Paraguay's Partido Colorado (20 per cent) and Partido

Revolucionario Febrerista (30 per cent) (Htun, 1999). See also note 110.

79. As Phillips (1993) argues, the other major problem concerns the principle on which recognition is given to collectivities, that of identity. In the case of women, on the basis of one of their identities (women, 'black', and so on), individuals are 'frozen' into them and encouraged to think of their interests in narrow terms. If the politics of identity is the only basis for political action, she argues, there is the danger that it may serve to essentialise and dehistoricise difference.

79. As has been repeatedly said, individuals have a multiplicity of identities, ones that are 'fractured' and unstable, and their interests are correspondingly variable.

80. Laclau and Mouffe (1985).

81. Jones (1997).

82. Mouffe (1992) expressed the point thus: 'the limitations of the modern conception of citizenship should be remedied not by making sexual difference politically relevant to its definition, but by constructing a new conception of citizenship where sexual difference should become effectively non-pertinent'.

83. Phillips has noted that feminism has, since its inception, 'contained within itself a double impetus towards both equality *and* difference' (Phillips, 1992 p. 10).

84. Jelin (1997).

85. One of the campaigners' speeches to the Congress began: 'Notice citizens that we are not talking about women. We are speaking without bias about the law which protects families' (Friedman, forthcoming, 2001).

86. Bock and James (1994).

87. Ruth Lister has proposed the concept of a 'differentiated universalism' to capture this idea (Lister, 1997).

88. Barrios de Chungara (1978), Menchú (1983).

89. It is also worth pointing out that Domitila's politicisation occurred through solidarising with her husband's struggle for better wages and conditions, in which she argues that women are entitled to some reward for their unpaid labour in the home.

90. Alvarez (1998).

91. The first UN Decade for Women's Conference in 1975 was attended by 6000 women; this rose to 8000 in 1980 in Copenhagen, 15 000 in Nairobi in 1985 and more than 30 000 in Beijing in 1995. In the NGO Forum of the latter there were 1800 participants from Latin America.

92. See, for example, León 1994.

93. Goetz (1997).

94. Interview with Ana Criquillón (Managua, 1998).

95. Anderson describes the problems associated with NGOs lack of connection with or leverage on governments, something which weakened their overall effectiveness. She remarks: 'as self-enclosed bubbles of change, many projects quickly burst' (in Nijeholt et al., 1998, p. 84).

96. Alvarez (1990).

97. Vargas and Wieringa refer to this alliance building as the 'triangle of empowerment' (in Nijeholt et al., 1998).

98. See Macaulay (2000).

99. As Harrington (1992) has argued, the feminist critique of liberalism has hypothesised one version – contractarian – at the expense of an engagement with other forms, such as social or welfare liberalism.

100. Vargas (1998).

101. The Mar del Plata ECLAC meeting in 1994 saw a confrontation between conservative Church-supported positions and feminist lobbies.

102. This came to be seen as all the more essential given the urgent need to tackle the social and gendered consequences of economic policies. The gender analysis of macroeconomic policy-making gradually entered the policy process, generating an awareness of the social consequences of public priorities. The 1996 Beijing Conference gave voice to the need to place the sphere of reproduction within the planning process, not just to acknowledge *women's* invisible labours, but to identify social needs more generally. Issues such as the feminisation of poverty also raised important questions of policy which need urgent debate and resolution.

103. The government of Eduardo Frei (1994) included equal opportunities in his political platform, while Peru's Fujimori took the unprecedented step for a male Latin American president of attending the Fourth World Conference on Women in 1995.

104. A survey of Latin American attitudes towards gender roles and women's participation in institutional politics was underway in Peru in 1999: interim results were announced at a conference held in Lima in November of that year (*Hombres y Mujeres en en Siglo XXI*). See also Blondet (1999) on changing Peruvian attitudes on these issues.

105. See the account of this process in Guatemala and in Mexico by Blacklock and Jenson (1998) which draws out interesting differences between Mexican and Guatemalan appropriations of rights discourses.

106. The National Coordinator of Guatemalan Widows.

107. Surveys carried out in a range of Latin American countries in the 1990s showed that in Mexico, Chile, Costa Rica and Ecuador, around 60 per cent of women had suffered physical violence at the hands of a male intimate (Htun, 1999).

108. By 1998, 15 Latin American countries had human rights ombudsman offices, and in six of these there was a specific body charged with women's issues (Htun, 1999).

109. This is examined in Molyneux and Lazar, 1999.

110. In the 1990s, women's representation in the Chambers of Deputies was as follows: (per cent of women) Argentina, 27.6 per cent (1997); Brazil, 6.6 per cent (1994); Chile, 10.8 per cent (1997); Colombia, 11 per cent (1994); Costa Rica, 19.3 per cent (1998); Cuba, 27.6 per cent (1998); Dominican Republic, 11.7 per cent (1994); Ecuador, 5.2 per cent (1994); El Salvador, 16.7 per cent (1997); Mexico, 17.4 per cent (1997); Peru, 10.8 per cent (1995); Uruguay, 7.1 per cent (1994). Average for all Latin American countries: 12 per cent. Female representation in Senates was lower, with a mean of 7.6 per cent. (Data compiled from Inter-Parliamentary Union sources cited in Craske 1999).

111. This is Goetz's formulation; see Goetz (1997), p. 1.

112. In this context, 'role-based' is preferable to 'identity-based' as it suggests the social materiality *and* the attendant identifications of the sexual division of labour.

113. Held et al. (1999), Yuval Davis (1999).

Bibliography

Abad de Santillán, D. (1930) *El movimiento anarquista en la Argentina* (Buenos Aires: Argonauta).

Aguilar, C., Popowski, P. and Verdeses, M. (1994) 'El período especial y la vida cotidiana: Desafío de las cubanas de los 90' (Havana: FMC), mimeo.

Alexander, S. (1995) *Becoming a Woman* (New York University Press).

Alvarez, S. (1990) *Engendering Democracy in Brazil. Women's Movements in Transition Politics* (Princeton, NJ.: Princeton University Press).

Alvarez, S. (1998) 'Latin American Feminisms "Go Global": Trends of the 1990s and Challenges for the New Millennium', in S. Alvarez, E. Dagnino and A. Escobar (eds), *Cultures of Politics/Politics of Cultures: Revisioning Latin American Social Movements* (Boulder, CO: Westview Press), pp. 93–115.

Alvarez, S., Dagnino, E. and Escobar, A. (eds) (1998) *Cultures of Politics/Politics of Cultures: Revisioning Latin American Social Movements* (Boulder, CO: Westview Press).

Alvarez Junco, J. (1976) *La ideología política del anarquismo español 1868–1910* (Mexico City: Siglo XXI).

AMNLAE (1981) *Documentos de la Asamblea de AMNLAE* (Managua).

Anderson, J. (1992) *Intereses o justicia* (Lima: Entre Mujeres).

Angel, A. and Macintosh, F. (eds) (1987) *The Tiger's Milk* (London: Virago Press).

Arendt, H. (1977) 'What is Freedom?', in *Between Past and Future* (Harmondsworth: Penguin)

Baker, H.D.R. (1979) *Chinese Family and Kinship* (Basingstoke: Macmillan).

Bareiro, L. and Soto, C. (eds) (1997) *Ciudadanas: Una memoria inconstante* (Caracas: Centro de Documentación y Estudios, CDE Editorial, Nueva Sociedad).

Barricada (15 November 1985).

Barricada (9 December 1987).

Barricada International (1987), vol. 7, no. 251 (27 August).

Barrig, M. (1998) 'Female Leadership, Violence and Citizenship in Peru', in J. Jaquette and S.L. Wolchik (eds), *Women and Democracy: Latin America and Central and Eastern Europe* (Baltimore, MD: Johns Hopkins University Press).

Barrios de Chungara, D. (1978) *Let Me Speak!: Testimony of Domitila, a Woman of the Bolivian Mines* (New York: Monthly Review Press).

Basu, A. (1992) *Two Faces of Protest: Contrasting Modes of Women's Activism in India* (Berkeley, CA: University of California Press).

Basu, A. (ed.) (1995) *The Challenge of Local Feminisms* (Boulder, CO: Westview Press).

Bauman, Z. (1976) *Socialism: The Active Utopia* (London: Allen and Unwin).

Bebel, A. (1988) *Women in the Past, Present and Future* (London: Zwan).

Bengelsdorf, C. (1994) *The Problem of Democracy in Cuba: Between Vision and Reality* (Oxford: Oxford University Press).

Bengelsdorf, C. (1995) '(Re)considering Cuban Women in a time of Troubles', mimeo.

Benton, E. (1981) '"Objective" Interests and the Sociology of Power', *Sociology*, vol. 15, no. 2.

Benton, E. (1982) *Realism, Power and Objective Philosophy* (Cambridge: Cambridge University Press).

Berman, M. (1985) *All That Is Solid Melts Into Air: The Experience of Modernity* (London: Verso).

Besse, S.K. (1996) *Restructuring Patriarchy: The Modernization of Gender Inequality in Brazil, 1914–1940* (Chapel Hill and London: University of North Carolina Press).

Blacklock, C. and Jenson, J. (1998) 'Citizenship: Latin American Perspectives', *Social Politics* (Summer), pp. 127–131, and in S. Rai (ed.) (1999), *International Perspectives on Gender and Democratisation* (Basingstoke: Macmillan).

Blondet, C. (1995) 'Out of the Kitchens and onto the Streets', in A. Basu (ed.), *The Challenge of Local Feminisms* (Boulder, CO: Westview Press), pp. 251–75.

Blondet, C. (1999) *Percepción ciudadana sobre la participación política de la mujer* (Lima: Instituto de Estudios Peruanos).

Bock, G. (ed.) (1992) *Beyond Equality and Difference: Citizenship and Female Subjectivity* (London and NY: Routledge).

Boff, L. (1984) *The Maternal Face of God* (London: Collins).

Bourdé, G. (1974) *Urbanisation et immigration en Amérique Latine* (Paris: Aubier).

Brasileiro, A.M. (ed.) (1996) *Building Democracy with Women* (New York: UNIFEM/UNDP).

Bridenthal, R. and Koontz, C. (1977) *Becoming Visible, Women in European History* (Boston, MA: Houghton Mifflin).

Brus, W. (1972) *The Market in a Socialist Economy* (London and Boston: Routledge and Kegan Paul).

Buckley, Mary (1989) *Women and Ideology in the Soviet Union* (London: Harvester Wheatsheaf).

Bukharin, N. and Preobrazhensky, E. (1969) *The ABC of Communism* (Harmondsworth: Penguin).

Caldeira, T. (1990) 'Women's Daily Life and Politics', in E. Jelin (ed.), *Women and Social Change in Latin America* (London: Zed Books), pp. 47–78

Callinicos A. (1987) *Making History* (Cambridge: Cambridge University Press).

Campbell, B. (1995) 'Old Fogeys and Angry Young Men: A Critique of Communitarianism', *Soundings*, issue 1 (Autumn), pp. 47–64.

Carranza Valdés, J. et al. (1995) *Cuba: La restructuración de la economía: Una propuesta para el debate* (Havana: Editorial de Ciencias Sociales).

Connell, R.W. (1987) *Gender and Power* (Cambridge and Oxford: Polity Press and Blackwell). Oxford. 1987

Coole D.H. (1993) *Women in Political Theory, from Ancient Misogyny to Contemporary Feminism* (Brighton, Sussex: Wheatsheaf Books).

Corraggio, José Luis (1983) 'Posibilidades y límites de la política en los procesos de transicíon: el caso de Nicaragua'. Paper presented at the Amsterdam Latin American Centre (CEDLA) Conference on Nicaragua.

Craske, N. (1999) *Women and Politics in Latin America* (Cambridge: Polity).

Craske, N. and Molyneux, M. (eds) (forthcoming, 2001) *Gender and Justice in Latin America* (Basingstoke: Macmillan).

Croll, E. (1978) *Feminism and Socialism in China* (London: Routledge and Kegan Paul).

Croll, E. (1995) *Changing Identities of Chinese Women* (Hong Kong and London: Hong Kong University Press and Zed Books).

Dahl, R.A. (1982) *Dilemmas of Pluralist Democracy* (New Haven, CT: Yale University Press).

Davies, C. (1997) *A Place in the Sun?: Women Writers in Twentieth Century Cuba* (London: Zed Books).

De Beauvoir, S. (1953) *The Second Sex* (London: Jonathan Cape).

Deere, C.D. (1983) 'Co-operative Development and Women's Participation in Nicaragua's Agrarian Reform', *American Journal of Agrarian Economics* (December).

Deighton, J., Horsley, R., Stewart, S. and Cain, C. (1983) *Sweet Ramparts* (London: War on Want/Nicaragua Solidarity Campaign).

Democratic Republic of Afghanistan (1979) *Decrees of the DRA* (Kabul: Ministry of Information and Culture, Afghanistan Publicity Bureau).

Diamond, I. and Hartsock, N. (1981) 'Beyond Interests in Politics: A comment on Virginia Sapiro's "When are Interests Interesting?"' *American Political Science Review*, vol. 75, no. 3, pp. 717–23.

Dietz, M. (1985) 'Citizenship with a Feminist Face', *Political Theory*, vol. 13, no. 1 (February), pp. 19–38.

Dietz, M. (1987) 'Context is All: Feminism and Theories of Citizenship', *Daedelus*, vol. 116, no. 4, pp. 1–24.

Dilla, H. (ed.) (1995) *La democrácia en Cuba y el diferendo con los Estados Unidos* (Havana: Ediciones CEA).

Dilla, H. (ed.) (1996) *La participación en Cuba y los retos del futuro* (Havana: Ediciones CEA).

Eckstein, S. (1991) 'More on the Cuban Rectification Process: Whose Errors?', *Cuban Studies*, vol. 21, pp. 187–92.

Einhorn, B. (1993) *Cinderella Goes to Market* (London: Verso).

Eisenstein, Z. (ed.) (1978) *Capitalist Patriarchy and the Case for Socialist Feminism* (New York: Monthly Review Press).

Elsentein, Z. (1983) 'Women as a Sexual Class'. Paper presented at 'A Marx Centenary Conference', Winnipeg, Canada.

Elshtain, J.B. (1981) *Public Man, Private Woman* (Princeton, NJ: Princeton University Press).

Elshtain, J.B. (1983) 'Antigone's Daughters', in I. Diamond (ed.), *Families, Politics and Public Policy* (Harlow: Longman).

Espín, V.G. (1991) *La Mujer en Cuba* (Havana: Editorial de la Mujer).

Etzioni, A. (1993) *The Spirit of Community: Responsibility and the Communitarian Agenda* (New York: Crown Publishers Inc.).

Evans, H. (1997) *Women and Sexuality in China* (Cambridge: Polity Press).

Evans, M. ed. (1994) *The Woman Question* 2nd edn (London: Sage).

Evans, P. (ed.) (1997) *State–Society Synergy*, Research Series no. 94 (Berkeley, CA: University of California Press).

Feijoó, M. (1982) *Las Feministas* (Buenos Aires: Centro Editorial de América Latina).

Feijoó, M. (1997) *La Voz de la Mujer* (Buenos Aires: Universidad de Quilares).

Feijoó, M. (1998) 'Democratic Participation and Women in Argentina', in J.

Jaquette and S.L. Wolchik (eds), *Women and Democracy: Latin America and Central and Eastern Europe* (Baltimore, MD: Johns Hopkins University Press), pp. 29–46.

Ferns, H.S. (1960) *Britain and Argentina in the Nineteenth Century* (Oxford: Oxford University Press).

Fierlbeck, K. (1995) 'Getting Representation Right for Women in Development: Accountability, Consent, and the Articulation of "Women's Interests"', *IDS Bulletin*, vol. 26, no. 3, pp. 23–30.

Fisher, J. (1993) *Out of the Shadows: Women, Resistance and Politics in South America* (London: Latin American Bureau).

Fisher, J. (2000), 'Gender and the State in Argentina: The Sindicato Amas de Casa', in E. Dore and M. Molyneux (eds), *Hidden Histories of Gender and the State in Latin America* (Durham, NC: Duke University Press).

FLACSO (1995) *Mujeres latinoamericanas en cifras. Tomo comparativo* (Santiago Instituto de la Mujer Espana)/FLACSO).

FMC (1975) *Memoria: II Congreso Nacional de la Federación de Mujeres Cubanas* (Havana: Editorial Orbe).

FMC (1995) *Estadísticas sobre las mujeres cubanas* (Havana: Federación de Mujeres Cubanas).

Foweraker, J. (1997) *Citizenship Rights and Social Movements: A Comparative and Statistical Analysis* (Oxford: Oxford University Press).

Franco, J. (1973) *Spanish American Literature since Independence* (London: Ernest Benn).

Franco, J. (1989) *Plotting Women: Gender and Representation in Mexico* (New York: Columbia University Press).

Fraser, N. (1989) *Unruly Practices* (Oxford: Polity Press).

Fraser, N. and Navarro, M. (1980) *Eva Perón* (London: André Deutsch).

Frazer, E. and Lacey, N. (1993) *The Politics of Community: A Feminist Critique of the Liberal-Communitarian Debate* (New York and London: Harvester Wheatsheaf).

French, J.D. and James, D. (eds) (1997) *The Gendered Worlds of Latin American Women Workers: From Household and Factory to the Union Hall and Ballot Box* (Durham, NC: Duke University Press).

Friedman, E. (forthcoming, 2001) 'Getting Rights for those without Representation: The Success of Conjunctural Coalition-Building in Venezuela', in N. Craske and M. Molyneux (eds), *Gender and Justice in Latin America* (Basingstoke: Macmillan).

FSLN (1987) *Women and the Sandinista Revolution* (Managua: Vangardia).

Funk, N. and Mueller, M. (eds) (1993) *Gender Politics and Post-Communism: Reflections from Eastern Europe and the Former Soviet Union* (New York and London: Routledge).

Galer, N., Ruiz Bravo, P. and Guzman, V. (1990) *Mujer en el desarrollo: Balance y propuestas* (Lima: Flora Tristán).

García-Guadilla, M.P. (1995) 'Gender, Environment, and Empowerment in Venezuela', in Lesser Blumberg, R. et al. (eds), *Engendering Wealth and Well Being: Empowerment for Global Change* (Boulder, CO: Westview Press).

Gaspar Pereira, H. (1996) *The Viva Rio Movement: The Struggle for Peace*, ILAS Research Paper no. 45 (London: Institute of Latin American Studies).

Gellner, E. (1994) *Conditions of Liberty* (Harmondsworth: Penguin).

Giddens, A. (1990) *The Consequences of Modernity* (Cambridge: Polity Press).

Gilligan, C. (1982) *In a Different Voice* (Cambridge, MA.: Harvard University Press).

Goetz, A.M. (1997) *Getting Institutions Right for Women in Development* (London: Zed Books).

Guo, J. (1999) 'Resisting Modernity in Contemporary China: The Cultural Revolution and Postmodernism', *Modern China*, vol. 25 no. 3 (July), pp. 343–76.

Guzman, V., Portocarrero, P. and Vargas, V. et al. (eds) (1992) *Una nueva lectura: Género en el desarrollo* (Peru: Entre Mujeres/Flora Tristán).

Hahner, J. (1978) 'The Nineteenth-Century Feminist Press and Women's Rights in Brazil', in A. Lavrin (ed.), *Latin American Women* (Westport, CT: Greenwood Press), pp. 254–85.

Hahner, J. (1990) *Emancipating the Female Sex: The Struggle for Women's Rights in Brazil, 1850–1940* (Durham, NC: Duke University Press).

Halliday, F. and Molyneux, M. (1982) *The Ethiopian Revolution* (London: Verso/NLB).

Hansson, C. and Liden, K. (1983) *Moscow Women* (New York: Pantheon).

Harding, N. (ed.) (1984) *The State in Socialist Society* (Basingstoke: Macmillan).

Harrington, M. (1992) 'What Exactly is Wrong with the Liberal State as an Agent of Change?', in V. Spike Peterson (ed.), *Gendered States: Feminist (Re)Visioning of International Relations Theory* (Boulder, CO: Lynne Rienner Publishers), pp. 65–82.

Harris, H. (1987) Introduction, in A. Angel and F. Macintosh (eds), *The Tiger's Milk* (London: Virago Press).

Heitlinger, A. (1979) *Women and State Socialism. Sex Inequality in the Soviet Union and Czechoslovakia* (Basingstoke: Macmillan).

Held, D. et al. (1999) *Global Transformations* (Cambridge: Polity Press).

Hindess B. (1982) 'Power, Interests and the Outcomes of Struggle', *Sociology*, vol. 16, no. 4, pp. 498–511.

Hola, E. and Portugal, A.M. (eds) (1997) *La ciudadanía: A debate* (Santiago de Chile: Isis International).

Htun, M. (1999) 'Women's Rights and Opportunities in Latin America', in R. Feinberg and R. Rosenberg (eds). *Civil Society and the Summit of the Americas* (Miami: The North–South Center Press). See also Report of the Women's Leadership Conference of the Americas, http://www.icrw.org/

Hufton, O. (1971) 'Women in Revolution, 1789–1796', *Past and Present*, no. 53, pp. 90–108.

Instituto Nacional de Investigaciones Económicas (1995) *Situación social en el ajuste económico* (Havana), mimeo.

Jackson, C. and Pearson, R. (eds) (1998) *Feminist Visions of Development: Gender Analysis and Policy* (London: Routledge).

Jancar, B. (1978) *Women under Communism* (London: Johns Hopkins University Press).

Jaquette J. (ed.) (1994) *The Women's Movement in Latin America*, 2nd edn (Boulder, CO: Westview Press).

Jaquette, J. and Wolchik, S.L. (eds) (1998) *Women and Democracy: Latin America and Central and Eastern Europe* (Baltimore, MD: Johns Hopkins University Press).

Jayawardena, K. (1986) *Feminism and Nationalism in the Third World* (London: Zed Books).

Jelin E. (ed.) (1987) *Ciudadanía e identidad: Las mujeres en los movimientos sociales latinoamericanos* (Geneva: UNRISD).

Jelin, E. (ed.) (1990) *Women and Social Change in Latin America* (London: Zed Books).

Jelin, E. (1997) 'Igualdad y diferencia: Dilemas de la ciudadanía de las mujeres en América Latina' *AgorA*, no. 7 (Winter), pp. 189–214.

Jelin, E. and Hershberg, E. (1996) *Constructing Democracy: Human Rights, Citizenship, and Society in Latin America* (Boulder, CO: Westview Press).

Johnson, K.A. (1983) *Women, the Family and Peasant Revolution in China* (Chicago and London: University of Chicago Press).

Jonasdottir, A.G. (1988) 'On the Concept of Interests, Women's Interests and the Limitations of Interest Theory', in K.B. Jones and A.G. Jonasdottir (eds), *The Political Interests of Gender* (London: Sage), pp. 33–65.

Jones, K.B. and Jonasdottir A.G. (eds) (1988) *The Political Interests of Gender* (London: Sage).

Jones, M. (1997) 'Cupos de género, leyes electorales y elección de legisladoras en las Americas' *Revista de Ciencia Political* (November).

Kabeer, N. (1992) 'Triple Roles, Gender Roles, Social Relations: The Political Subtext of Gender Training', IDS Discussion Paper 313 (Brighton).

Kandiyoti, D. (1988a) 'Bargaining with Patriarchy', *Gender and Society*, vol. 3, pp. 274–90.

Kandiyoti, D. (1988b) *Women and Rural Development Policies: The Changing Agenda*, IDS Discussion Paper 244 (Brighton).

Kandiyoti, D. (1991) *Women, Islam and the State* (London: Macmillan).

Kandiyoti, D. (1996) 'Modernization without the Market? The Case of the Soviet "East"', *Economy and Society*, vol. 25, no. 4 (November), pp. 529–41.

Kaplan, T. (1971) 'Spanish Anarchism and Women's Liberation', *Journal of Contemporary History*, vol. 6.

Kaplan, T. (1977) *Anarchists of Andalusia, 1868–1903* (Princeton, NJ: Princeton University Press).

Kaplan, T. (1982) 'Female Consciousness and Collective Action: The Case of Barcelona, 1910–1918', *Signs*, vol. 7 (Spring), pp. 546–66.

Kollontai, A. (1972) *Sexual Relations and the Class Struggle* (London: Falling Wall Press).

Koonz, C. (1988) *Mothers in the Fatherland: Women, the Family and Nazi Politics* (London: Methuen).

Kumar, R. (1992) *A History of Doing. An Illustrated History of the Indian Women's Movement* (New Delhi: Kali for Women).

Kymlicka W. and Norman, W. (1994) 'Return of the Citizen: A Survey of Recent Work on Citizenship Theory', *Ethics*, vol. 104 (January), pp. 352–81.

Laclau, E. and Mouffe, C. (1985) *Hegemony and Socialist Strategy: Towards a Radical Democratic Politics*, translated by Winston Moore and Paul Cammack (London: Verso).

Lancaster, R. (1992) *Life is Hard: Machismo, Danger, and the Intimacy of Power in Nicaragua* (Berkeley, Los Angeles and Oxford: University of California Press).

Lapidus, G. (1978) *Women in Soviet Society. Equality, Development, and Social Change* (London: University of California Press).

Lavrin, A. (1996) *Women, Feminism and Social Change in Argentina, Chile and Uruguay, 1890–1940* (Lincoln, NB: University of Nebraska Press).

Lechner, N. (1990) *Los patios interiores de la democracia* (Santiago: Fondo de Cultura Economica/FLACSO).

Lenin, V.I. (1970) *Selected Works in Three Volumes,* vol. 2 (Moscow: Progress).

León, M. (ed.) (1994) *Mujeres y participación política* (Bogotá: TM Editores).

Levi, M. (1996) 'Social and Unsocial Capital: A Review Essay of R. Putnam's *Making Democracy Work', Politics and Society,* vol. 24, no. 1 (March).

Lister, R. (1995) 'Dilemmas in Engendering Citizenship', *Economy and Society,* vol. 24, no. 1.

Lister, R. (1997) *Citizenship: Feminist Perspectives* (Basingstoke: Macmillan).

Little, C.J. (1978) 'Education, Philanthropy, and Feminism: Components of Argentine Womanhood 1860–1926', in A. Lavrin (ed.), *Latin American Women* (Westport, CT: Greenwood Press), pp. 235–53.

Lobato, Z. (1997) 'Women Workers in the "Cathedrals of Corned Beef": Structure and Subjectivity in the Argentine Meatpacking Industry', in J.D. French and D. James (eds), *The Gendered Worlds of Latin American Women Workers: From Household and Factory to the Union Hall and Ballot Box* (Durham, NC: Duke University Press), pp. 54–71.

López, S. (1997) *Ciudadanos reales e imaginarios: Concepciones, desarrollo y mapas de la ciudadanía en el Perú* (Lima: Instituto de Diálogo y Propuestas).

Lora, C. (1996) *Creciendo en dignidad: Movimiento de comedores autogestionarios* (Lima: Instituto Bartolomé de las Casas).

Lovibond, S. (1989) ' Feminism and Postmodernism', *New Left Review,* no.178 (November–December), pp. 5–28

Lutyens, S. (1994) 'Remaking the Public Sphere: Women and Revolution in Cuba', in M.A. Tétrault (ed.), *Women and Revolution in Africa, Asia and the New World* (Columbia, SC: South Carolina Press), pp. 366–94.

Lutyens, S. (1995) 'Reading between the Lines', *Latin American Perspectives,* vol. 85, no. 2, pp. 100–24.

Macaulay, F. (2000) 'Getting Gender on the Policy Agenda: A Study of Feminist Lobbying in Brazil', in E. Dore and M. Molyneux (eds), *Hidden Histories of Gender and the State in Latin America* (Durham, NC: Duke University Press).

McCauley, A. (1981) *Women's Work and Wages in the USSR* (London: George Allen and Unwin).

McIntyre, A. (1981) *After Virtue. A Study in Moral Theory* (London: Duckworth).

McIntyre, A. (1988) *Whose Justice? Which Rationality?*(London: Duckworth).

MacKinnon, C. (1982) 'Feminism, Marxism, Method and the State: An Agenda for Theory', *Signs* (Spring).

MAGÍN (1994) *Programa de Desarrollo* (Havana), mimeo.

Mahon, E. (1987) 'Women's Rights and Catholicism in Ireland', *New Left Review,* no. 166.

Maier, E. (1980) *Nicaragua. La mujer en la revolución* (México: Ediciones de Cultura Popular).

Markus, M. (1976) 'Women and Work: Emancipation at a Dead End', in A. Hegedus et al. (eds), *The Humanisation of Socialism* (London: Alison and Busby).

Marotta, S. (1960) *El movimiento sindical Argentino: su genesis y desarrollo* (Buenos Aires: Lacio).

Marques-Pereira, B. and Carrier, A. (eds) (1996) *La Citoyenneté sociale des femmes au Bresil* (Brussels University, L'Harmattan).

Marshall, T.H. (1950) *Citizenship and Social Class and Other Essays* (Cambridge: Cambridge University Press).

Marx, K. (1956) *The Holy Family* (Moscow: Foreign Languages Press).

Marx, K. (1973) *The Revolutions of 1848, Political Writings,* vol. 1 (Harmondsworth: Penguin).

Marx, K. (1974) *The First International and After* (Harmondsworth: Penguin).

Marx, K. (1975) *Early Writings* (Harmondsworth: Penguin).

Marx, K. and Engels, F. (1970) *Selected Works* (London: Lawrence and Wishart).

Mass, B. (1975) *The Political Economy of Population Control in Latin America* (Montreal: Women's Press).

Massel, G. (1974) *The Surrogate Proletariat. Moslem Women and Revolutionary Strategies in Soviet Central Asia: 1919–1929* (Princeton, NJ: Princeton University Press).

Menchú, R. (1983) *I, Rigoberta Menchú: An Indian Woman in Guatemala,* edited by E. Burgos-Debray (London: Verso/NLB).

Menéndez-Carrión, A. and Bustamente, X. (1995) in Peter Smith (ed.), *Latin America in Comparative Perspective: New Approaches to Methods and Analysis* (Boulder, CO: Westview Press).

Mill, J.S. (1861) *The Subjection of Women* (New York: Prometheus Books, 1986).

Miller, F. (1991) *Latin American Women and the Search for Social Justice* (Hanover and London: University Press of New England).

Mitchell, J. (1965) 'Women: The Longest Revolution', *New Left Review,* no. 40.

Moghissi, H. (1994) *Populism and Feminism in Iran: Women's Struggle in a Male-Defined Revolutionary Movement* (Basingstoke: Macmillan).

Moller Okin, S. (1991) *Justice, Gender and the Family* (New York: Basic Books).

Molyneux, M. (1981) 'Women's Emancipation under Socialism: A Model for the Third World?' *World Development,* vol. 9, nos 9/10, pp. 1019–37. Revised and reprinted as 'Women in Socialist Societies: Problems of Theory and Practice' in K. Young, C. Wolkowitz and R. McCullagh (eds), *Of Marriage and the Market* (London: Routledge and Kegan Paul).

Molyneux, M. (1982) *State Policies and the Position of Women Workers in the PDRY* (Geneva: ILO).

Molyneux, M. (1985a) 'Mobilisation Without Emancipation? Women's Interests, State and Revolution in Nicaragua' *Feminist Studies* vol. II pp. 227–54.

Molyneux, M. (1985b) 'The Role of Women in the Revolution', in T. Walker (ed.), *Nicaragua: The First Five Years* (New York: Praeger).

Molyneux, M. (1986a) 'Legal Reform and Social Revolution in Democratic Yemen', *International Journal of the Sociology of Law,* no. 13.

Molyneux, M. (1986b) 'Prologue', in G. Omvedt, *Women in Popular Movements: India and Thailand during the Decade of Women* (Geneva: UNRISD).

Molyneux, M. (1990) ' "The Woman Question" in the Age of Perestroika', *New Left Review,* vol. 183, pp. 23–49.

Molyneux, M. (1995) 'Women's Rights and Political Contingency: The Case of Yemen, 1990–1994', *Middle East Journal,* vol. 49, no. 3 (Summer). Reprinted in R. Wilford and R.L. Miller (eds), *Women, Ethnicity and Nationalism. The Politics of Transition* (London: Routledge, 1998).

Molyneux, M. (1996) 'Women's Rights and the International Context in the Post-Communist States', in M. Threlfall (ed.), *Mapping the Women's Movement: Feminist Politics and Social Transformation in the North* (London: Verso), pp. 232–59.

Molyneux, M. (1998) 'Comunitarismo, moralidad y políticas de identidad', in E. Hola and A. M. Portugal (eds), *La ciudadanía: A debate* (Chile: ISIS Internacional), Ediciones de las Mujeres no. 25.

Molyneux, M. (1999) 'The Politics of the Cuban Diaspora in the United States', in V. Bulmer-Thomas and J. Dunkerley (eds), *The United States and Latin America. The New Agenda* (London: Institute of Latin American Studies, and Cambridge, MA: David Rockefeller Center for Latin American Studies).

Molyneux, M. (2000a) 'State Formations in Latin America', in E. Dore and M. Molyneux (eds), *Hidden Histories of Gender and the State in Latin America* (Durham, NC: Duke University Press).

Molyneux, M. (2000b) 'Gender and Citizenship in Comparative Perspective', in J. Cook, J. Roberts and G. Waylen (eds), *Towards a Gendered Political Economy* (Basingstoke: Macmillan).

Molyneux, M. and Lazar, S. (1999) *Rights, Citizenship and Participatory Development.* DFID (Department for International Development) Report on ESCOR Research Project R1783.

Molyneux, M. and Steinberg, D. (1995) 'Mies and Shiva's *Ecofeminism*: A New Testament?', *Feminist Review*, no. 49.

Moser, C.O.N. (1989) 'Gender Planning in the Third World: Meeting Practical and Strategic Needs', *World Development*, vol. 17, no. 11, pp. 1799–825.

Mouffe, C. (1988) 'Towards a New Concept of Democracy', in C. Nelson and L. Grosberg (eds), *Marxism and the Interpretation of Culture* (Urbana, IL: University of Illinois Press).

Mouffe, C. (ed.) (1992) *Dimensions of Radical Democracy* (London: Verso).

Mulhall, M.G. and Mulhall, E.T. (1892) *Handbook of the River Plate* (London: Kegan Paul, Trench).

Najmabadi, A. (1999) 'Feminism in an Islamic Republic', in Y. Haddad and J. L'Esposito (eds), *Islam, Gender, and Social Change* (Oxford: Oxford University Press).

Nelson, B. and Chowdhury, J. (eds) (1994) *Women and Politics Worldwide* (New Haven, CT: Yale University Press).

Nettlau, M. (1971) *Histoire de l'anarchie* (Paris Editions du Cercle).

New, C. (1996) 'Man Bad, Woman Good? Essentialisms and Ecofeminisms', *New Left Review*, vol. 216 (March/April), pp. 79–93.

Nicholson, L. (ed.) (1989) *Feminism/Postmodernism* (New York and London: Routledge).

Nijeholt, G. Lycklama à, Vargas, V. and Wieringa, S. (eds) (1998) *Women's Movements and Public Policy in Europe, Latin America and the Caribbean* (New York: Garland).

Nussbaum, M. and Glover, J. (eds) (1995) *Women, Culture and Development* (Oxford: Clarendon Press).

O'Donnell, G. (1993) 'On the State, Democratization and Some Conceptual Problems: A Latin American View with Glances at Some Post-communist Countries', *World Development*, vol. 21, no. 8, pp 1355–69.

Oduol, W. and Kabira, W.M. (1995) 'The Mother of Warriors and her Daughters: The Women's Movement in Kenya', in A. Basu (ed.), *The Challenge of Local Feminisms* (Boulder, CO: Westview Press), pp. 187–208.

Oficina de la Mujer (1986) 'Informes: Diéz años de investigaciones sobre la mujer en Nicaragua 1976–1986' (Managua).

Olivares, C. (ed.) (1996) *Memoria: Foro género y ciudadanía* (CIDEM/RIPEM).

Omvedt, G. (1986) *Women in Popular Movements: India and Thailand during the Decade of Women* (Geneva: UNRISD).

Oved, I. (1978) *El anarquismo y el movimiento obrero en Argentina* (Mexico City: Siglo XXI).

Paidar, P. (1995) *Women and the Political Process in Twentieth-Century Iran* (Cambridge: Cambridge University Press).

Pastor, M. and Zimbalist, A. (1995) 'Waiting for Change. Adjustment and Reform in Cuba', *World Development*, vol. 23, no. 5, pp. 705–20.

Pateman, C. (1988) *The Sexual Contract* (Cambridge: Polity Press).

Pearson, R. (1997) 'Renegotiating the Reproductive Bargain: Gender Analysis of Economic Transition in Cuba in the 1990s', *Development and Change*, vol. 28, no. 4, pp. 671–706.

Pensamiento Propio (1985) November/December.

Phillips, A. (1991) *Engendering Democracy* (Cambridge: Polity Press).

Phillips, A. (1992) 'Universal Pretensions in Political Thought', in M. Barrett and A. Phillips (eds), *Destabilizing Theory* (Stanford, CA: Stanford University Press).

Phillips, A. (1993) *Democracy and Difference* (Cambridge: Polity Press).

Putnam, R. (1992) *Making Democracy Work* (Princeton, NJ: Princeton University Press).

Quesada, F. (1979) *Argentine Anarchism and 'La Protesta'* (New York: Gordon Press).

Quinn, S. (1977) 'Mother of a Revolution'. *Guardian* (Manchester and London), 14 April.

Radcliffe, S. and Westwood, S. (1993) *Viva!: Women and Popular Protest in Latin America* (London: Routledge).

Rai, S. (ed.) (1999) *International Perspectives on Gender and Democratisation* (Basingstoke: Macmillan).

Ramírez-Horton, S. (1982) 'The Role of Women in the Nicaraguan Revolution', in T. Walker (ed.), *Nicaragua in Revolution* (New York: Praeger).

Ramos, C. et al. (eds) (1987) *Presencia y Transparencia: La Mujer en la Historia de México* (México: El Colegio de México).

Ramos Escandón, C. (1998) 'Women and Power in Mexico', in V.E. Rodríguez (ed.), *Women's Participation in Mexican Political Life* (Boulder, CO: Westview Press), pp. 87–102.

Randall, M. (1978) *Inside the Nicaraguan Revolution* (Vancouver: New Star Books).

Randall, M. (1982) *Sandino's Daughters* (London: Zed Books).

Randall, M. (1994) *Sandino's Daughters Revisited* (New Brunswick, NJ: Rutgers University Press).

Rock, D. (1975) *Politics in Argentina 1890–1930* (Cambridge: Cambridge University Press).

Rodríguez, E. (ed.) (1997) *Entre silencios y voces: Género e historia en América Central (1750–1990)* (San José: Centro Nacional para el Desarrollo de la Mujer y la Familia).

Rooper, A. (1987) *Fragile Victory: A Nicaraguan Community at War* (London: Weidenfeld and Nicolson).

Rose, G. (1995) *Love's Work* (London: Chatto and Windus).

Rowbotham, S. (1972) *Women, Resistance and Revolution* (London: Allen Lane).

Rowbotham, S. (1973) *Hidden from History* (London: Pluto Press).

Rowbotham, S. (1992) *Women in Movement: Feminism and Social Action* (New York and London: Routledge).

Ruddick, S. (1980) 'Maternal Thinking', *Feminist Studies*, vol. 6, no. 2.

Ruvira, G. (1971) *Orígines del anarquismo en Buenos Aires 1886–1901* (Valencia: Universidad de Valencia).

Safa, H.I. (1990) 'Women's Social Movements in Latin America', *Gender and Society*, vol. 4, no. 3, pp. 354–69.

Salinas, G.A. (1986) 'The Barzolas and the Housewives Committee', in J. Nash and H. Safa (eds), *Women and Change in Latin America* (South Hadley, MA: Bergen and Garvey).

Saporta Sternbach, N. et al. (1992) 'Feminism in Latin America: From Bogota to San Bernardo' in A. Escobar and S. Alvarez (eds), *The Making of Social Movements in Latin America* (Boulder, CO: Westview Press).

Schild, V. (1998) 'New Subjects of Rights? Women's Movements and the Construction of Citizenship in the "New Democracies"', in S. Alvarez, E. Dagnino and A. Escobar (eds), *Cultures of Politics/Politics of Cultures: Revisioning Latin American Social Movements* (Boulder, CO: Westview Press), pp. 93–115.

Schirmer, J. (1989) 'Those who Die for Life Cannot Be called Dead: Women and the Human Rights Protest in Latin America', *Feminist Review,* vol. 32 (Summer), pp. 3–29.

Schumaher, M.A. and Vargas, E. (1993) 'Lugar no governo: Alibi ou conquista?, *Estudos Feministas*, vol. 1, no. 2 (São Paulo).

Scott, J. (1988) *Gender and the Politics of History* (New York: Columbia University Press).

Segundo censo de la República Argentina (1898) (Buenos Aires: Taller Tipográfico de la Penitenciaria Nacional).

Sen, G. and Grown, C. (1987) *Development Crises and Alternative Visions: Third World Women's Perspectives* (London: Earthscan).

Showstack Sassoon, A. (ed.) (1987) *Women and the State: The Shifting Boundaries of Public and Private* (London: Hutchinson).

Skocpol, T. (1992) *Protecting Soldiers and Mothers: The Political Origins of Social Policy in the United States* (Cambridge, MA, and London: Harvard University Press).

Slater, D. ed. (1985) *New Social Movements and the State in Latin America.* (Amsterdam: CEDLA).

Smith, L. and Padula, A. (1996) *Sex and Revolution: Women in Socialist Cuba* (Oxford: Oxford University Press).

Solberg, C. (1970) *Immigration and Nationalism in Argentina and Chile: 1890–1914* (Austin, TX: University of Texas Press).

Stacey, J. (1983) *Patriarchy and Socialist Revolution in China* (Berkeley and London: University of California Press).

Stepan, A. (1978) *The State and Society: Peru in Comparative Perspective* (Princeton, NJ: Princeton University Press).

Stepan, N. (1991) *The Hour of Eugenics* (Ithaca, NY: Cornell University Press).

Stephen, L. (1998) *Women and Social Movements in Latin America: Power from Below* (Austin, TX: University of Texas Press).

Stone, E. (1981) *Women and the Cuban Revolution: Speeches and Documents* (New York: Pathfinder).

Stoner, K. L. (1991) *From the House to the Streets. The Cuban Women's Movement for Legal Reform* (Durham, NC: Duke University Press).

Stubbs, J. (1994) 'Cuba: Revolutionising Women, Family and Power', in B. Nelson and N. Chowdhury (eds), *Women and Politics Worldwide* (New Haven and

London: Yale University Press), pp. 189–209.

Szporluk, R. (1988) *Communism and Nationalism: Karl Marx Versus Friedrich List* (Oxford: Oxford University Press).

Tarrés, M.L. (1992) 'Perspectivas analíticas en la sociología de la acción collectiva', *Estudios Sociológicos*, vol. X, no. 30, pp. 735–57.

Tétrault, M.A. (1994) *Women and Revolution in Africa, Asia, and the New World* (Columbia, SC: University of South Carolina Press).

Threlfall, M. (ed.) (1996) *Mapping Women's Movements* (London: Verso).

Tilly, C. (1978) *From Mobilization to Revolution* (Reading, MA: Addison/Wesley).

Ting, L. (1975) 'Thoughts on 8 March', *New Left Review*, no. 92 (July–August).

Tronto, J.C. (1993) *Moral Boundaries: A Political Argument for an Ethic of Care* (New York and London: Routledge).

Trotsky, L. (1967) *History of the Russian Revolution*, vol. III (London: Sphere).

Trotsky, L. (1970) *Women and the Family* (New York: Pathfinder Press).

Turgeon, L. (1989) *State and Discrimination. The Other Side of the Cold War* (London: M.E. Sharpe Inc.).

Turner, B. (1986) *Citizenship and Capitalism: The Debate over Reformism* (London: Allen and Unwin).

Valdés, T. and Gomariz, E. (eds) (1992) Report on Cuba, *Mujeres latinoamericanas en cifras* (Santiago: Instituto de la Mujer/FLACSO).

Vargas, V. (1991) 'The Women's Movement in Peru: Streams, Spaces and Knots', *European Review of Latin American and Caribbean Studies*, vol. 50 (June).

Vargas, V. (1993) 'Los intereses de las mujeres y los procesos de emancipación' (Programa Universitario de Estudios de Género, Universidad Nacional Autonoma de México), pp. 1–18.

Vargas, V. (1996) 'Women's Movements in Peru: Rebellion into Action', in S. Wieringa (ed.) *Subversive Women: Women's Movements in Africa, Asia, Latin America and the Caribbean* (London: Zed Books).

Vargas, V. (1998) *Caminos a Beijing* (Lima: Flora Tristán).

Vaughan, M.K. (2000) 'Modernising Patriarchy: State Policies, Rural Households and Women in Mexico, 1930–1940', in M. Molyneux and E. Dore (eds), *Hidden Histories of Gender and the State in Latin America* (Durham, NC: Duke University Press).

Vaz Ferreira, C. (1945) *Sobre Feminismo* (Buenos Aires: Editoria Losada).

Vilas, C.M (1986) 'The Mass Organisations in Nicaragua', *Monthly Review*, vol. 38 (November), pp. 20–31.

Villavicencio, M. (1992) *Del silencio a la palabra: Mujeres peruanas en los siglos XIX–XX* (Lima: Ediciones Flora Tristán, Centro de la Mujer Peruana).

Walker, T. (1985) (ed.) *Nicaragua: The First Five Years* (New York: Praeger).

Watson, P. (1993) 'The Rise of Masculinism in Eastern Europe', *New Left Review*, no. 198, pp. 71–82.

Waylen, G. (1996) *Gender in Third World Politics* (Milton Keynes: Open University Press).

White, S. (n.d.) 'Making Men an Issue: Gender Planning for "the Other Half"', (Sussex University: Institute of Development Studies), mimeo.

Wieringa, S. (1994) 'Women's Interests and Empowerment: Gender Planning Reconsidered', *Development and Change*, vol. 25 (The Hague), pp. 829–48.

Wieringa, S. (ed.) (1995) *Subversive Women: Women's Movements in Africa, Asia, Latin America and the Caribbean* (London: Zed Books).

Wilde, A. (1999) 'Irruptions of Memory: Expressive Politics in Chile's Transition to Democracy', *Journal of Latin American Studies*, Vol 31, pp. 473–500.

Wolchik, S. (1979) 'The Status of Women in a Socialist Order: Czechoslovakia, 1948–1978', *Slavic Review*, vol. 38 (December).

Wolchik, S. (1994) 'Women and the Politics of Transition in the Czech and Slovak Republics', in M. Rueschemeyer (ed.), *Women in the Politics of Postcommunist Europe* (London: M.E. Sharpe Inc.).

Women in Central America (1987) Year 1, no. 2, 2 March.

World Bank (1985) *Development Report* (Oxford: Oxford University Press).

World Bank (1997) *Development Report* (Oxford: Oxford University Press).

Young, I.M. (1990) *Justice and the Politics of Difference* (Princeton, NJ: Princeton University Press).

Young, K. (1993) *Planning Development with Women* (Basingstoke: Macmillan).

Young, K. et al. (1984) *Of Marriage and the Market: Women's Subordination in International Perspective*, 2nd edition (London: Routledge).

Yunque, A. (1941) *La literatura social en la Argentina* (Buenos Aires: Claridad).

Yuval Davis, N. (1999) 'The Multi-Layered Citizen: Citizenship in the Age of "Globalization" ', *International Feminist Journal of Politics*, vol. 1 (June), pp. 119–36.

Yuval Davis, N. and Werbner, P. (eds) (1999) *Women, Citizenship and Difference* (London: Zed Books).

Zetkin, C. (1934) *Reminiscences of Lenin* (New York: International Publishers).

Index

CPSIA information can be obtained
at www.ICGtesting.com
Printed in the USA
LVHW11s0142101018
593046LV00001B/32/P

9 781900 039581